COSTUME DESIGN

SECOND EDITION

Barbara and Cletus Anderson
Carnegie Mellon University

THOMSON

WADSWORTH

Australia • Canada • Mexico • Singapore • Spain • United Kingdom • United States

Publisher	Earl McPeek
Developmental Editor	Steve Stembridge
Project Editor	Claudia Gravier, Michele Tomiak
Art Director	Don Fujimoto
Production Manager	Diane Gray

ISBN: 0-15508379-1

Library of Congress Catalog Card Number: 98–86089

Wadsworth Group/Thomson Learning
10 Davis Drive
Belmont CA 94002-3098
USA

For information about our products, contact us:
Thomson Learning Academic Resource Center
1-800-423-0563
http://www.wadsworth.com

For permission to use material from this text, contact us by
Web: http://www.thomsonrights.com
Fax: 1-800-730-2215
Phone: 1-800-730-2214

Printed in the United States of America
10 9 8 7 6 5 4 3

Preface

Costume design is both an art form and a practical craft, a duality that makes the field somewhat difficult to master and equally elusive to explain to others. The craft cannot be defined in absolutes, nor can the costume designer indulge in the complete freedom of expression available to the fine artist. But an intelligent, sensitive, informed method of working can help those interested in the field develop the design ideas for a production. *Costume Design* offers a logical approach, from the beginnings of costumes and the psychology of clothes through the development and sketching of ideas to the actual building of costumes.

The first three chapters—"Costume Design: What It Is and What It Does," "The Costume Approach," and "Developing the Basic Concept"—help the novice designer understand the field and develop costume ideas. We urge designers to communicate creatively with others on any project so that ideas can be exchanged and encouraged to grow. This interchange of ideas is a unique aspect of the performing arts, for it is through the collaboration of a number of artists with expertise in different areas of the production that an exciting piece is created for the audience. This book presents a way of working that will be creative and constructive, one that will lead to effective collaborations and rewarding experiences. Costume ideas cannot exist solely in the designer's head, so chapters 4, 5, and 6—"Developing the Line," "Designing the Costume: Color Control," and "Costume Presentation: Rendering or Final Sketch"—offer the beginner ways to present the work. They provide a basic guide to the figure, suggest and show examples of different presentation techniques, and explain the basic principles of line and color and how to apply them to costumes. The purpose of *Costume Design* is to open doors to myriad possibilities, and to develop a designer who is effective because he or she has a mind and imagination that can adapt to any challenge. Today many doors lead to work in film and television, so Chapter 7, "Designing for Film and Television," gives a brief approach to working in these areas.

The final two chapters, "Costume Construction" and "Patterning and Building the Costume," provide a basis for converting a sketch to an actual costume. A handsome sketch can communicate ideas to others involved with the production, but the final result must be an effective costume presented to the audience. The brief guide to the history of clothing and list of source books and artists at the end of the book can be used as a springboard when the designer begins research for a project.

Many people encouraged and helped us as we set about getting these ideas onto paper, on both this edition and its predecessor, and we are very grateful to them all. We wish particularly to thank Phillip Graneto of Rowan University for his time, patience, and wonderful ability to clarify a thought; Ainslie Bruneau for her assistance in developing the patterns and checking over the original manuscript; and Melinda Eshelman for her thoughts on Chapter 7. We also wish to thank all of the colleagues and students, both past and present, who allowed us to use some of their work, and Stacy Eddy and Kevin Ritter for their assistance with the pictures for Chapter 9. And we are very grateful to those reviewers who read and critiqued the manuscript: Alan Armstrong, UCLA; Alexandra Bonds, University of Oregon; Leon Brauner, Indiana University; Gail Crellin, University of Minnesota; Alicia Finkel, University of Connecticut; Barbara Mendlicott, University of Houston; Paul Reinhardt, University of Texas, Austin; and Al Tucci, West Virginia University, and those who reviewed the book for the second edition: Barbara Cox, University of North Texas; Carson Eddy, Tufts University; Margaret McCubbin, Bowling Green University; and Ritchie Spenser, University of Southern California.

Contents

◆ *Chapter 3*
Developing the Basic Concept

◆ *Chapter 4*
Developing the Line

◆   *Chapter 5*
Designing the Costume: Color Control

◆   *Chapter 6*
Costume Presentation: Rendering or Final Sketch

◆   *Appendix A*
A Guide to the History of Clothing

◈ Introduction

There are no absolutes in costume design, but there is certainly a logical way to approach the work so designers can develop a basic understanding of the field and guidelines that will allow them to grow and expand their capabilities with each project. Talent is important, but in a collaborative art knowing how to get the job done efficiently and effectively is a tremendous asset. And a well-balanced combination of talent, know-how, dependability, positive attitude, and skill in communicating is almost unbeatable. This book is designed to help develop this combination of skills.

Good costume designers must know a tremendous amount about a great many subjects including the literature of the performing arts and the physical spaces in which performances take place. They must understand people and be familiar with drawing and painting and the history of art. They must be knowledgeable about social history, be aware of many types of fabrics, and be ready to develop ideas from the sublime to the ridiculous. They must constantly be open to all kinds of stimuli; a designer never knows what information will be valuable when embarking on a new project.

This book presents practical information in the areas mentioned above, some discussed briefly, others explored in depth. It provides a working knowledge of the field, a foundation that can open doors for designers to use as they develop and learn with each new project in a wide variety of fields.

Costume Design gives the designer a basic understanding of what costumes are and what they do, beginning with a brief description of how costumes developed in the past. Since costumes are based on the clothing people wear, designers must think about what is worn, why it is worn, and what others think about it. We believe that the primary function of the costume is to enhance the characterization of a role. "Nobody ever goes away humming the costumes"—nor should they, but well-thought-out costumes can certainly add great zest to a production.

There is more than a little craziness in the clothes of everyday life and costumes in the performing arts, so a well-developed sense of humor will never hurt any designer. Directors have many things to think about, and designers who can keep their wits and wit about them make much better collaborators. Actors are usually quite concerned with their physical appearance in a role, and an open, friendly approach can often soften rough

A practical approach to designing can help make creating a costume such as this one for Beulah in *Merton of the Movies*, a fun and satisfying experience. Design for a 1982 production at Carnegie Mellon University by Cletus Anderson. Pencil sketch.

High fashion is not always sensible, offstage or on. A 1780 "Anglo-American bonnet."

spots. Fellow workers in a costume shop will feel a lot more like working for a designer who is enthusiastic and cheery than for a cloud of doom that descends on the cutting table.

Perhaps there is one absolute after all: Costume designers who know how to approach their work and know what they should do to achieve the goals decided on for a production will instill confidence in all those who work with them. The first three chapters of this book present a step-by-step method of approaching the project, defining the objectives, and determining the methods that can best be used to achieve the goals.

The ability to put ideas down almost effortlessly is a basic tool the designer must master. Actually putting pencil to paper to begin drawing the costumes is a step that is sometimes difficult to take. We have provided a guide to the figure and the basic design principles and how they apply to the body and the costume. Designers can get to work when they are confident that they can develop the ideas on paper. They must believe in what they do and not try to hedge their bets. A sketch cannot be presented with the old dodge: "Well, what I really wanted was. . . ." What is really wanted should be there. It does not have to be a work of art; it should be a clear

A costume sketch may indicate the mood of the play but must clearly show the costume. Jean in John Whiting's *The Devils* produced at Carnegie Mellon University in 1970. Done in acrylic by Cletus Anderson.

Soldiers in *Macbeth* wore quilted tunics and gauntlets in costumes designed by Cletus Anderson for the 1980 Pittsburgh Public Theater production. The quilting and helmet-mask added bulk and menace to the figure.

presentation of what the costume will be, one that can be easily read by the director, actors, and those in the shop who will build it.

Producing costume sketches and renderings requires an understanding of materials and color theory. Color control is a primary factor in costume design. The designer must know what range of color is available, what effect it may have, and how it reacts to other colors around it.

In today's market the designer may find that much of the work that is available is in film and television. The approach to designing a valid costume is the same for any field, but the way the work is organized does vary, so a short explanation of the differences is included.

An effective costume rendering is indeed a wonderful thing, but it can be a mere academic exercise if the designer doesn't know how to translate it into an actual costume. We explain how to develop a point of view for

The Purple Panda in *Mister Rogers' Neighborhood* wore this dinosaur suit designed by Barbara Anderson. Photo by Lilo Guest. Courtesy Family Communications, Inc.

building the show and how to take the costume plate and accurately interpret the areas to three-dimensional form. We also explore the world of fabric, for it is the backbone of the costume realization. Even while putting down the first quick impression, designers can sense the idea growing as they think of how it will work in a heavy, tweedy wool or a lightly flowing chiffon.

Most people who regularly attend some form of performing arts never consider the fact that to build a costume you first have to develop the pattern for it. We explain the basic principles of developing the pattern and include layouts for the basic shapes of the most-used elements with illustrations of what they will look like when assembled. This book gives designers a way to work so they can tackle any problem because they understand what fabric can do and aren't afraid to keep trying different approaches, including both flat patterning and draping, until they achieve the shape they want. Within a space of a few months we designed and built a production of

The costume for Nathan Grantham after he has been dead for seven years required a somewhat unorthodox approach. Designed for the George Romero film *Creepshow* by Barbara Anderson. Makeup by Tom Savini. Photo courtesy Laurel Show, Inc., New York.

Macbeth for the Pittsburgh Public Theater that included intricate quilting and draping; a dinosaur costume for a man in a purple panda suit for *Mister Rogers' Neighborhood;* and the costumes for the motion picture *Knightriders,* which included an entire motorcycle gang doing elaborate stunts clad in medieval armor. This certainly required variation in approach and a willingness to try new things.

The best research material for a designer to use involves primary sources—sources created during the span of the historical period—but it is often difficult to know just what is being presented in these sources. The appendices in this text provide a guide to the history of clothing presenting the basic shapes of each period—a concise starting point for understanding the history of clothes and a period-by-period list of sources for a more in-depth look at any era.

Costume design is a delightful and challenging field. It certainly isn't an area for those of faint heart who yearn for a serene life and 10 hours of sleep a night. Problems run rampant, deadlines are always too near, and just as one need is met another jumps up to take its place. But the rewards can outweigh all these, for it is a field that keeps one involved, communicating, thinking, and growing. And it can be exciting and fun.

◆ Chapter 1

Costume Design:
What It Is and What It Does

Preceding page: This costume design instantly tells the audience that the young man has just motored to the country house. Costume design for *Hay Fever* produced at the Pittsburgh Public Theater. Watercolor by Cletus Anderson.

Costume design must encompass both the past and the present and be based on a knowledge of the art form and the world from which it springs. It must be predicated on an understanding of characters created for the entertainment of others and of the actual people who are the resource for the presentation and its roles. Any developing designer needs an awareness of these influences, so this book begins with a brief look at the development of theatrical costuming and defines what a costume is. Since the characters in a presentation may be recognized by their garments, a knowledge of the psychology of clothing gives designers a background that will help them explore the dramatic ideas and find ways that costumes will help develop the characters and present the ideas of the script. Costume designers can bring a great deal to any production, but they do not work on their own. The world of the performing arts is made up of many people exchanging ideas and combining talents to produce an event for the audience. This chapter explains how to develop this collaboration.

Hand in hand with the development of drama, the desire to create a heightened dramatic effect through physical adornment has made the theatrical experience increasingly more exciting to the audience. Costuming for theatrical effect is as old as drama itself, but costume design as an element planned to help delineate the character and further the interpretation of the production as a whole is a relatively new development. Today's costume designer is an artist who enriches the production by selecting the underpinnings, garments, and accessories that will best suit the actors in their roles and at the same time reinforce the flavor of the whole presentation.

◆ Early Theatrical Costuming

A style of costume that added importance to the figure and gave more visibility to the actor was well established by the time of Aeschylus (525–456 B.C.) and the great Greek tragedies. Performing in a huge outdoor amphitheater, the actor became larger than life with the aid of spacious, padded robes, thick-soled boots called *cothurni*, and masks constructed to amplify the voice. The masks were not only practical; they did much to heighten the spectacle and the appearance of the actors, for often they were adorned with the *onkus*, a lofty headdress. Stock character masks were common in Greek and Roman tragedies and comedies, allowing the audience to identify with ease the type of role played by the actor. In the comedies much humor came from these exaggerated headpieces, and the colorful costumes were made ludicrous by dangling appendages.

Costuming began cautiously as drama slowly reemerged in Western Europe at the end of the early Middle Ages (roughly A.D. 475–1000). The

Figure 1.1 Greek and Roman actors became larger than life with the aid of *cothurni*, mask, and *onkus*. This ivory statuette of a tragic actor, probably Roman, is in the Musée du Petit Palais, Paris.

Figure 1.2 Comedy and Tragedy. Masks in a mosaic now to be seen in the Capitoline Museum, Rome.

mystery and miracle plays started in the church, and the costumes for these were inspired by church vestments, which have always had a certain theatricality. As presentations moved from the church precincts to the marketplace the scope of the pageants widened and more contemporary characteristics and flair were incorporated into the performance to help capture the attention of the gathered populace. Much of the art of the early Middle Ages was based on religious themes, with the artists depicting the biblical characters in robes with simple lines. The style of these illustrations influenced the garments first used for the drama, but this trend was soon reversed. The presentations became more theatrical, the characters acquired more extraordinary accoutrements that would heighten the dramatic effect, and the visual artists soon followed along, depicting the figures in their paintings in a much more theatrical manner. The human desire to adorn the body and entertain others won out again. This was particularly evident in the character of the Devil who, aided by fantastical masks, costumes, and accessories, tended to run away with the show.

The desire for extravagant and lavish costuming in presentations was quite compatible with the richness of the extraordinary fashions of the nobles of the time of the Italian Renaissance. This delight in spectacle was paramount, though to the modern eye it might seem a bit misplaced, as in the case of a production of *Oedipus Rex* staged at the Teatro Olimpico at Vicenza in 1585, with the king's retinue of 24 archers dressed in Turkish fashion. This excerpt from Sabbattini's *Practica,* published in 1638, expresses the philosophy behind the rich presentations of the time:

> **Veridico:** I tell you especially that I make efforts to dress the actors always in as noble a fashion as is possible for me, but in such a manner that there is a sense of proportion among them, in view of the fact that the rich costume . . . particularly in these times when pomp is at its highest peak, adds much reputation and beauty to comedies, and even more to tragedies. I would not hesitate to dress a servant in velvet or colored satin, as long as his master's costume were embroidered or decorated with gold, so rich that there would be maintained the proper proportion between them. But I would not clothe a housemaid with a torn old skirt, or a servant with a torn doublet; on the contrary, I would have her wear a nice skirt and him a showy jacket, and I would add so much nobility to the clothes of their masters as to allow for the beauty of the servants' costumes.
>
> **Massimiano:** There is no doubt that the sight of the rags which others put on a miser's back, or on a servant's, detracts much from the dignity of a play.
>
> **Veridico:** One can very well clothe a miser or even a peasant with costumes which have a certain degree of richness about them, without being unnatural.

Often spectacle was also the primary function of costumes in Elizabethan and Jacobean England, particularly in the court masques shown in the sketches of Inigo Jones (1573–1652). The basic silhouette was that of the Elizabethan costume, with bits of fancy and fantasy added to give a particular flavor. This style of costuming was prominent for a great many years. The clothes of the performers were based primarily on the daily attire worn at the time and place of the production, and only slight additions or subtractions were made to give a feeling of the character, situation, or location of the play. With few exceptions presentations were staged in this manner until the nineteenth century. Thus a Scottish thane killing his king, a Greek maid frolicking on a midsummer night, a goddess blessing a wedding, and a Roman orator could have many costume pieces in common.

Ballet and opera costumes evolved along more opulent lines, while those used in the theater tended to be less extravagant, though still given to excess. Many of the costumes of a theatrical company were actually hand-me-downs, acquired from patrons who would bestow discarded garments on the group or give an outfit to a favored performer. It was also common practice for leading actors and actresses to select their own costumes, basing their choice on the accepted conventions of the times, which certainly did dictate an imposing look for the primary characters. Joseph Addison (1672–1719) described the traditional heroic costume in an issue of *The Spectator* of 1711:

> The ordinary method of making a hero is to clap a huge plume of feathers on his head which rises so very high that there is often a greater length from his chin to the top of his head than to the sole of his foot. One would believe that we thought a great man and a tall man the same thing. This very much embarrasses the actor, who is forced to hold his neck extremely

Figure 1.3 Spectacle was a primary function of the court masque costumes designed by Inigo Jones in Elizabethan England. This sketch is for Tethys or a Nymph in Daniel's *Tethys Festival*, 1610. Devonshire Collection, Chatsworth Library, Derbyshire, England.

Figure 1.4 Macbeth appears much more the Restoration gentleman than an early Scottish thane in this eighteenth-century production. Engraving from Nicholas Rowe's edition of Shakespeare, 1709. Courtesy Billy Rose Theater Collection, New York Public Library at Lincoln Center.

stiff and steady all the while he speaks; and not withstanding any anxieties which he pretends for his mistress, his country, or his friends, one may see by his action that his greatest care and concern is to keep the plume of feathers from falling off his head. . . . As these superfluous ornaments upon the head make a great man, a princess generally receives her grandeur from those additional encumbrances that fall into her tail. I mean the broad sweeping train that follows her in all her motions and finds constant employment for a boy who stands behind her to open and spread it to advantage. . . . It is, in my opinion, a very odd spectacle to see a queen venting her passion in a disordered motion, and a little boy taking care all the while that they do not ruffle the tail of her gown.

Figure 1.5   The celebrated Mrs. Sarah Siddons' hairstyle as The Grecian Daughter (right) is very 1782 English.

Historical accuracy or careful delineation of character was given little thought when costuming productions during the seventeenth and early eighteenth centuries, so some steps taken toward more realism in selecting costumes caused particular comment in the mid-eighteenth century. In his *Source Book in Theatrical History* A. M. Nagler refers to a noted French actress of the time, Mlle Clairon. Performing in a small theater in the 1750s, she

Figure 1.6   Hairstyle and dress shape place Mrs. Bunn's Queen Elizabeth (above) squarely in the early 1820s.

Figure 1.7   Mr. and Mrs. Berry appeared in traditional heroic costumes as Bajazet and Selima in Nicholas Rowe's *Tamerlane* in June 1776. He wore a high plume of feathers and she a broad, sweeping train. His line: "Now, now thou Traitress."

was thought quite daring when she presented her role of a sultana without hoops and also toned down her declamatory acting style to fit the acting space. The effect was received enthusiastically by the audience. Diderot exclaimed "A courageous actress, Mlle Clairon, has just discarded her hoops, and no one thinks it wrong. She will go even further, I say. Ah! what if she dared, one day, to appear on the stage in all the nobility and simplicity of dress that her parts demand!"

Realizing that her change in acting style required a change in her entire presentation, Clairon complained to a friend: "Ah! . . . Don't you see that it ruins me? In all my characters, the costume must now be observed; the truth of declamation requires that of dress; all my rich stage wardrobe is from this moment rejected; I lose twelve hundred guineas worth of dresses; but the sacrifice is made." She went on to perform Electra "in the simple habit of a slave, disheveled, her arms loaded with chains" and was declared admirable in the role. This "simple habit" was still relatively elaborate, but it seemed quite innovative at the time.

Figure 1.8 Costume sketch by James Robinson Planché for Charles Kemble's much-publicized "historically accurate" revival of Shakespeare's *King John* in 1823. Courtesy Stark Collection, University of Texas Library, Austin.

The cry to let the character dictate the costume also came from others in this era, including John Hill. In his treatise *The Actor,* written in 1750, he indicated that he did not expect unnecessary extremes:

> One great source of these abuses in the parts of the waiting maids is that the authors of our farces in general have made persons of that rank the principal characters of the piece, while their mistresses have been little better than cyphers. But we are apt to believe that the authors of those pieces intended that the superiority of character in the servant should be discovered in the course of performance, not by the habit; and that the whole would have somewhat more the air of nature, if when they are both to appear often together upon the stage, the maid were at least not better dress'd than the mistress. . . . We would not desire things to be carry'd so far indeed on this occasion, as to expect a beau to enter in dirty boots, because he is to mention his having come a journey, but then we would not have an Orestes return from the temple, where at the instigation of Hermione he has been causing Pyrrhus to be assassinated, without one curl of his peruke out of order. Let the look of reality be kept up; and when the actor tells us of some dreadful bustle he has been in, we would have him shew some marks of it by the disorder of his person.

Desire for historical accuracy began to grow in the nineteenth century. The first notable production of this movement was a revival of Shakespeare's *King John* by Charles Kemble in 1823. It was designed by James Robinson Planché, a man who was both designer and historian and the author of *A History of British Costume.* Playbills proclaimed that the production was to be done "with an attention to Costume never equalled on the English Stage. Every Character will appear in the precise HABIT OF THE PERIOD, the whole of the Dresses and Decorations being executed from undisputable Authorities." Allardyce Nicoll points out in *The Development of the Theatre* that "Planché put on what was undoubtedly the first completely 'historical' production of Shakespeare's drama, for he paid attention not only to the hero's costume but to those of the meanest underling." Coordinating the costumes of the complete production was an entirely new idea. The lead costumes had often received special attention, but costumes for the extras were usually anything that happened to be handy at the time.

Historical accuracy and character meaning in costumes continued to develop throughout the nineteenth century. One theater group, the Meiningen Company, working out of the small German principality of Saxe-Meiningen in the last quarter of the century, was particularly noted for historical presentation of both sets and costumes and for its ensemble acting. This group greatly influenced both André Antoine (1858–1943), who proclaimed a doctrine of stage realism at his Théâtre Libre in Paris, and Konstantin Stanislavski (1863–1938) and his work at the Moscow Art Theatre. Stanislavski's reforms toward naturalism and ensemble acting are recognized by theater history as milestones, even though he tended to extremes at times. Theodore Komisarjevsky reports in *The Costume of the Theatre:*

> On the opening night in the production of the poetical and historical Russian play *Tzar Fyodor Ivanovitch,* the costumes of the Tzar, of the boyars,

Figure 1.9 Antony speaks over the body of Caesar in the Meiningen Company's production of *Julius Caesar* in London in 1881. The German company was noted for historical accuracy of both sets and costumes as well as for ensemble acting. From *The Illustrated London News*. Courtesy Theatre Museum, Victoria & Albert Museum, London (Crown Copyright).

and of the Moscow people were exact replicas of historical documents and made as far as possible of the genuine old materials. The long bejeweled brocade coats of the boyars had fur collars and were lined throughout with fur, which made them so heavy that it seemed almost impossible for the actors to breathe, let alone move in them. In the production of Julius Caesar the stage was so filled with brass armor, helmets, weapons, ample togas,

Figure 1.10 Gordon Craig, a leader in the movement against realism in both costume and stage setting, wanted to transform theater into "a place for visions." Craig's set and costumes for *Hamlet* at the Moscow Art Theatre in 1911.

and various minute details of costume and properties that Shakespeare's play was completely drowned.

A reaction against such slavish attention to historical detail arose by the end of the nineteenth century. The cry was for scenery and costumes that were evocative rather than descriptive, a simplicity that would suggest rather than reproduce. Both Adolphe Appia (1862–1928) and Gordon Craig (1872–1966) were leaders in this movement against realism. In Germany Max Reinhardt (1873–1943) became a primary influence with his desire for a visual interpretation that would reinforce the play's main themes and thus add an accent or viewpoint to the dominant flavor without unquestioning devotion to historical accuracy. This type of approach is still prevalent in theater today. The costume designer is the artist who specifically plans costumes to heighten the visual impact of the play and reinforce the flavor established for the production. Costumes in film and television tend to be more realistic, but there, too, the design concept is an important part of the whole presentation. It should not be an afterthought left to the whims of the actors, director, wardrobe mistress, or anyone who happens to walk through the auditorium.

◆ The Visual Impact

As a scene is revealed, impressions are created before a word is said. The visual impact of the setting or character is the first influence on the audience. It is the responsibility of the costume and scene designers to provide the proper atmosphere for the presentation and perhaps impart information that may not be explicit in the text.

Figure 1.11   Costume and set affect the audience before a word has been spoken. The opening picture of Haydn's opera *House Afire*, produced at Yale University in 1963. Costume design by Barbara Anderson. Set design by Lewis A. Crickard.

Figure 1.12 A costume can be layers of clothing, with very little of the body showing. Nun's costume for *The Devils,* produced at Carnegie Mellon University, 1970. Acrylic sketch by Cletus Anderson.

Figure 1.13 A costume can be nothing at all—or almost nothing, as in the case of these designed by Cletus Anderson for George Romero's film *Knightriders.* Photo by James Hamilton. Courtesy Laurel-Knights, Inc., New York.

◆ What Is a Costume?

Anything worn in a production is a costume, whether it be layers of clothing or nothing at all. A costume is technically defined as dress in general, including underpinnings, accessories, hairdressing, and makeup. It can be the distinctive style of a people, class, locality, or period. There is no such thing as a show without costumes, despite the fact that the desire to forgo this essential element is often proclaimed. A production to be done "in rehearsal clothes" is a production costumed as though the actors were rehearsing. A scene certainly can be presented in whatever the actors happen to be wearing at the time, but these clothes then become costumes and will have an influence on the audience. Obviously a woman portraying a young girl full of innocence and purity will have trouble convincing the audience of her sincerity if she is clad in a short-skirted, low-cut red knit dress and red patent leather sandals that lace to the knee. An actor in bare feet, no shirt, and fringed Levis can probably not overcome the obstacles in his way to be believed as an establishment businessman. Denying costumes by having the actors wear leotards and tights is not eliminating the costume effect at all; the uniformity itself makes a strong statement, as does the shape of the body revealed by these garments. While these are some obvious examples, there are also many subtle ways the visual impact can influence the audience, ways that reinforce the need for careful selection. The audience sees—and reacts, consciously or subconsciously. Anything worn in a production is a costume and should be as appropriate and meaningful as possible.

◆ The Psychology of Clothing

Any study of costume design entails a basic understanding of the psychology of clothing and how styles develop through various periods. The logical question that arises is "Why do styles develop as they do?" There are no definite logical answers. Quentin Bell has written an excellent book on the subject, *On Human Finery*. He bases much of his work on *The Theory of the Leisure Class* by Thorstein Veblen. According to Bell, Veblen found the study of clothes to be the study of monstrosities and absurdities, and Bell himself says, "We are dealing here not with abnormal, but with normal behavior, and when we begin to reflect upon it we discover our normal behavior is crazy."

In his book *Clothes*, James Laver postulates the idea that clothes are worn for three main reasons. The least important of these is the Utility Principle: garments are selected to counteract the effects of the cold or damp. Stronger motivation is found in the Hierarchical Principle: clothes are selected because they lend social status to the wearer and display his or her importance to the world. The third motivation cited by Laver is the Seduction Principle: clothes are donned to make the wearer look as attractive as possible, within the framework of what is considered attractive at any particular time in history. Laver applies the Hierarchical Principle more to men and the Seduction Principle more to women, though a combination of the two often comes into play. The Utility Principle is equally important to both sexes, but "The question of modesty hardly enters into the matter at all."

Figure 1.14 This 1914 Paris fashion could have been the sort of high style that led clothing theorist Quentin Bell to conclude "our normal behavior is crazy."

Figure 1.15 James Laver's Seduction Principle could very possibly lurk behind this advertisement for Arrow collars in a 1910 issue of *The Review of Reviews*.

Figure 1.16 This elegant *toilette de ville* would have cost a great deal of money in 1875. Conspicuous Consumption?

Bell and Veblen agree that styles of clothes are not really determined by such logical factors as climate and comfort. They feel that change in fashion is the result of the struggle of the classes, a way in which the aristocracy can declare its superiority. Social pressures can be very strong influences on behavior, and a means of maintaining social superiority is to dress properly according to the unwritten rules of society. For many years what was considered "socially proper" would keep the members of society in their appropriate niches independent of laws. Governments, in fact, attempted to legislate social status by means of sumptuary laws, which regulated dress by specifically stating who could wear what. Many such laws were enacted because their predecessors had not been effective—the old law didn't work, a new law was passed, it in turn proved ineffective, and another took its place. Where laws were ineffective, social pressure held sway. A woman once commented to Ralph Waldo Emerson that "a sense of being perfectly well dressed gives a feeling of inward tranquillity religion is powerless to bestow." Lord Chesterfield observed, "Dress is a very foolish thing, yet it is foolish for man not to be well dressed, in accordance with his rank and way of life."

Humans use clothing to express social superiority in a number of ways. Some of the categories posited by Bell and Veblen are:

1. *Conspicuous Consumption.* We adorn ourselves with clothes that cost a great deal of money. Because we can afford to do this and others cannot, we are therefore better than they.

Figure 1.17 Fox hunting—elitist, expensive, and useless—qualifies for Quentin Bell's category of Conspicuous Waste. Queen Alexandra, Queen Mary, and the Queen of Norway at a foggy meet of the West Norfolk Foxhounds.

2. *Conspicuous Leisure.* We dress in clothes that make it impossible to do practical work. For hundreds of years this was a sign of the nobility who could hire others to toil for them.
3. *Conspicuous Waste.* Based on the theory that practical things are not beautiful, we show our superiority by indulging in pastimes that have no useful purpose but are expensive to maintain. The most elite sports are polo, fox hunting, and yachting. Football is much too plebeian to be a style-setter. The military officer of the old-fashioned war was the epitome of waste—glorious to see but useless in battle.
4. *Vicarious Consumption.* This method of exhibiting supremacy developed with the Industrial Revolution. The merchant barons were not like the aristocrats who were born to money, and had neither the time nor the inclination to participate in the first three categories. They could express their superiority however, by ensuring that those connected to their households—their wives, children, and servants—were presented to the world in the most costly way possible.

Alison Lurie agrees with the Bell-Veblen theories and expands on them in her *The Language of Clothes.* Conspicuous consumption implies not only expensive clothes but also more of them. While the actual working peasants and servants require few garments, the person of status will often wear many layers. In addition to those layers, the wealthy male might be physically larger, for a man's girth could be associated with wealth, status, and power. This was particularly true in the latter part of the nineteenth century. Lurie speculates that when the world is hungry the physical ideal tends toward fat, and when food is more plentiful the physical ideal is thin. A quantity of clothes worn consecutively rather then simultaneously can also attest to the social importance of the wearer. For example, a Savile Row

Figure 1.18 The old-fashioned military officer has been characterized as the epitome of waste—glorious but useless. This splendidly mustachioed specimen was posted to the Bombay Lancers. Musée de l'Armée, Parigi.

Figure 1.19 Brill Brothers offered a large helping of Vicarious Consumption in the April 1920 *Harper's Bazaar.*

tailor in 1908 displayed a poster that depicts the 16 different costumes needed for an Edwardian gentleman to be correctly attired for every high-status activity. And just to get through the day his wife might need a morning costume, afternoon costume, tea gown, motoring outfit, and evening dress. Today this type of consumption is evident in the sports specialties, for in certain levels of society one must have the proper togs for tennis, hiking, golf, aerobic exercise, skiing, bicycling, swimming, scuba diving, and so forth—correct in both brand name and model. Conspicuous labeling has also become a status factor, in case the observer should miss the value of the garment. Actually, the garment is valuable because of the label, not necessarily because of any better quality in material or workmanship.

Lurie adds the category of theatrical consumption, which she terms the triumph of extravagance. Theatrical extravagance has a long history. Louis XIV of France, for example, did not stint at his festivities at Versailles, and fifteenth- and sixteenth-century masques were often quite sumptuous although performance times were relatively brief. Today, however, stage costumes are made to be worn many times and, if the play is successful, can be used more often and more vigorously than actual real-world garments. Film costume, on the other hand, continues the tradition of extravagance, for months of work and thousands of dollars can be expended on garments that will be seen for only a few moments.

It is the nature of fashion to evolve from one form to another, seldom taking any drastic new departures, often retaining atrophied parts. For example, the codpiece developed in the late fourteenth century to cover the opening in the front of men's hose when they changed from being separate pieces for each leg to one whole unit. For years it was a practical flap

Figure 1.20   A man's girth might be thought to reflect his wealth at certain periods, according to Alison Lurie. Above is James Buchanan ("Diamond Jim") Brady about 1913. (Compare Figure 1.24.)

Figure 1.21   Fashion is slow to discard atrophied parts. The codpiece, a practical clothing element when it developed in the late fourteenth century, stayed on as a decorative focus long after it was functional. Titian's portrait of Carlos V, painted about 1530, is in the Prado, Madrid.

that untied, but when the styles of trunk and leg covering changed this was no longer necessary. Rather than disappearing, the codpiece remained for more than 50 years as a padded-out and embroidered decorative element. In the eighteenth century buttons were used to fasten up the large cuffs of the coat sleeves and one was sewn on each side of the back of the coat to control the heavy pleats that sprang from the hip. To this day buttons can be found on men's coat sleeves, and one is still placed at the waist of the side back seam of the formal tailcoat, though the pleat has diminished to no more than a slight fold in the fabric. No proper gentleman would consider wearing an outfit without these details, though he probably has no idea why they are there.

Fashion dictates with no regard for the individual and no concern for how the style will look on many who copy it. It declares what will be considered beautiful and, therefore, what will be thought ugly by reason of no longer being fashionable. The immediate past is often thought the most ugly, for time usually softens what is considered unacceptable.

Figure 1.22 We see the past through the eyes of the present. Roman bath in Cecil B. DeMille's 1932 epic *The Sign of the Cross.*

The past is always seen through the eyes of the present, and the appreciation of the styles of the past is influenced by the style currently in vogue. This is often quite evident in purportedly historical productions, which can reflect more of the current period of the production than the period being reproduced. Nowhere is this more easily observed than in historical cinema created during this century: a Roman orgy filmed in the 1930s certainly has a different flavor than one done in the 1940s, 1950s, or 1960s. The closer the historical line is to that of the present period, the more it will be thought acceptable and attractive.

Since the thirteenth century the West has had an ever-changing concept of beauty as fashion has shifted, for fashion dictates the taste of the society. Many elements influence fashion, and it is probably not possible to pinpoint the absolute prime factor in every change. Occasionally prominent individuals, designers or laypeople, may have a strong influence on a style. As Henry VIII got wider he greatly influenced the bulky, horizontal, aggressively masculine style of his time. Marie Antoinette's love of extravagance certainly encouraged some of the extremes of the 1770s. Jacqueline Kennedy Onassis did more for the pillbox hat and the A-line dress than any ad campaign could have. Human nature, with its desire for change and its

Figure 1.23 Katharine Hepburn was a lovely queen in RKO's 1936 *Mary of Scotland*, but her silhouette has little in common with that of the real sixteenth-century Mary, Queen of Scots, shown here in a portrait now in the Uffizi Gallery, Florence. Photograph of Miss Hepburn by Bruehl-Bourges. Courtesy *Vogue*. Copyright ©1936 (renewed 1964) by The Condé Nast Publications Inc.

Figure 1.24 Henry VIII's girth probably influenced the styles of men's clothing in his time. The portrait is by Hans Holbein.

boredom with current styles, can give impetus to these fluctuating modes. A country that is politically strong and expanding will export its styles to others and will pick up external fashions as trade and influence are exchanged. Political and spiritual events often influence fashion; wars in particular affect the modes of a country. Religion, nationalism, and climate may also leave their mark on what is worn and why it continually changes.

One of the strongest determinants in the ever-changing face of fashion, and possibly the most consistent throughout history, is class struggle: the fight of the upper class to maintain its place. This struggle to uphold status and to keep one step ahead of those considered socially inferior causes an incessant fluctuation, a perpetual striving for improvement. Quentin Bell says that this can only happen in a society in which status has the possibility to change, where a middle class is always nipping at the heels of the upper, seeking to take that last step to the high plateau of fashion. When too many arrive, the plateau is moved, for fashion exists when it consists of a select number and is destroyed when too many are part of its elite world. In his *On Fashion* (1818), William Hazlitt explains, "[Fashion] exists only by its being participated among a certain number of persons, and its essence is destroyed by being communicated to a greater number. It is a continual struggle between 'the great vulgar and the small' to get the start of or keep up with each other in the race of appearances. . . ." Hazlitt describes how a style is adopted by the great, copied by "the slavish herd of imitators," then allowed to "sink without any further notice into disrepute and contempt. Thus fashion lives only in a perpetual round of giddy innovation and restless variety."

Fashion is not easily explained. The costume designer can be aware of the general theories and understand how garments may reveal many things about the people they adorn. He or she must deal with all the vagaries of fashion, take a firm grasp on the "normal behavior that is crazy" and the "perpetual round of giddy innovation and restless variety," and make it meaningful to an audience. Costume design is a world of challenges, and these challenges make it a stimulating, ever-changing, often difficult but seldom boring field of endeavor. It must interpret ideas that could defy explanation, distill them so a few strokes say a great deal, blend them with the innovations of many others, and produce a result that is at once individually creative and integrated so firmly into a whole that it cannot be extracted as a separate entity.

Figure 1.25   Marie Antoinette, at home in the extreme styles of the 1770s, may have encouraged greater excesses. Portrait by Marie Vigée-Lebrun.

◆ The Meaning of Clothes

There may be no overall logic to the way fashion moves through history, but clothes worn within any specific time period can reveal a great deal about the wearer. Whether modern or period, garments make a statement that is perceived and interpreted by an audience. Objectively, clothing can easily convey information about sex, age, occupation, social status, geography, season, time of day, action, and period. On a more subjective level the personality and attitudes of the wearer may be indicated by his or her garments. Since anything the actor wears is a costume that will communicate information to the audience, the designer should consider all these variables in order to select the correct message.

◆ What the Costume May Reveal

Figure 1.26   Fashion designer Rudi Gernreich promoted the unisex look at the beginning of the 1970s. Here his models Tom and Renée wear caftans.

Sex

For most of history, clothing indicates sex immediately and obviously, though the second half of this century has seen the introduction of more unisex garments. The manner in which clothing emphasizes or de-emphasizes the sex of the wearer can be very telling. A woman in a man-tailored suit with her hair in a bun affects others differently than one with long curls wearing a low-cut, frilly dress.

Age

Each era has its own symbols for youth and age. In general and logically, young people tend to reveal their figures because they are usually in better shape, while older people tend to cover themselves up—though the dictates of fashion in certain periods may negate this. Clothing in the twelfth century was bulky, loose, and flowing; good for the older figure but not particularly advantageous to the youthful one. In the fourteenth century clothing became extremely tight-fitting; youth was in its prime and age could look somewhat uncomfortable. In any period color, cut, and fit can suggest the age of the wearer and may give clues to how he or she feels about age. Should another age seem preferable, a person might wear clothes that are more suitable to someone either younger or older.

Occupation

Workers in many occupations can be instantly categorized by what they wear, and this recognition can cause an emotional response. The uniforms of the military and the police are easily recognized and act as symbols of the authority behind them. The costume of the priest and nun elicit a

Figure 1.27   Every era has its own symbols for youth and age. Fashion kept Victorian children very much in their place until they were considered old enough to assume adult apparel. An illustration from *La Mode Illustrée*, Paris, 1881.

Figure 1.28 Members of the medical profession often are recognized by their garments, no matter what the period. Nurses in training at Bellevue Hospital, New York, about 1900.

reaction to the church hierarchy they represent. The garb of the mail carrier, nurse, bellhop, chef, and many others proclaims a specific manner of making a living. Some clothes only give an indication of occupation. A man in jeans and a T-shirt does different work than a man in a business suit. Coveralls could indicate a mechanic, a painter, or someone cleaning his garage, but probably not a bank teller or a shoe salesman. Time can also vary the occupational meaning. A man in elaborate particolored clothes in the fourteenth century would most likely be a noble; in the fifteenth century he would be the court jester.

Social Status

For many years, a primary means of indicating social status was the practicality (or, more accurately, the impracticality) of the garments worn. The upper classes tended to wear clothes that made it impossible for them to do any work. Combinations of corsets, voluminous gowns, and hoops kept the noblewomen isolated and aloof from the workaday world. The cost of the garment was also commensurate with social status. The lower class had garments with fabric of lower quality, and in earlier periods with less decoration, fewer accessories, and simpler colors, as the cost of dye was prohibitive. While there are some general rules to be made about clothes and status, much depends upon the period in which the fashion functions. In the 1770s the woman of fashion had a high, elaborate coiffure and a gown with much color and fullness and plenty of ruffles and bows; her maid was drabber in color, plainer in fabric and style, and coifed simply. In the 1950s

Figure 1.29   There can be no visual question that these are members of a Scots regiment, the Forty-Second Highlanders. Musée de l'Armée, Parigi.

the lower-class girl might have worn a beehive, bouffant hairdo with full, ruffly, colorful clothes, while the society matron wore a basic black dress, simply but beautifully cut of fine fabric, adorned only with a gold circle pin or a string of pearls.

Geographic Area

The country in which a person lives always affects the way he or she dresses, but in the modern world the variations may not be strong. Small differences can be very significant, however, in creating a special effect. A woman's kerchief tied under the chin might seem European. Tied behind the neck it might be American suburban. Reversed to tie on top of the head it appears West Indian. Historically the costumes of the last six centuries in the Western world might differ more between classes than countries, though some national characteristics and climatic influences may be present. Specific national costumes, or elements of them, have strong recognition value, and the costumes of the Eastern world are very different from those of the West.

Figure 1.30　Although the shapes of the gowns are quite similar, it is easy to see which ladies are strolling in winter and which are about to embark on a spring walk. From *La Mode Illustrée,* 1880 and 1881.

Season and Weather

Clothing usually changes with the seasons in a very logical way. Hot weather brings out fewer garments of lighter fabrics; cold weather means more and heavier clothing. Historically the difference tended to be more in the weight of the fabric than in the shapes or number of garments. Women could be encased in layers of corsets, hoops, petticoats, and gowns in summer as well as winter. Logic is not always king in the fashion world, even in our enlightened modern age. The miniskirt in midwinter can leave little to the imagination and much to medication.

Time of Day and Occasion

Although a bathrobe, housedress, cocktail dress, evening gown, or nightgown might be worn at any time of the day, each tends to suggest a specific time. If a garment is worn at a time other than that usually accepted by society as proper, an even stronger statement is made. Any garment worn at an inappropriate time calls attention to itself. A person entering in pajamas when everyone else is dressed for a cocktail party must have a very specific reason for the incongruity.

Activity

Wearing certain clothes may imply that a specific activity is connected with the wearer, whether it has happened, is going on at the moment, or will happen in the future. A nightgown could lead to bed; a white sweater, shorts, socks, and athletic shoes may indicate a tennis game is in the offing. Enveloping black capes may imply a secretive meeting, and the buckling on of armor connotes an impending battle.

Historical Period

The shape of the clothes provides the first identification of a historical period, for each era casts its own shadow and has its own ideals of beauty. Historical costumes may not be exact replicas of what was actually worn. History may be the base, with a theatrical reality created that is more meaningful to the staged situation in which the costume will be presented.

Psychological Factors

In the areas discussed above, fairly objective decisions about wearing apparel can be made. There are specific clothes a middle-age, lower-class scrubwoman would have worn on her way to work in England on a snowy winter morning in 1870. She would most likely have worn heavy practical skirts and petticoats with a slight fullness to the back, sturdy shoes, a loose top, and a large, shapeless shawl. But if for some reason she were trying to pretend to her neighbors that she was really a lady's maid, a new world of costuming possibilities would open up. She might have gone to work and come back home in something with much more style—garments that were more fitted, a real bustle, and better shoes—to give the impression that her work gave her some status and let her mingle with a better class of people.

Figure 1.31   Rebellion has its own strict dress conformity. Hell's Angels, 1982. Wide World Photo.

Figure 1.32 Modart's ad in the November 1, 1921, *Vogue* appeals to the desire to be attractive, claiming the credit can go to the corset "when your appearance is admired."

Then when she got to her place of business and could no longer be seen by those who lived near her, she would have changed into the more practical garments.

Clothes express people's attitudes toward themselves and their society, both what they wear and how they wear it. A certain type of clothing can be worn to conform to a particular society or to rebel against it. If enough people rebel in the same direction, a new society is formed—with rules of conformity as strong as those of the old, but along slightly different lines. Should a person rebel only slightly, he or she may have the "proper" garments but wear them differently; absolute conformists might wear only those articles that would ensure their blending into the crowd at all times.

Clothes can be used to try to change an existing condition. Those who wish to move up the social ladder could dress not as their peers but as those in the group to which they aspire. On the emotional level, a person in a gloomy state of mind might deliberately choose clothes that appear more cheerful, while another might select clothes that reinforce the gloom and broadcast it to the world. The extrovert may wear something outlandish for the pure joy of causing a stir; the introvert may wear only what others are wearing for the security of being part of the crowd.

People often select clothes to fulfill the desire to be attractive to the opposite sex. Items can be chosen because they are thought to have sex appeal, though this may be an illusion perpetrated by the advertising firms of the world. The desire to be considered attractive is present in all age groups, and the parts of the body thought to be most alluring have varied considerably throughout history. What was once considered attractive in a specific historical setting must be considered along with the standards of beauty accepted by a contemporary audience.

Objective and subjective factors work together to determine why people clothe themselves as they do. Without an understanding on both levels a costume designer cannot fully develop the possibilities presented by the characters in a given situation. This understanding comes from extensive observation and research.

◆ Interpreting the Script and Enhancing the Characterization

The beginning of a theatrical presentation is a dramatic idea that may take the form of a script or merely a scenario. From this either the producer or director establishes the major focus of the interpretation. The actors and

Figure 1.33 A great many possibilities were explored to produce this character costume for Peachum in *The Threepenny Opera* by Brecht and Weill. It suggests a period in history, Peachum's class, and his place in the world. Design by S. Scott Welborn.

Figure 1.34 The costume for Saint Michael was more a decorative symbol than based on character. His wings were part of the set and not attached to his body at all. Design by Frank Bevan for a production of *Faust* at Yale University in 1949. Beinecke Rare Book and Manuscript Library, Yale.

designers help fill out this concept. Designers work within an established frame and add as much as they can to produce a specific dramatic result without placing undue emphasis on their particular aspect. Performing art is collaborative. Selfish goals might produce a grand effect, but the quality of the total production can suffer unless everyone works toward the common goal. As part of the team, the costume designer, as well as everyone else, should know as much as possible about all production areas. Unity is best achieved through knowledge, understanding, and good communication.

Costume interpretation draws from both the written material and the directorial approach. The costume designer studies the script thoroughly to understand its emotional tone and its physical requirements. The designer must look for the primary and secondary themes of the production and develop an understanding of the characters and their interrelationships. By carefully reading and rereading the script the designer should see how the plot flows, where the important moments are, which characters hold the primary focus, which are minor but have important input, and which merely fill out the scene. He or she can discern what changes occur as the story progresses. The director will probably offer an interpretation of the script to the designers. The ideal interaction occurs when the director and designers exchange ideas, discuss possible objectives, and together evolve the goals for the production. The director should be the focal point of these discussions: it is usually the directorial approach that balances all the elements and acts as the guide for the working relationship. The costume designer can develop an approach that considers both the impact of each individual costume and all the costumes seen as a whole, maintaining a balance between the two. If a costume operates on only one level, it will not work for the production. The problems that arise from this lack of integration may be most evident in the "star" costume, which can be designed with the wishes of one person in mind, often with little regard for the overall production concept.

It is possible for the costumes in a production to be simply decorative or symbolic if they contribute to telling the story, but the character costume is more common and grows out of the interpretation of the dramatic elements present in a certain role. The decorative costume is often no more than an extension of the scenic elements. The coronation robes of Richard III are not just typical symbols of a king but special garments selected because of a unique dramatic situation; the pages who stand behind his throne may be necessary only to fill out the scenic picture.

◆ Script Influence on the Character Costume

The character costume develops from what the characters say and do and what others say about them. It may or may not deal with what the writer has indicated in the stage directions, depending upon the specific director's approach. Just as people dress according to the many influences on them in daily life, so does the dress of the actor reflect the influences of the script. Sometimes the character is not well delineated and remains two-dimensional and obvious. The characters in the musicals *L'il Abner* and *Superman* are never any deeper than the two-dimensional comic-strip characters on which they are based. A clichéd villain may very well wear a black hat. An ingenue might be costumed in a dress with frothy yellow ruffles, conforming to stereotyped audience expectations; but if she is trying too hard to make an impression her character takes on another dimension, and too many ruffles or too much jewelry may help to show this.

As the character progresses through a production, so can the costumes progress to underline the change. Costumes can indicate differences of location or time, emotional modifications within the character, or mood

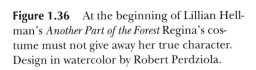

Figure 1.36 At the beginning of Lillian Hellman's *Another Part of the Forest* Regina's costume must not give away her true character. Design in watercolor by Robert Perdziola.

Figure 1.35 A "small-town boy goes to the big city" cliché costume was just what was needed for the title character in a Carnegie Mellon University production of *Merton of the Movies* in 1982. Pencil sketch by Cletus Anderson.

variations of the script. When Blanche first appears in Tennessee Williams' *A Streetcar Named Desire* she is a strong figure trying to maintain a foothold on reality. As the play progresses this foothold weakens and the strength crumbles. This should be evident in what Blanche wears and how she wears it. For her first entrance her clothes are appropriate for the situation and worn with confidence; as she exits in the final scene she appears lost and uncertain. While the costume can be a great aid in underscoring character development, the design must be considered carefully so that it will not anticipate an action. It must show what the actor is when he begins the scene, not predetermine the outcome of an interchange that will take place. Regina in Lillian Hellman's *Another Part of the Forest* must seem a lovely, charming, dutiful daughter. The audience must not immediately recognize her as the cold, hard, calculating woman the play later reveals her to be.

◆ Symbolizing the Role

The costume should give as much meaning to the character as possible, but this does not necessarily mean it should symbolize the role. There may be good reasons not to dress a woman of ill repute in a tight-fitting, leg-revealing red satin dress. A jealous wife need not necessarily wear green; nor should young lovers both appear clad in pale blue so the audience knows at once that they will end up together. The actor, not the costume, is the primary means of communication to the audience. The costume designer should not try to do the actor's job. There are, of course, occasions when blatant symbols are just right. This usually happens when the character itself is not well defined and the action requires instant symbolic recognition. In Jean Giraudoux's *The Madwoman of Chaillot,* the costume designer has a wonderful opportunity for careful individualized character delineation in the costumes of the four elderly women because the script tells a great deal about each; but the presidents, prospectors, and press agents sent to oblivion are presented by the playwright only as symbols and must be easily identifiable to the audience.

◆ Subjective Character Indications

Even the more subtle subjective indications of character must be effective on two levels. They can enrich the costume by a careful attention to detail that expands the understanding of the character, but the costume must seem appropriate to the situation whether the subjective indications come across to the audience or not. The designer might decide an actor playing a conservative part should wear a dark blue suit and lighter blue shirt; the addition of a red paisley tie and handkerchief can indicate that he secretly wishes to break out of the boring mold that confines him, adding subtle dimension to the effect. If this works within the context of the scene, so much the better. If, however, the tie and handkerchief become the misplaced focus of attention, they must change no matter how strongly the designer and actor feel about the innermost desires of the character. It's possible for the designer, actor, or even director to become more subjective than the production can stand by bringing too many subtle nuances to a character through what he wears and how he wears it. This can prove confusing to the audience guided solely by what is presented to it. If the extras reinforce the primary interpretation, fine; should they start off in a direction of their own, they must change.

◆ The World of the Production

Costume in any production is used to help create a reality for a specific situation. This reality is removed from the everyday world because it is intended for presentation to an audience. The degree of difference from the real world varies immensely with the type of production and the manner in which it will be presented, and the costume style should reflect this. The script will give the first indication of the world to be created. Both the subject matter and style of language can guide the designer to an effective approach. Costumes for Shakespeare's *Hamlet* differ from those of Arthur Miller's *Death of a Salesman,* though both plays are tragedies. Elsinore is peopled with characters who speak in iambic pentameter, are confronted with monumental problems, and must fill the vast spaces that suggest the castle around them. Willy Loman lives in a small, middle-class world full of the problems that could beset almost any man, though even here the designer

Figure 1.37 The world of *Hamlet* suggests heightened feelings; sketches can be made with a broad stroke. Costume for Claudius. Watercolor by Cletus Anderson.

Figure 1.38 Willy Loman's *Death of a Salesman* world is small; his costume should reflect attention to small details. Pencil sketch by Cletus Anderson.

must search for those things that make Willy special and help the audience want to cry out with his wife "So attention must be paid!"

The type of physical presentation can also greatly affect the style of costumes that will best fit into this world. Costumes designed for a production of *Hamlet* to be presented in a 2,000-seat auditorium with a proscenium stage would be different than those created for an arena that seats 200 or for a television production. In the large proscenium house most of the audience is at a distance from the actors and the impact of the costumes must carry across that distance; in the smaller arena most audience members are near enough to the actors to see even delicate detailing; and in the world of television production the camera brings the viewer right to the performer. Extensive scenic elements can contribute to the atmosphere framing the costumes on the proscenium stage; an arena eliminates many background pieces and focuses more on the actors themselves; and film and television can use both effects in the same presentation.

The amount of money available to mount a production also greatly affects the type of world that can be created. As nice as it would be to consider art only for art's sake, ten costumes that can be made with a $200 budget differ greatly from ten that cost $2,000. This does not mean the former will necessarily be of poorer quality than the latter, but they will be different. Limitations can be parlayed into ways of exploring new possibilities and discovering new and exciting solutions.

Figure 1.39   Time and money must be considered when designing. The single costume for Beulah will take more than twice as much of both than the costumes for all four bathing beauties. Designs in pencil by Cletus Anderson for *Merton of the Movies.*

◆ Costumed Groups and Movement

Many productions use the costume as a decorative element not based on character development but still founded on the basic interpretation or approach to the piece. Even many serious dramas have scenes based on spectacle where some of the actors are really part of the scenery and basically help create an appropriate environment in which the action takes place. Unlike the set, which is more stationary, here the concern is with a moving visual impact that may shift many times during the scene. The character of

Figure 1.40 A group will be much more interesting if each member is given individual characteristics. Pencil sketch by Cletus Anderson for the Simsbury Gents in *Merton of the Movies.*

the individual actor does not concern the designer in this case; what is important is the character of the scene and the total feeling of all the costumes. A thorough discussion must take place with the director to clarify the blocking and determine the color effect of the mass of costumed actors.

There are instances where groups of costumed actors add to the overall atmosphere of the production, though the individuals within the groups may not be well delineated. The crippled masses of Bertolt Brecht's *Mother Courage* create a specific visual effect, as do the nymphs and reapers in the masque scene of Shakespeare's *The Tempest.* The inherent characterization of the chorus line of a 1950s musical may be only skin-deep, but some sort of group characteristic does define its presence. In *Guys and Dolls* the Hot Box girls differ from the Salvation Army team, who in turn are not like the boys of Nathan Detroit's floating crap game, yet the costume scheme must encompass the groups and present a unified production along with the more specifically characterized principals. Designing a group of costumes for a specific effect often takes a special approach. The group characteristic must be clearly defined, and within this the costumes that make up the group should be designed for specific people. These may not be differentiated in the script, but the designer can give to each person attributes that make him or her unique within the group. Given a "crowd of townspeople" the result can be bland and uninteresting for both the designer and the audience if a group of miscellaneous clothes are assembled and distributed merely to cover bodies. If the designer sees the crowd as an assembly of individuals—the town drunk, the busybody, the shoe salesman, the piano teacher, the mailman—these people are more real and make up a crowd with more vitality, thereby enriching the production.

Costumes create a constantly shifting pattern of colors, textures, and sculptural shapes, so the visual impact of a group of costumes must be effective in numerous compositions. Each costume should be planned in relation to the total effect. The picture may shift; the focus remains. A certain idea might be perfect for a particular moment, but unless it also works with the prior and following action, it can't be used. One example might be found in *Macbeth*. Lady Macbeth is at home, reading her husband's letter telling her of the witches, their prophecy, and the promotion he has already received. A messenger comes, Macbeth enters, and husband and wife are reunited. A designer might wish to costume Lady Macbeth in something casual and intimate to accentuate the sexual bond between the couple. In just a few moments, however, she must return to greet King Duncan and his retinue and take center stage amid a group of nobles. Her costume, with only minor changes, must accommodate both situations.

Figure 1.41   The fashion plate can be quite elegant but does not necessarily deal with character or dramatic interpretation. Figure from a Bergdorf Goodman ad in *Vogue*, October 1976.

◈ Costume Design and Fashion Design

Costume design is quite different from fashion design and experience in one area may be of little help in the other. Costume design concerns itself with dramatic interpretation and character; it deals with the overall production concept first, the costumes as a whole, then the individual costume. Fashion design need not be collaborative, nor is it concerned with character relationships. Certain trends are set that may or may not be followed; a unity may be established for a particular show but it is not governed by the thoughts and actions of others; a reaction is sought from the finished garment, but a reaction based solely on the garment and not on its relationship to the wearer. Even the method of presentation of the idea differs greatly. The fashion plate is elegant, characterless, often de-emphasizing sex. The costume plate strives for character, life, and a flavor of the production.

◈ Costume Design and Collaboration

Performing art is collaborative. Costume design is only one element of the whole—it blends with the actors, sets, and lights to fill out a director's interpretation of a writer's idea. But within these confines costume design can be an art in itself, given the right preparation and execution. Costumes that "just happen" might not actually detract from the performance, but an opportunity would have been missed to enrich the production. The current trend in theater is toward using more selective scenery and prop pieces and letting the costumes carry a greater responsibility for creating the visual atmosphere. By their very nature thrust and arena stages are quite costume- and property-oriented. The television and film camera focuses on the actor and costume more intimately than ever before. As the emphasis on the costume grows, so does the responsibility of the costume designer, but it is a responsibility with very specific limitations. Once the script or scenario is selected and the direction for the interpretation chosen, everything used to realize the goal must work for a unified production.

◆ Chapter 2
The Costume Approach

Preceding page and Figure 2.1 Designer Allison Achauer was amused by the thought of creating costumes for an impoverished theater group presenting an 1830s version of *The Threepenny Opera* using inexpensive items that could easily be found but that were also appropriate for the characters. Polly Peachum reflects the proletariat image her father cultivates in athletic socks, tablecloths, and boxer shorts. Macheath's gang wears elements they might have looted from houses: curtains, rugs, tufted upholstery, wicker, plant pots, and garden hose.

Figure 2.1

The beginning of a project can be a very exciting time for a designer. A new challenge is present; a new world waits to be researched, probed, and developed. Even if the designer is working on a familiar script, this is a fresh approach involving different people and another opportunity for the exchange of ideas. The costume designer should be eager to develop concepts that will reinforce the interpretation that grows from this collaboration. The creative urge should remain strong even though there are many steps that must be taken before pencil is set to paper to draw a costume.

◆ First Impressions

The costume designer's first concern is to read the script and become thoroughly familiar with the problems and challenges at hand. The initial readthrough should determine the emotional impact of the piece; dealing with specific costume problems will come later. The designer should discover the aesthetic needs and overall mood, which may bring to mind colors, textures, fabrics, silhouette, and detail treatment. Within the overall feeling some scenes will have their own emotional requirements, as will certain characters. Thoughts should be jotted down during this initial reading; more specific questions and observations noted during a second or third time through. These ideas can then be taken to the director, with whom they can be discussed to clarify the interpretation that will be used for the entire production.

Take, for example, Molière's *Le Bourgeois Gentilhomme*. The immediate impact is one of bright frivolity and surface lushness, color at fairly high intensity, crisp rather than heavy fabrics. Monsieur Jourdain, the would-be gentleman, is the broadest character in a broadly treated comedy. There are three sets of lovers who must reflect differences in their ages and stations. A number of visual aspects can be considered to advance the spectacle, climaxing with the Turkish scene, in which Jourdain is gulled by his disguised friends as they perform a ridiculous ceremony to make him a "*mamamouchi.*" Written at the time of the French Baroque, a period of much excess, Molière is having fun at the expense of the "stylish" element of his society. The designer should be familiar with the excesses of the time, record any ideas that come to mind, and review these ideas frequently to keep the creative process in motion. Not just words, but pictures, fabrics, rough sketches, and any other visual aids should be gathered together. Words conjure up different images to different people. Anything that actually can be seen and discussed will help establish a more solid common ground for the entire production staff. The designer will also be better prepared for an intelligent interchange of ideas if he or she is knowledgeable about the writer, understands something of the cultural milieu in which the writer lived and worked, and is familiar with the social history behind the piece.

Figure 2.2   Quick sketches can be used to suggest ideas to the director. These were done for Molière's *Le Bourgeois Gentilhomme,* produced at the Great Lakes Shakespeare Festival, Lakewood, Ohio, 1969. Designs by Cletus Anderson.

◆ Determining the Basic Interpretation

A discussion between the director and the designers should clarify the basic concepts and settle the interpretation to be used. In most theatrical productions and films the director establishes the guiding concept and sets the lead to be followed by all others working on the show; in television this may be done by the producer. The world of the performing arts is collaborative, but each production needs one guiding hand. The director or producer should function as a leader, however, not as an absolute dictator. All the designers should contribute ideas that might enrich the production.

The success of the visual aspects of the project depends upon good coordination between the sets, lights, and costumes. The shapes and colors to be used to establish specific moods must be agreed upon by all, for each visual element must interact with the others to enhance the total effect and create a unique world for the production.

The director may have one central theme that will stand as the key. From this will come a choice of period. The degree of reality to be used is established, although it may not be maintained at the same level for all the

Figure 2.3   These costumes for *A Little Night Music* by Stephen Sondheim were designed for a production at Carnegie Mellon in 1989, and are based on the clothing of the period in which the play is set. Watercolor sketches by Cletus Anderson.

different design elements. For example, a production of *A Little Night Music* done on an arena stage would most probably use costumes influenced strongly by the actual clothes of the time, but the set could give just a suggestion of the architecture and properties that would create the numerous locations. Variations in approach can mesh together well if those involved clearly understand the aims set forth. Scenery entails more than recreating a specific place; it requires a selection of elements that define a point of view, all the while keeping in mind the limitations of the performing space. This can lead to a degree of stylization. The costume, based on the human figure, is more limited, but still may not need to be absolutely authentic or realistic. A stylized set can lead to arbitrary lighting, in which light is used to its best dramatic advantage without the need for a motivating source of illumination (such as the moon, a chandelier, or an incandescent bulb).

◆ Coordinating Sets and Costumes

Ideas for either costumes or sets can come first. There is no rule that one has to follow the other. If the dramatic values of one are more important to the production, then they may receive first consideration.

Some of the areas that need a common understanding are:

Period and Source Material. One design element may need to be more realistic than another, but both can be based upon the same background material. Often specific painters or books are used as key references. Such visual inspiration can vary widely, from the paintings of Michelangelo to the drawings of Aubrey Beardsley to the Sears Roebuck catalog. The best feeling for a period often comes from sources contemporary to the period in which the work is set: statues, illustrated manuscripts, paintings, photographs, etchings, catalogs, magazines, and so on. The basic guide to a color scheme often can be found in a painting. *A Midsummer Night's Dream* might be staged basing sets and costumes on a pastoral scene by Fragonard or the shadowy atmosphere of *Hamlet* on a painting by Rembrandt.

Color and Contrast. A limited palette can produce a specific dramatic effect. An entire production could be based on one color, or specific colors could be assigned to various scenes. There are three types of contrast to consider. The contrast of all the elements can be kept close: the set can be darker with lighter costumes, or the set lighter with darker costumes. If the light-to-dark ratio is close, color can be used to separate the actors from the sets. Light will usually mold the actor, but if the costume and set colors are too similar the actor will tend to blend into the background. There are instances, of course, where this is desirable. If the set is dark and light costumes are used, the lighting can easily highlight the figure. Light sets with dark costumes present certain problems, however, for the details of the face and figure tend to blur and a high light level may accent the set too strongly.

Type of Detail.   The approach to the detailing of the set and properties might well influence the costumes, and vice versa. If one is scaled up and the other kept at a realistic level, the realistic element will lose importance. When the set is to be quite detailed and busy, the costume approach must separate the actors from the active background. If one element approaches the detailing as a means to comment on the period, this will influence the audience and the way it perceives the other elements.

Movement and Performance Space.   Any potential movement and blocking problems should be considered and a feeling for the desired pictures should be explored. The set and costume designers and director must deal with such questions as: How will the movement of the actors be affected by the performance space? Must the costume be designed to permit

Figure 2.4   The scale of the detail is heightened in this costume for one former wife in Béla Bartók's one-act opera *Bluebeard's Castle*, produced at Carnegie Mellon University in 1976. Design by Cletus Anderson.

easy movement? Must the costumes be scaled to work within space determined by the sets, or will the costumes determine the scale of the sets?

Textures and Fabrics. A realistic production may dictate the types of textures and fabrics that will be used, but designers often deliberately decide to let a specific style predominate. The choice could be for heavy nubby textures; deep, rich piles; shiny, reflective fabrics; or a light, airy, floating treatment. If the designers' ideas about textures and fabrics are not well coordinated an imbalance could result. *A Midsummer Night's Dream* done in heavily encrusted, realistic Elizabethan costumes against a chiffon-swagged forest will never mesh properly. Different types of textures and fabrics can be deliberately mixed, but this should be done for a specific result, not just by accident.

Figure 2.5 Coarse textures are indicated in this sketch for the Parade Master in the film *Knightriders*, directed by George Romero. Design by Cletus Anderson.

◆ Establishing Needs

When the general trends have been set, the costume designer can get down to specifics with the director to establish a clear understanding of what is to happen. Quick sketches or pictures from source books provide a concrete reference that will minimize the possible confusion of verbal description. The designer should find out how the director wishes to use the costumes, make sure the director knows how they will affect the actors, and explain the limitations they may impose on the production. The director should provide a scene breakdown that details who will be in what scene. The two should also settle the time sequences involved and what costume changes might be necessary to indicate them. If the sequencing of the script is to be changed, this should be discussed. Moving scenes around or eliminating intermissions can affect the costume treatment. With this information the designer can now go back to the script and organize his or her work.

◆ The Costume Lists

Once the preliminary approach is set the costume designer can define the task at hand as concretely as possible and determine the actual physical needs of the production. It should be possible to lay the groundwork in a systematic way that will enable the designer to express ideas artistically and develop a costume sketch that will satisfy both the dramatic and the practical needs of the project.

The preliminary costume tally should include every costume or part of costume that will be needed. The designer must go through the script, listing every character in each scene with an indication of what he or she is wearing, even if it is a repeat of something worn before. If a coat is added or a garment taken off, this must be noted. Any extras, crowds, servants, armies, or the like must be tallied. On the same list any action that will affect the costumes should be included, plus any color or costume prop references in the script, annotated to indicate whether these are necessary to the action or can be changed to accommodate a different scheme. Notes should be made where any costume changes occur to anticipate any possible problems involved. Routine information is not the only objective at this time, and clues to the characterizations and imagery found in the script can also be assembled. This is often a long list, unwieldy in its original form, but a necessary step on the path to the actual working outlines.

From these preliminary notations come two essential charts: the Costume List (page 54) and the Costume Scene Breakdown (page 55). These may need to be established simultaneously since decisions made about one may affect the other. The costume scene breakdown lists each character and each scene in chart form, as shown in the example following the scenario. Each character is listed under the scenes in which he or she appears, with an indication of the appropriate clothes. The costume list indicates each character and each different costume he or she will wear. Each costume is numbered consecutively so at the end of the list the total number of costumes in the show is easily seen, and each costume for a particular character is numbered so that the quantity of costumes for any given character is readily available. The list is broken down into men's costumes and women's costumes, or in larger productions principal men, principal women, chorus men, chorus women, and so forth.

The following scenario is taken from Tennessee Williams' *Summer and Smoke,* Part One of the original Broadway version. This extremely brief indication of the plot may help explain how the costume lists are compiled, but this example will be more useful to the designer who reads the actual script. The scene for *Summer and Smoke* is a simultaneous setting, showing a fountain and angel in the town park or square, the parlor of the Episcopal rectory, and the office in the neighboring doctor's home. The action is continuous.

Prologue   *Dusk, an evening in May in the first few years of this century.* John Buchanan and Alma Winemiller, 10-year-old children, are playing near the fountain. Alma already has "the dignity of an adult; there is a quality of extraordinary tenderness or spirituality in her."

Scene 1   *July 4th, shortly before the First World War.* The scene moves from fading sunlight to dusk at the fountain and town square. The Reverend and Mrs. Winemiller, Alma's parents, sit on the bench. Mrs. Winemiller has "slipped into a state of perverse childishness. She is known as Mr. Winemiller's 'cross.'" Alma sings offstage as John enters. He is "brilliantly and restlessly alive in a stagnant society." A couple, Dusty and Pearl, stroll by. Dr. Buchanan, John's father, confronts him, then leaves. Alma enters, flustered after her song, now "prematurely spinsterish," "dressed in pale yellow and carrying a yellow silk parasol." She asks her father to open her bag for her to get her handkerchief. The others leave and Alma and John talk. Rosa Gonzales crosses to the fountain, dressed "in almost outrageous finery, with lustrous feathers on her hat, greenish blue, a cascade of them, also diamond-and-emerald earrings." Nellie Ewell, a girl of 16, stops to chat with John and Alma. John leaves and Roger Doremus, "a small man, somewhat like a sparrow," comes to walk Alma home.

Scene 2   *Inside the Rectory.* It is obviously some time later. Mrs. Winemiller has a white plumed hat she has stolen from a shop in the town, concealing it in her parasol. Later in the scene this hat gets torn in a fight with Alma. Mr. Winemiller passes through the room, concerned about the cost of the hat and the embarrassing situation in which his wife has placed them. Alma is getting ready for her group meeting, to be held that evening. She invites John, who is seen in his house. Nellie comes by for her singing lesson.

Scene 3   *Inside the Rectory.* The meeting is in progress, attended by Roger; Vernon, "a willowy younger man with an open collar and Byronic locks"; Mrs. Basset; and Rosemary, "a wistful older girl with a long neck and thick-lensed glasses." John enters, "immaculately groomed and shining," carrying a jacket he leaves behind when he hastily departs.

Scene 4   *Inside the Doctor's Office.* John's arm is wounded and he and Rosa are bandaging it. Alma enters, ostensibly to ask old Dr. Buchanan to give her something to calm her nerves. John loans her his handkerchief, takes her pulse using his pocket watch, then unbuttons and speaks of the "little pearl buttons" on her blouse when he listens to her heart. He also comments on her topaz ring.

Scene 5   *Inside the Rectory.* A few days later; Alma and her parents are in the parlor. Alma is going out with John and before she leaves picks up a hat, gloves, and veil.

Scene 6   *An arbor at the Moon Lake Casino, a few moments later.* John, in a white suit, and Alma stand in the arbor because Alma refuses to enter the Casino. A waiter, Dusty, brings some wine. John lifts her veil to kiss her, then offends her and leaves to call a taxi.

The scenario for Part Two is not included here, but two important costume references in the second half of the play should be mentioned. In Scene 7, John is "dressed, as always, in a white linen suit." In the following scene John says ". . . every evening I put on a clean white suit. I have a dozen. Six in the closet and six in the wash."

The preliminary list for a production of this play might read as follows:

Prologue.   Early twentieth century, town square and fountain.

ALMA WINEMILLER, age 10. Adult dignity, tenderness, spirituality.
JOHN BUCHANAN, age 10.
} Both in school clothes.

I.1.   *Just before World War I, town square and fountain.*

REV. WINEMILLER Episcopalian.
MRS. WINEMILLER Childish and stubborn.
JOHN Brilliant and restlessly alive.
PEARL
DUSTY } Strolling couple.
DR. BUCHANAN
ALMA Prematurely spinsterish. Pale yellow dress and yellow silk parasol. Bag and handkerchief.
ROSA GONZALES Outrageous finery, hat with greenish blue lustrous feathers, diamond-and-emerald earrings.
NELLIE EWELL Age 16.
ROGER DOREMUS Small, like a sparrow.

} All rather dressed up for the Fourth of July

I.2.   *Some time later, Rectory and Doctor's house.*

MRS. WINEMILLER White plumed hat (gets torn) and parasol.
REV. WINEMILLER As before.
ALMA Preparing for company. QUICK CHANGE IN AND OUT.
JOHN At home.
NELLIE Regular everyday wear.

I.3.   *That evening, the Rectory.*

ROGER Dressed for meeting.

VERNON Willowy, open collar, Byronic locks.

MRS. BASSETT Dressed for meeting, widow.

ROSEMARY Wistful, long-necked, thick-lensed glasses.

ALMA Dressed for meeting. Small buttons on blouse. QUICK CHANGE IN.

JOHN Immaculately groomed and shining. Carrying jacket and hat.

I.4.   Later that evening, Doctor's office.

JOHN Wounded arm, bandage. Shirt and trousers rather messed up. Handkerchief and pocket watch. MEDIUM-QUICK CHANGE.

ROSA Has come from Casino.

ALMA As before. Blouse unbuttons, line "little pearl buttons." Topaz ring referred to by line.

I.5.   A few days later, the Rectory.

ALMA Dressed to go out, picks up hat, gloves, veil. QUICK CHANGE IN.

REV. WINEMILLER As before, perhaps sweater instead of suitcoat.

MRS. WINEMILLER At-home dress.

I.6.   A few minutes later, the arbor outside the Moon Lake Casino.

JOHN White suit.

ALMA As before, hat, veil, and gloves on.

DUSTY Waiter.

From this preliminary list can come the Costume Scene Breakdown (page 55) and the Costume List on page 54. Not every item of the costume needs to be listed at this time, for until the actual designing is done, all the parts may not be known. Color indications and costume pieces specified in the script should be considered carefully to discern if they are necessary or merely a suggestion of the writer. In this case John's white suits are quite important in delineating his character, but Alma's yellow dress could possibly be a different color if that seems more appropriate to the production. The description of Rosa's costume helps the reader understand the playwright's intentions, but the actual costume could vary from those indications if the spirit of Williams' description is retained. On the other hand, Alma's blouse should have the little buttons John refers to as he listens to her heart. Any specific mention of costumes in the script should be noted so it can be discussed by designer and director.

The discussion should also clarify when costume changes occur, any quick-change problems, and any extras that might be needed but are not mentioned in the script. For example, in *Summer and Smoke* the director might find it unnecessary for Mrs. Winemiller to have two different day dresses and at the same time decide that there should be ten extra townspeople onstage in Scene 1. The costume count has just changed from 25 to 34: one costume cut and 10 added. An unanticipated advantage could come from the added people. The director could use them to dress the stage atmospherically for a few moments after Alma and Roger leave, thus allowing Alma a bit more time for her quick change.

◆ Costume List

Principal Men
1. JOHN, age 10 school clothes
2. JOHN I white suit
3. JOHN II at home casual
4. JOHN III dirty shirt and pants.
   MEDIUM-QUICK CHANGE IN
5. REV. WINEMILLER Clerical suit, add sweater
6. ROGER DOREMUS I summer dressy suit
7. ROGER II medium dressy
8. DR. BUCHANAN good work suit

Principal Women
9. ALMA, age 10 school clothes
10. ALMA I good dress (yellow?), purse, parasol
    QUICK CHANGE OUT
11. ALMA II day skirt and blouse. QUICK CHANGE
    IN & OUT
12. ALMA III meeting outfit. QUICK CHANGE IN
    & OUT
13. ALMA IV dressy dress, hat with veil, gloves
    QUICK CHANGE IN
14. MRS. WINEMILLER I good dress
15. MRS. WINEMILLER II day dress, parasol, plumed
    hat (breakaway)
16. MRS. WINEMILLER III day dress
17. ROSA I very dressy, plumed hat
18. ROSA II medium dressy
19. NELLIE I dressy, young
20. NELLIE II everyday dress
21. MRS. BASSETT medium dressy, widow

Featured Men
22. VERNON medium dressy
23. DUSTY I working-class dressy
24. DUSTY II waiter

Featured Women
25. ROSEMARY medium dressy
26. PEARL working-class dressy

◆ Time Considerations and Changes

The director may not wish to have intermissions where they are indicated in the script. A play written in four or five acts is now often done with only one or two intermissions, the other breaks being dealt with as though they were pauses between scenes. This may create a situation in which only a few moments are available for a costume change. Double-casting may also pose time problems. If an actor is playing more than one role, special attention must be paid to the time between his exit as one character and his entrance as another, particularly if the audience is not intended to be aware of the double casting (which may well involve time-consuming makeup and hair changes).

◆ The Flexible, Confident Designer

Though many decisions may have been made, the designer must bear in mind that a production is always a work in progress. Seldom, if ever, are things finalized in the preliminary stages. As the work progresses from beginning ideas to final presentation, many changes take place. Good designers know when it is necessary to compromise and when they should be firm, but the attitude must remain cooperative. The designer must feel

◆ Costume Scene Breakdown

	Prologue	Pt.1, Sc.1	Pt.1, Sc.2	Pt.1, Sc.3	Pt.1, Sc.4	Pt.1, Sc.5	Pt.1, Sc.6
Alma, Age 10	School clothes						
John, Age 10	School clothes						
Alma		1 Good dress	II Day skirt and blouse QUICK	III Meeting outfit QUICK	Repeat III	IV Dressy QUICK	Repeat IV
John		I White suit	II Casual	Repeat I			Repeat I
Rev. Winemiller		I Clerical suit				Repeat I add sweater	
Mrs. Winemiller		I Good dress	II Day dress plumed hat			III Day dress	
Rosa		I Very dressy			II Medium dressy		
Nellie		I Good dress	II Everyday dress				
Dr. Buchanan		Good worn suit					
Roger		I Summer dressy		II Medium dressy			
Mrs. Bassett				Medium dressy			
Vernon				Medium dressy			
Rosemary				Medium dressy			
Dusty		I Working-class dressy					II Waiter
Pearl		I Working-class dressy					

Figure 2.6   Original ideas for the costume of Bedelia in the film *Creepshow*, led to the sketch at left above. But costumes often change as characters develop through conferences and casting. The photograph shows Bedelia as played by Viveca Lindfors. Design by Barbara Anderson. Photo courtesy LaurelShow, Inc., New York.

confident in what he or she is doing and relay that confidence to the director so that a good exchange of ideas can continue to take place. Nothing can be more debilitating to creative energies than the feeling that a battle must be fought with every new decision. Fewer problems arise if a director has had time to prepare for the production and has carefully thought through the guiding concepts. Often, however, work begins on a show before much of the groundwork has been laid. Preliminary ideas may change significantly as work progresses. As a partner in a collaborative venture, the designer should have a feeling for the director's method of working and must prepare for whatever will come. Practically any problem can be solved with enough time and enough money. Difficulties arise when either or both are in short supply, as is too often the case.

◆ Assessing the Work

The number of costumes in a show may be quite easy to determine, but the number alone does not indicate the scope of the challenge facing the designer. Four other elements are equally important. The five critical questions that must be answered are:

1. How many costumes are there?
2. How complex are they?
3. How much time is there to build them?
4. How much skilled help is available to build them?
5. How much money can be spent on them?

To answer these questions take into account the following:

1. When arriving at the final costume tally, consider every possibility. It is always much easier to cut than to add when time and cash budgets have already been set. Consider overcoats and large capes as a second costume, for they cost money and take time to build. Consider underclothes that are visible to the audience as a separate costume for the same reason: they require more time and money than undergarments that are not seen, which may be pulled from stock or the actor's private wardrobe. Check carefully for second costumes that may be needed because the actor appears first neat and all together and later, in ostensibly the same costume, in a distressed condition. Kate appears in her wedding dress at the time of the ceremony (Figure 2.7, left). A short time later she is seen after Petruchio has dragged her through the mud and mire (Figure 2.7, right). The same costume could not be used, for it could never be sufficiently cleaned for the next night's performance. A duplicate that is always in the wretched condition must be made.

Figure 2.7 In *Kiss Me Kate* when Kate is married her dress is in good condition (above left), but soon after the ceremony the wedding gown is much the worse for wear. Double costumes are a must in such situations. Design by Cletus Anderson for the Carnegie Mellon production, 1977. Set design by Eduardo Castro.

2. Consider carefully the period to be used and the social class revealed by the costumes. Two Elizabethan court costumes may be much more difficult to build and more expensive than costumes for a dozen medieval peasants. Ball gowns are more of a problem than bathing suits. It is often useful to break down the costume list in terms of classes of costumes: Type A for those most expensive in terms of time and money (e.g., formal ladies and liveried servants); Type B, which are middle-of-the-road (rented men's formal attire, spinster aunts, and the upstairs maid); and Type C for those easily acquired or made (a chimney sweep, grape pickers, and participants in a girls' pajama party). See examples, Figures 2.8 and 2.9.

3. The time available to build the show can have a great influence on how it is designed. A production to be done in two weeks with 40 costumes presents one problem. One to be mounted in three weeks with 10 costumes is entirely different.

Figure 2.8   The complex trims and shapes of this costume for Petruchio in *Kiss Me Kate* make it a Type A costume. Design by Cletus Anderson.

Figure 2.9 Gremio's *Kiss Me Kate* costume (left), easier to pattern and executed in less expensive fabric than Petruchio's, is a Type B costume. The Servant's costume, which has simple pieces and does not require much fabric, is a Type C. Designs by Cletus Anderson.

4. The amount of help available must be considered concurrently with the allotted time. This involves more than just the number of bodies available in the costume shop; the level of skill of those working is also of utmost importance.

5. The money available for the costumes may be last on the list, but this is not because it is of least importance. It weighs heavily on what can be done in all the other areas. And although money can't buy more time, it can pay for more people to make the time more productive.

All of these elements must be considered together if the designer is to develop a valid, integrated concept for the show.

◆ Budgeting

Budgeting a production is not an easy matter, for there are no absolute rules one can apply. The first step is to know how many costumes of what type will be needed and then to establish an average cost for each type of costume. This cost will depend largely on the circumstances involved in acquiring the costume and the economy of the area in which the production is being mounted. If built today in a New York costume house, the cost of a Type A costume might be $5,000; a Type B $2,000; and a Type C $1,000. Since most costumes are not built in the New York houses, a more accurate budgeting assessment can be reached by considering a typical costume in each grouping and assessing a probable materials cost to each costume element. Consider the following:

Type A Costume	**Lady of 1895 (Afternoon Suit)**	
Suit	10 yd. Wool @ $20/yd.	$200
Jacket lining	3 yd. @ $4/yd.	12
Patterning fabric	10 yd. @ $2/yd.	20
Blouse	3 yd. @ $5/yd.	15
3 petticoats	15 yd. @ $3/yd.	45
Corset	fabric, bones, fastening	25
Shoes		30
Hose (5 pair)		10
Hat	fabric, feathers, flowers	25
Braid	skirt and jacket 12 yd. @ $2/yd.	24
Buttons		5
Parasol	frame and fabric	20
Gloves		10
Notions	thread, fastenings, etc.	5
	Total	$446

An idea of the potential cost of the costume is now established. If part of the costume is available from stock (usually such items as shoes, petticoats, corset, gloves are) the cost is lowered, in this case by $110. This cost breakdown can be done for each costume if individual items vary a great deal and this seems necessary, or one representative costume from each grouping can be examined and the budget determined by multiplying this costume cost by the number of similar costumes. The development and maintenance of a good stock will be discussed later in this chapter.

The cost and availability of different types of fabric vary widely throughout the country. Costume designers should thoroughly explore the areas in which they are working, locate all possible sources, find the best suppliers, and get an idea of the prices of various types of items that will be used. A shop foreman or buyer can be very helpful in laying this basic groundwork. A comprehensive stock of up-to-date catalogs of items that are not available in many areas or items that are more easily and less expensively purchased in quantity is another important resource.

Yardage Estimates

While the actual dollar value of the different elements of a costume can vary too widely to be listed, a chart giving the approximate yardages used should be helpful. The following chart lists these yardages using a fabric width that is common for a fabric typically used for the garment. Following the chart is a conversion list for fabric widths.

◆

Garment	Yardage Needed	Fabric Width (in Inches)
Women		
Blouses and bodices		
Tight-fitting, sleeveless	1½	45
Full-bodied, sleeveless	1½	45
Fully pleated sleeveless	3	45
Sleeves		
Long, tight	1	45
Long, full	1¾	45
Short	½	45
Very full, leg-o-mutton	2¼	45
Funnel to knee	2¼	45
Funnel to floor	3½	45
Hanging straight to floor	3	45
Skirts		
Below knee, straight	1	54
Below knee, moderate A-line (2-yard hem)	1, 1¾*	54
Below knee, full (5-yard hem)	3, 4*	54
Floor-length, fairly straight (2-yard hem)	1¾	54
Floor-length, medium full, general fullness (5-yard hem)	4½, 5¾*	54
Floor-length, medium full, shaped gores (5-yard hem)	5¾, 6¾*	54
Floor-length, full, general fullness (7-yard hem)	5¾, 7	54
Floor-length, full, shaped gores (7-yard hem)	7½, 8½*	54
	For moderate trains add ⅔ yard	
Jackets		
Fitted to hip sleeveless (8 piece)	2½	45
Full to hip, sleeveless	3½	45

Gowns—combine amounts for bodice style, skirt style, and sleeve style, subtracting yardage if it will be possible to cut the smaller bodice and sleeve pieces from the areas left after cutting the skirt gores.

Ruffles and flounces—These can add a great deal of yardage, particularly if they are fairly wide. For example, 2⅔ yards of fabric are needed for a 10-inch finished ruffle with 200 percent fullness on the hem of a 5-yard skirt (360 inches of ruffle needed, 8 widths of 45-inch fabric, each 12 inches wide = 2⅔ yards).

	Yardage Needed	Fabric Width (in Inches)
Men		
Shirts and bodices		
Tight-fitting, sleeveless	2	45
Full-bodied, sleeveless	2	45
Fully pleated, sleeveless	4	45
Sleeves		
Short	½	45
Long, tight	1	45
Long, full	2	45
Medium leg-o-mutton	2	45

Bagpipe	2	54
Funnel, to knee	2	54
Funnel, to floor	3 ½	54
Hanging straight, to floor	3	45

Tunics and robes

To thigh, fairly straight	2½	54
To thigh, pleated	3¾	54
To knee, fairly straight	3	54
To knee, pleated	4½	54
To floor, fairly straight	4	54
To floor, pleated	6	54

Trousers

Full-length	1½, 2½*	54
Knee breeches	1, 1¾*	54

Men and Women

Capes

To waist, circle cut	1½	45
To hip, 1/2 circle (2 3/4-yard hem)	2, 2½*	45
To hip, 3/4 circle (4-yard hem)	3, 3¾*	45
To calf, 1/2 circle (4 1/2-yard hem)	3, 4½*	54
To calf, 3/4 circle (7-yard hem)	4½, 6*	54
To floor, medium fullness (gored 5-yard hem)	4, 7*	54
To floor, full (gored 8-yard hem)	6, 10½*	54

*indicates yardage needed if fabric has a nap or pattern that can only be cut one way.

Fabric Conversion Chart

The chart below uses the equivalent fabric area at each width, rounded to the nearest yard or fraction of a yard that is commonly sold in fabric stores. In converting from one width to another consider the number of large pieces that must be cut. Often a certain length of fabric is needed to accommodate these pieces and a few extra inches of width make no difference.

Costume Stock

A good costume stock is an invaluable asset to a designer and a production company. It should be built carefully, organized well, and guarded religiously. Items should be made with enough seam allowance for later alteration, as long as this can be done without affecting the fit of the costumes in the production for which they are constructed. Items that are pulled from stock and reused should be handled sensibly to prolong their longevity and continued usefulness. For example, it is not sensible to pull a full-length skirt from stock and cut it down to make a short skirt; the cost of the fabric alone in the full-length skirt might have been $120, and

◆

Fabric required	Yardage needed in other widths					
	36″	42″	45″	48″	54″	60″
½ yard × 36″	½	½	½	½	⅓	⅓
× 42″	⅝	½	½	½	½	⅜
× 45″	⅔	⅝	½	½	½	½
× 48″	⅔	⅝	½	½	½	½
× 54″	¾	⅔	⅝	⅝	½	½
× 60″	⅞	¾	⅔	⅔	⅝	½
1 yard × 36″	1	⅞	⅞	¾	⅔	⅝
× 42″	1¼	1	1	⅞	⅞	⅔
× 45″	1¼	1⅛	1	1	⅞	¾
× 48″	1⅓	1¼	1⅛	1	⅞	⅞
× 54″	1½	1⅓	1¼	1⅛	1	1
× 60″	1⅔	1½	1⅓	1¼	1⅛	1

the short skirt might be made for $20. Retrimming a garment is often desirable, although this is impossible if glue has been used. Taking a costume apart merely to reuse the fabric may be foolish. The time involved may offset any money saved and a stock item has been lost. In accumulating a costume stock, concentrate on those elements that can be used over and over again, saving everyone much time and money. The integrity of these costumes should be maintained if at all possible so they will continue to be available when they are needed. The time may come when an item is essential for a show and must be used in such a way that it can never be reclaimed. Bid it a fond farewell and hope that the stock is now extensive enough for another garment to take its place.

Stock shrinks not just because items are used badly. If a stock is not well organized, items often cannot be used because they cannot be found. Space is always limited, but careful planning should make the best possible use of available space. A good costume stock must also be guarded jealously. Too often, "souveniritis" causes valuable pieces to disappear. This problem cannot be completely solved, but the security of the costumes must be considered carefully in both the storage areas and the dressing rooms.

Labor. Thus far, discussion of budgeting the show has involved only the cost of the costume materials. When labor costs are included in the budget the total amount needed will increase considerably. Much depends on the style and complexity of the production, but labor costs can often account for one-half to two-thirds of the total budget. For example, a show that budgets $2,000 for fabrics and the like may add an additional $2,000 to $4,000 for labor costs.

◆ The Design Interpretation and the Actor

While the designer is determining the basic interpretation of the script and assessing the work to be done, he or she must always keep in mind the relationship of the actor to the costume. The job of setting the style of the production belongs first to the director, then to the designers. The actors ultimately present the writer's work to the audience, but they do so following the lead of the script and the interpretation the director has chosen.

Part of this interpretation is the visual aspect provided by the designers, who are responsible for both the overall feeling of the production and the individual elements of which it is composed. Many of these ideas may be well under way before the actors are involved in the production. The actors are also most immediately involved with the problems of the characters they are playing, and while they may often want to be involved in developing costume ideas for those characters, they cannot be fully aware of the overall picture and how their costumes must fit into it. The designer, who should have ultimate control over the costumes to be used, needs as much cooperation and understanding from the actors as possible; the costume and the actor should be two inseparable components of a single visual effect. If the two cannot work together, the desired effect will not be achieved. For the actor the costume is an externalization of the character, an extension of his or her interpretation of the role. By the time the production opens the actor should feel that the costume is the real clothing of the character.

At the beginning of the rehearsal period the designer should present the sketches to the cast, explain the ideas that led to this approach, and clarify the effect the costumes are intended to create in the production. Some form of work must be shown at this point, even if the finished renderings are not available. The designer should clearly explain the choices that were made for each character, and why. If it is a period show, some historical background would be helpful: Why did people wear the clothes common in a particular period? How did they feel about them? What bearing does this have on this particular production? The designer should explain shapes, fabrics, and any necessary underpinnings. Any changes that are to be made should be discussed, focusing the discussion on why they are to occur.

If there is not sufficient time at the first presentation to communicate with each actor individually, this can be done when measurements are taken or at the first fitting. Each piece should be explained: how it can be used; what restrictions or freedoms it will allow; what is practical in terms of pockets, buttons, and so on; what accessories are included; and any special problems that might arise. The total costume should be discussed in terms of the effect it will have on the character. If some of the garments are unfamiliar to the actors, they should be taught how to dress, sit, stand, and move in them. The actors should understand their costumes well enough to "wear" them mentally in rehearsal. It might be very useful for both the actors and the director to have copies of the costume designs displayed in the rehearsal area to serve as a reminder of what will actually be worn.

◆ The Rehearsal Costume

Mentally donning the costume is a great aid to rehearsal and to preparation for the first costume runthrough. So is the proper rehearsal costume. The designer must talk with the actors about what they should wear for rehearsal, provide garments they may need, and explain the type of movement their garments will require.

It is extremely important that the actors rehearse in the same type of footwear they will wear in performance. The footwear is the basis for the stance and movement; a woman wearing heels has a completely different bearing from a woman wearing flats; a man in boots moves quite differently from a man in sneakers and men's period high-heeled shoes may require an extensive adjustment period.

Any actor who will wear a long gown in performance needs a rehearsal skirt of comparable length and weight to provide the correct quality of movement. Any hoops or trains to be used should be simulated for rehearsal so the blocking can account for the actual space an actor will need. A designer knows from experience that a woman of 1860 wearing a large hoop cannot move between a chair and settee placed two feet apart, nor can a woman wearing a train back up easily. The earlier these problems are faced and solved, the more comfortable the actor will be in the final costume.

Corsets and padding should also be provided early in the rehearsal phase. A corset is used not so much to create a tiny waist, although this illusion may be achieved, as to give the torso the shape of the period and to give the actress a feeling of the restriction that was so much a part of the time. Modern woman is not subjected to rigid figure control and must become accustomed to the manner in which a corset modifies movement. Padding, too, may place restrictions on movement by adding bulk in places strange to the actor, bulk which must be incorporated into the actor's whole movement pattern.

Rehearsal pieces should be available for any costumes that are removed or put on during the performance to enable the actor to become quite familiar with the necessary action. In the theater quick offstage changes should be thoroughly rehearsed as soon as all the garments are ready so that both the actor and the crew will know exactly what is to happen. In film and television the problem may be solved in the shooting schedule.

Everything that can be done before the dress rehearsals or filming begin to help the actors prepare will be an asset to the outcome of the production. The designer should view the rehearsals periodically and help the director and actors arrive at the fullest possible understanding of the costumes and their use.

◆ Reducing Actor–Designer Conflicts

While there could be conflicts between actors and costume designers, good costume designers do everything possible to reduce them. Letting the actor in on preliminary design plans is the best way to begin. The actors are ultimately the ones before the audience and are rightfully concerned about the image they will project. The designer must be always ready to assure them that the costume provides the proper image for the production. The greatest costume sketches in the world are useless if they cannot be turned into actual costumes on actors in performance—and if the actors are not confident in what they are wearing, the costumes most likely will not be fully effective.

There are many ways to help actors understand the costumes. Actors may wish to wear costumes in particular colors or styles because they feel more comfortable in them. The designer should try not to react negatively to suggestions. After consideration, if a suggestion proves unsuitable the designer should explain carefully why it does not fit into the scheme being used. If an actor's ideas are ineffective because they are outside the line of the period, do not work well with the set, or perhaps will not show up properly in the lighting that will be used, this can be explained in a way that will help the actor see the overall planning of the show and realize that design decisions are the result of a serious consideration of many elements and any changes must take into account a number of factors. Actors may indeed have some costume ideas that the designer finds quite acceptable. An actor who really understands the costume will be able to relay information about business that is established during rehearsal: "I have to hide a notebook on my person, but I don't think I have a pocket"; "The director has decided he wants me to do a somersault here—do you think I can, wearing a bustle?"

There are situations in which a conflict between actor and designer cannot be resolved without conferring with the director, and the designer may not always be happy with the outcome. The designer must be able to take the new information and work it into the scheme in the best possible way. If an established star is involved in the production, a preliminary meeting during the design period might be desirable. There are actors who have very specific ideas about what they wish to look like and if their position in the company is such that they are going to have a great deal to say about what happens, this should be considered at the very beginning. The actor's actual input into the designing of the costumes is not usually extensive, but the influence of the actor on the costume cannot be underestimated. Fitting the actor in the costume is discussed in Chapter 9.

Chapter 3

Developing the Basic Concept

The costume designs grow out of a basic concept that is developed from a thorough understanding of the objectives of the production, the director, and the other designers. There is seldom enough time to develop the project to everyone's satisfaction, but if the work progresses from a solid understanding of what is to be done and why it is to be done decisions at every step will be clearer and surer. A carefully considered, well-planned basic concept is invaluable. It permits the designer to exchange ideas confidently with the director and the scene and lighting designers and to present sound ideas to the cast and to the crew.

◆ Developing the Character Costume

In the process of designing the production the designer must establish a clear understanding of the characters for whom costumes will be created. He or she does not interpret the script alone. The writer has given the groundwork, the designers and director have discussed this particular production. The interpretation continues to grow as the actors bring their skill to the roles. Director, actors, and designers all help the character evolve during the rehearsal period.

Obvious indications of character—age, physical stature, occupation, social position, and the like—are often excellent ways to enhance a memorable and accurate depiction of character. The designer should not be reluctant to reinforce visually information the audience receives from the script. Revealing the character's psychological state and relationship to his or her world is more tricky because the designer is working more with interpretation than given facts. The audience may not completely understand the designer's motivation for a particular costume, yet the costume must still seem valid and perfectly acceptable for the dramatic moment. And there is also the possibility that the audience will understand too much and the designer will give away the plot. If a boy and girl enter both clothed in the same shade of powder blue, even if they don't know each other at first and spend most of the act fighting, chances are awfully good they will kiss and go off into the sunset together before the final curtain.

Careful study of the script will enable the designer to answer the following questions effectively:

- When do the crucial moments occur in the production, and how should they be staged?
- What type of line, color, and texture will best express these moments?
- What is the motivation of each character?
- How does each character fit into the framework of the entire production?

Figure 3.1 Sagramore's character called for a costume that would make him large and menacing but not totally evil. Pencil sketch; design by Barbara Anderson for *A Connecticut Yankee in King Arthur's Court*, one of the Once Upon a Classic series produced by the Public Broadcasting System.

- Does the character go through changes as the action progresses, and if so, how should this evolution be expressed?
- What did the character do before the action begins, and what will he or she do after the action ends?

It is through this attention to detail and character development that the costume designer makes a strong contribution to the production. The actor, the costume, and the situation all fit together to tell the story.

Figure 3.2   These sketches for Algie in Wilde's *The Importance of Being Earnest* not only show the clothes that clearly help define his character, they also tell the viewer something about his attitude toward life. Watercolors by Susan Tsu for a 1995 production at the Alley Theatre in Houston.

Figures 3.3 through 3.6 are examples of how costumes help delineate the character. These four costumes were created for characters in *The Leatherstocking Tales,* dramatized on the Once Upon a Classic series produced by the Public Broadcasting System. These characters lived in the wilderness of northern New York in the mid-eighteenth century. James Fenimore Cooper's novel *The Deerslayer* inspired the television scripts and was valuable background material for the designer. Since the designer could not assume that the audience would be familiar with Cooper's novel, costume designs were based on the presentation of the characters in the shooting script. Hawkeye (Figure 3.3) is the young hero. He is accepted by both Indians and whites, so he must relate to both worlds. He presents an ideal image of a resourceful and honest woodsman. His costume consists of a handmade linen hunting shirt and rough cotton shirt, fringed leather

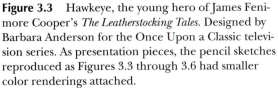

Figure 3.3　Hawkeye, the young hero of James Fenimore Cooper's *The Leatherstocking Tales*. Designed by Barbara Anderson for the Once Upon a Classic television series. As presentation pieces, the pencil sketches reproduced as Figures 3.3 through 3.6 had smaller color renderings attached.

Figure 3.4　Harry March

Figure 3.5　Hutter

Figure 3.6　Rivenoak

breeches, Indian moccasins, and the powder horn, bag, knife, belt, and gun that were necessities in the wilderness. Lines were kept simple and the garments were made of homespun fabrics and leathers. The color scheme used tones in warm off-whites, tans, and medium browns.

Harry March (Figure 3.4) is a different case entirely, a blustering braggart, who takes advantage of any person or situation he can to turn an easy buck. He is flamboyant, careless, and lazy, always looking out for himself. His clothes must reflect his life in the woods, hence the handmade boots and Indian leggings, heavy belt, pouches, powder horn, and rifle. His shirt is homespun, but with more flair than Hawkeye's. His breeches and vest look very much lived in, and his hat is made dashing with an Indian feather trim. Harry's hair is unkempt, his face whiskery, and the actor who plays him would ideally have a hairy chest. The colors of his clothes are darker and dirtier than Hawkeye's, in shades of greens and green-browns.

Hutter (Figure 3.5) is an old pirate who lives on a barge with his daughter. An unpleasant man with an unsavory background, his greed soon leads to his death at the hands of the Indians. Though it has been a long time since he has really been at sea, he retains a bit of the flavor of the sailor, and so wears the jacket and scarf commonly worn by sailors. His clothes are worn but not torn; although he doesn't care what he looks like, he does have a daughter to look after him. His beard is scraggly and his hair is very casually tied back. The colors of his costume, grayed blues and browns, tie in with his maritime background.

Rivenoak (Figure 3.6) is a proud and vengeful Huron warrior chief. He is Hawkeye's enemy, but they oppose each other honorably according to the Indian code. His demeanor must reflect his heritage and the contact he has had with the French. He wears Huron clothing and trims, but he also wears a shirt of finer fabric and a double gorget that he has received from his benefactors. His Indian blanket is deep red to help give him stature and set him off from the rest of his warriors. Rivenoak's shirt is off-white, and the tones of his leather garments range from medium brown to muted orange to contrast with Hawkeye, who wears more yellowish browns.

In each of these costumes, every element was selected because it seemed psychologically right for the character and because it helped create a physical look that enhanced audience understanding of these people and their situations.

The Way of the World by William Congreve is a Restoration comedy that provides a more decorative means of presenting the characters. Lady Wishfort is an overripe grande dame, a foolish woman easily flattered and easily angered (Figure 3.7). She presents herself as an attractive coquette, though she is much past her prime. Lady Wishfort's costume shows her fondness for excess and her true lack of taste. All her choices are amusingly wrong for her age and figure: her overcurled hair, the bows and pearls worn at her neck, her extravagant ribbons and skirt trim all emphasize the width of her overabundant figure. She wears more ruffles than anyone needs at the elbow . . . and all is carried out in reds and oranges.

Lady Wishfort is attracted to Sir Rowland, who is really the servant Waitwell in disguise (Figure 3.8). His costume is also overdone, but in a more elegant way, for he has been created by Mirabell, the hero of the play.

Figure 3.7 Lady Wishfort, like the other three figures, is a character in Congreve's Restoration comedy *The Way of the World*. Designs executed in pencil by Cletus Anderson, 1972.

Figure 3.8 Sir Rowland

Figure 3.9 Petulant

Figure 3.10 Sir Wilfull Witwoud

Sir Rowland wears a rich, warm rust suit, a color Lady Wishfort would find attractive, trimmed with much gold braid and accented with a beribboned baldrick. His crowning glory is a strawberry-blond wig. Lady Wishfort cannot help but find him enticing.

Petulant is a fop, typical in Restoration comedy (Figure 3.9). He considers himself a man of much wit, learning, and good breeding. In reality he is a coward and a fool. The color of his costume is a delicate beige trimmed in gold and accented with precious lavender bows at the neck, shoulders, and knees. The sash at his waist accents the overly genteel feeling, as does his carefully curled wig and his hat, decorated with curly ostrich feathers.

Sir Wilfull Witwoud is fresh from the country and shows it in everything he wears (Figure 3.10). The fabric of his costume is coarser, the trim simpler, the cut less fashionable than the others. He wears boots and spurs, unacceptable to the gentleman of polite society where the proper turn of the calf was very important. Witwoud's linen is not refined, his wig hasn't been set in years, and the feathers on his hat were probably plucked from a bird he himself shot. The colors of his costume reflect the earth tones of his country surroundings.

Notice that the personality of each character is also expressed in the figure's attitude and posture. Lady Wishfort is overly coy, Sir Rowland is manly and elegant, Petulant is too, too genteel, and Sir Wilful is planted firmly on his heels as he surveys the unfamiliar territory.

The process of developing the character costume continues throughout the design process, from setting the limitations that will define the world of the production to the choice of line and color that will be used and even to the presentation style of the costume plate.

✦ Setting the Limitations

To establish limitations in a production, the designers and director must consider the historical period, geographic area, season and weather, and time of day of the production; and the social status, age, and sex of the characters. In Chapter 1, these categories were discussed in relation to the general meaning of clothes. They will now be reexamined to determine how they can be used for a specific production and cast.

Historical Period

Many productions have a very definite time frame set by the writer (for example, the summer of 1865 in Eugene O'Neill's *Mourning Becomes Electra*), and the director may decide to comply with this. The designer can then determine the span of years to be researched, which will provide a good understanding of the silhouette of the era. The designer should feel comfortable enough with the style of a period to design a costume as if he or she were actually living in that period, not just precisely reproduce garments found in sources. (See Figure 3.11.) In some cases, of course, a char-

Figure 3.11   A costume based on a historical source can be reworked by the designer to make it more suitable to the character. This costume for DeConde in John Whiting's *The Devils* for a 1970 production at Carnegie Mellon was based on Anthony Van Dyck's portrait of Viscount Grandison. Acrylic; design by Cletus Anderson.

acter must appear deliberately old-fashioned, a particular problem because the audience may not know enough about the costumes of a period to pick up on what is old-fashioned and what is merely strange.

In a production set in 1895, for example, the women's costumes cannot be designed from sources that include the entire 1890s, for there were three different silhouettes in style during this decade. The style in women's fashions dominant in 1895 was only in vogue from 1894 to 1896. For men's costumes, which were not as subject to the vagaries of fashion as women's, the period can be broader, encompassing the whole decade and perhaps a bit more. Generally, the farther back in history a piece is set, the wider the span of years available to use and still keep within the desired silhouette. Styles did not change as rapidly, source material is not as abundant, and the audience is not as familiar with the fashions. A production set in the fifteenth century whose action takes place in one afternoon can easily be designed with a strong feeling for the unity of style using sources from 1425 to 1475. This would be impossible for a more recent 50-year span—from 1900 to 1950, for example.

Geographic Area

The script may specify a geographic locale; the geographic setting can also be surmised by the writer's nationality. At times a specific country is not as important as a feeling for the general area, such as Scandinavia, Middle Europe, or the Mediterranean. At other times the perception of an area within a country must be more specific: New England, the South, or the West. (See Figure 3.12.) The amount of research material available varies greatly, so the designer must know how widely to range in search of inspiration and still capture the characteristics of the locale. The plays of Chekhov need the ambiance of nineteenth-century Russia, but sufficient source material might not be available. Since French and English fashions greatly influenced the styles adopted by upper-class Russians in the late nineteenth century, the designer might go to the original sources for basic silhouette ideas, but with enough understanding of Russian fashions to keep that flavor dominant. At times a production should not be identified with any specific country, and the designer must search for shapes that are universal and do not suggest a specific locale.

Season and Weather

In the most practical sense, the time of year must be established simply to ascertain whether the actors need overcoats. A production that takes place

Figure 3.12 The costume for the Rhode Island Kid from a production of *Merton of the Movies* at Carnegie Mellon portrays a humorous version of the Wild West of the United States. Design by Cletus Anderson.

in winter can be much more expensive to mount simply because more garments are needed to reveal this fact. Weather conditions can also be indicated by the costume. The actual time of year may be very important to the plot or may be quite incidental. The general mood of the piece may suggest a season without actually specifying one; a designer may decide to reflect this mood in the colors chosen for the costumes.

Time of Day

This information is usually given in the written directions, but might not be specifically mentioned in dialogue. If it is important that the audience know the time of day, the designer must select appropriate costumes. (See Figure 3-13.) Pajamas are a logical choice for early morning and night, formal wear usually suggests an evening function. In the Victorian era a fashionable woman might have changed often—a housedress for morning, a promenade costume for the midday walk or shopping, a tea dress for late-afternoon receiving, and an evening gown for dinner.

Social Status

Class differences should be clearly defined so that the proper contrast in clothing reflects differences in social status for the audience. For example, a production might include a well-to-do family, its servants, the poor relations

Figure 3.13 The dressing gown can suggest either coming from or going to bed, morning or evening. In this case Frederick's attire in *A Little Night Music* denotes both evening and coming from bed. Design by Cletus Anderson for a production at Carnegie-Mellon in 1989.

Figure 3.14 Different social levels are suggested by the costumes in these sketches by Frank Bevan for the 1949 production of *Faust* at Yale University. The two figures at left are upper-class; the one at right is definitely a peasant. (See also the sketch on page 67.) Beinecke Rare Book and Manuscript Library, Yale.

living in the household, and the tradesmen who perform services for them. The dress of the upper-class family members will obviously be more stylish than that of their poor relatives. The servants fall into two distinct levels as well: footmen, butlers, and chauffeurs, all of whom are meant to be seen, are clothed differently from cooks, kitchen maids, and gardeners. Tradesmen would probably resemble the "backstairs" domestics. The arrival of a group of afternoon visitors who come from a background of recently acquired wealth introduces another element and affords the designer the opportunity to show the age-old struggle between the establishment and the *nouveaux riches*.

Age

The script usually establishes a specific or general age for a character. How the age of the character is approached can often be influenced by the age of the actor who will play the role. Disguising the actual age may be an important part of the design. For example, telltale signs of age in a woman often appear in the upper arms and neck; a costume that does not expose these will greatly aid the illusion of youth for the older actress or advanced age for a younger one. A child's part may be cast with someone who is older and better able to fulfill the acting requirements of the role. The actual age of the actor may be more effectively disguised by selecting garments that seem more youthful than those worn by a real 10- or 11-year-old.

Sex

Gender is one area where the designer may have little creative leeway. The sex of the character is usually clearly determined by the author, and while it is possible for the gender to be changed, this is usually done by the producer or director and may involve rewriting of the script. The amount of "sexiness" that needs to be exhibited by a character may be of primary concern to the designer (Figure 3.15). How this is solved can be influenced by a number of factors, including what was considered sexy in the period in which the production is set and how this will be perceived by a modern audience. The actual appeal of the performer can be a strong factor, for the costume can enhance what he or she already has and try to provide what is missing.

Figure 3.15 Sex certainly has something to do with the occupation of Girl #3 in *Dracula, A Musical Nightmare,* designed by Susan Tsu for a production at Houston's Alley Theatre in 1993. Watercolor.

◆ Design Guidelines for Costume Unity

Realism Versus Stylization

With the practical considerations established the designer turns to the aesthetic decisions that must be made. A primary factor is the degree of realism or stylization to be used. In some productions the costumes may need to present realistic clothes of the period, such as those purchased at the corner store today or faithfully reproduced from the Sears Roebuck catalog for a story set in the 1920s. This is, however, not random realism, for the designer makes choices in colors and textures that influence the interpretation.

The degree of realism to be used may well be indicated in the language as well as in its subject matter. The very nature of a piece written in verse makes its characters different from those who inhabit our workaday world. In other cases, a more prosaic costume line is ideally suited. Consider, for example, the different costume approaches that would be taken for Joseph A. Walker's forthright protest drama *The River Niger,* set in the turbulence of the 1960s, and Maxwell Anderson's *Winterset,* a drama concerned with social unrest in the 1930s but written in eloquent verse.

Shakespeare's language creates an extraordinary world and presents an exciting opportunity for the designer to complement the eloquence in the design concept. *Hamlet* presented in a historical period can evoke images of lines and textures that make the figure of the actor seem heroic; detail can be suppressed in quantity but rich in terms of the elements that are used; and colors can range from vibrant jewel tones to the shadowy darkness of Elsinore (Figure 3.16). *Hamlet* done in modern dress might still tend toward these elements translated into modern garments. But a modern rewrite of *Hamlet*—such as Elmer Rice's *Cue for Passion,* set in southern California in the 1960s and told in modern prose—does not evoke the same images. The clothes would reflect contemporary reality, since the characters are as unassuming as their prosaic language.

The subject matter of the production can also help the designer set the degree of realism or stylization to be used. A kitchen drama filled with life's little moments of pathos and joy needs costumes detailed with the same attention to the little realities of life (Figure 3.17). A story of the struggle of man against the universe is concerned not with minutiae but with broader issues and requires a similar costume idea.

Unity through Line and Detail

The designer's goal is for costume unity, and all decisions about the clothes worn during a production must consider this. He or she is creating a world for this particular presentation. Compared with the multitude of variations in dress during any period, the designer has only a few opportunities to show the audience what this world is like. The feeling of the period must be captured by selecting its most typical and representative lines, not by introducing all the eccentric elements that are the exception rather than the rule. If a character needs to seem eccentric this can only be done in contrast to the other costumes. There can be no variations from the norm if the norm is not understood.

Figure 3.16 The costume at the left for the Ghost of Hamlet's Father grew from the eloquence of Shakespeare's language. Watercolor design by Cletus Anderson, 1966.

Figure 3.17 Small realistic touches are appropriate for Eva in Alan Ayckbourn's *Absurd Person Singular*, produced by the Carnegie Mellon Theatre Company in 1978. Design by Barbara Anderson.

Establishing the period and the most useful elements in it is one step toward a unified costume approach. The basic line of the chosen era may seem quite suitable as it is, but often an interpretation of the line may better reinforce the mood. In some cases the silhouette may need simplification. The bustle gowns of the 1870s and 1880s can be quite complex, with many puffs and swags (Figure 3.18). A costume for Mrs. Alving in Ibsen's *Ghosts* could come from this era with the bustle intact but with many of the overlays eliminated to give her an appearance of resolve and control (Figure 3.19). The women in Shaw's *Arms and the Man,* although contemporaries of Mrs. Alving, might be costumed using all the intricacies available. Through an exaggeration of the line and detail, the designer reinforces the personalities of these women, who wish to be considered extremely fashionable by contemporary Bulgarian standards.

The way the detailing is handled on the silhouette can make a strong statement in unifying the costume effect. Costumes of the early Middle

Figure 3.18 A bustle gown of the 1870s, designed by Gustave Janes to be worn in public during the daytime—*toilette de vine* or town dress.

Figure 3.19 Mrs. Alving in Henrik Ibsen's *Ghosts*. Pencil sketch by Cletus Anderson.

Figure 3.20 This Gothic costume has a long flowing line and very little trim, typical of the period of its source. Design for Judith in Bartók's *Bluebeard's Castle,* produced at Carnegie Mellon in 1976; watercolor sketch by Cletus Anderson.

Figure 3.21 Both fabric and trim are atypical of the Gothic in the costume for Morning from *Bluebeard's Castle*. The choices heightened the unreal quality needed for this character. Watercolor design by Cletus Anderson.

Ages are typified by a long, flowing line with very little trim. (Figure 3.20). If a great deal of ornamentation is added to the silhouette a definite style has been set (Figure 3.21). The period approach to Elizabethan detail is quite a contrast to that of the Middle Ages, for proliferation of detail is found in almost all areas and an overall exceedingly decorative effect is achieved (Figure 3.22). Here stylization by suppressing some of this detail lends significance to what is used and helps focus the costume (Figure 3.23).

Color and Fabric Control

An audience first reacts to the color revealed as the lights come up on a scene. Perception of forms and textures follows. This makes color control a primary tool available to the designer, for through the relationships of the colors within a costume and among costumes in the scene a strong unified statement can be achieved and individual character development reinforced. A visual unification will be present if all the characters are clothed in the same color, but unity without variation can be monotonous. The designer can creatively incorporate the element of color into the scheme of

Figure 3.22   This etching of Louise of Lorraine shows the period approach to Elizabethan detail.

production by selecting a range that seems most suitable to the mood, then developing variations within the range to delineate the characters. Color should be considered in terms of hue, value, and intensity or chroma, terms explained in detail in Chapter 5. *Hamlet* might be conceived with hues in high-intensity jewel tones producing a deep and rich color effect. Brecht's *Mother Courage* might be designed in predominantly neutralized earth tones to create a result that conveys a sense of affinity with the earth and a struggle for survival. Hues also can be used to clarify different factions in the production. In *Romeo and Juliet,* the Montagues might be clad in blue, green, and purple shades and the Capulets in reds, oranges, and yellows, contrasting hues but with value and intensity levels used to unify the total color effect.

The types of fabrics selected for the costume are an integral part of the overall design scheme. If the fabrics chosen are typical of those that might have been used in the period, a degree of naturalism is achieved (Figures

Figure 3.23   The detailing of a period costume might be suppressed for a particular effect. Pencil sketch by Cletus Anderson.

3.24 and 3.25); if the fabrics were not common, a step toward stylization has been taken (Figure 3.26). Costumes of the thirteenth century done in wools will seem more authentic to the audience, even if the line has been altered, than the same designs executed in chiffon. English Renaissance costumes constructed in shiny cottons create a world that would not have been familiar in Elizabeth's court. Fabric selection can be crucial to the success of a costume design, for proper tailoring, movement, and draping qualities must be present. A robe made of lining taffeta will never mesh in a scene where the other costumes are made of heavy satin and *peau de soie*. The designer may also decide to use plain fabrics instead of patterned ones; low, smooth surfaces instead of course textures; or a controlled combination of these treatments. The designer must always be concerned with visual balance, however. If all characters are costumed in plain fabrics except one extra in a busy print dress, much more attention will fall on this single contrast.

Costume unity, which is established with carefully conceived decisions, must take one more step before it can be given the final stamp of approval. It must also coordinate with the scenery and lights. Close communication

Figure 3.24   Realistic fabrics were used for this gown for *The Duel*, adapted from a short story by Chekhov. Design by Barbara Anderson.

Figure 3.25   These tailored suits seem quite at home in the early nineteenth century because they are made of the same types of wools that would have been used then. From the John Marshall series sponsored by the U.S. Judicial Commission. Design by Barbara Anderson. Photo by Norris Brock. © Metropolitan Pittsburgh Public Television, Inc., 1976.

Figure 3.26   An element of humor is added to this costume for *Kiss Me Kate* by the use of non-realistic fabric. Design by Cletus Anderson.

must be maintained during the design period so ideas can be discussed as they develop. The color decisions may be particularly crucial. The first dress rehearsal is not the time to discover that the leading lady disappears as she sits in a chair on the set, for it may well be too late to construct a new gown or do reupholstering.

◆ Considering Practical Limitations

Up to this point the designer has been making artistic and creative decisions about his or her approach. Before going too far in developing the actual costume designs, the designer should take one more look at the limitations that were discussed in Chapter 2 and evaluate them against the direction the production should now take. The number of costumes needed, their complexity and the amount of time it will take to construct them, and the crew and money available to build them can seriously affect design decisions. It is the responsibility of the designer to create sketches for costumes that can be realized. Costume unity cannot be achieved if three costumes are made of fine fabrics and exquisitely detailed while seven more are thrown together using unbleached muslin and ball fringe. Fabric and trim choices must be made to fall within both the scheme and the budget. If there is not enough time and skilled labor to achieve 10 intricately cut and detailed costumes, then an approach suitable for both the characters and the shop time available should be determined. If a number of costumes must be pulled from stock because of time and money constraints, the designer should look through the stock to determine what might be useful and how it can best be integrated. It is irresponsible to develop a concept that can only be realized for some of the costumes when more careful planning would result in a unified production.

Restrictions Caused by the Performance Space

Any restrictions that might be caused by the blocking or elements of the set should be considered as the costumes are designed, such as the amount of floor space a costume can take up in relation to the number of people, the rake of the stage, or the size of the stairs. The physical size of the performance space can also influence the design concept.

Costumes and the Body

Costume design has one general limitation: it must relate to the body of the actor, though for space aliens and mascots this relationship may not be too evident. Creative costumes can enhance an actor's physical stature or modify the body's appearance for a specific character. In either case the basic

Figure 3.27   The clown outfits use costume elements to change the shape of the body to produce a humorous effect. In one the hat, full jacket, and flaring pants create a pyramid; in the other the corselette provides contrast for the ballooning trousers. Designs for the Ringling Bros. and Barnum & Bailey Clown College characters by Howard Kaplan. Sketches done in colored markers.

shape of the actor usually sets the limits on what can be achieved. Corseting can be used to give a slimmer, more controlled figure, but there is a limit past which breathing and movement become impossible. Realistic padding can be added to a figure only to the degree that it will blend into the body behind it. A huge tummy that slopes up to a very thin neck or down to very small thighs can be humorous, but cannot be taken seriously. Padding can only go so far; it is impossible to create a believable extremely buxom woman from a flat-chested actress in a very low-cut dress.

Basic design lines can be used to reinforce an emphasis on certain body areas. Shoulders can be broadened by the treatment of the sleeve-head and by diagonal body lines, which also diminish the waist by stressing the V shape of the torso. A small waist can be emphasized by flaring the hip; large hips can be de-emphasized by stressing the vertical line. The mass of the costume itself can heighten the visual impact of the actor. But if the mass becomes too great it takes over; rather than making the actor seem bigger, it makes him appear small, insignificant, and lost within the bulk of the costume. Expensive special-effect techniques have been developed for film work that can produce an extremely realistic change in the body shape. These techniques include actual prosthetics, computer-enhanced images, or a combination of the two.

◈ The Actor's Experience with Costumes

If the designer is familiar with the actors who are cast in the production, it may be helpful to consider the experience they have had with costumes and how easily they are able to use them. Some costumes are quite difficult to wear and some actors do not deal easily with unfamiliar costumes. The designer should try to choose costumes that can be worn confidently by the actors and should expect cooperation from the cast, for most actors realize that developing a skill in wearing period costumes is one of the tools of their trade.

◈ Researching the Production

Once the approach is established, thorough research is needed to give substance and authenticity to the ideas. There are a great many sources to draw from for research, and not all involve time spent in a library. For some productions the best source material might be found while hanging out at the local all-night diner, or on the streets near a steel mill as the shifts change. The more common sources, however, are found in printed materials. Social histories and biographies can give the flavor of a period. Accounts of similar productions may expand the designer's thinking by presenting different viewpoints and different solutions. These should be approached as interesting background pieces that can increase awareness and not used as actual models.

Books on costume history furnish information that has been gathered from many areas, condensed, and presented in an easily used fashion. Although important sources, these books have limitations that must be

Figure 3.28   These two costumes are both based on the Holbein portrait of Jane Seymour (Figure 4.55, page 122), but each presents a different interpretation of the period feeling communicated in the original. (a) is from the early twentieth century *Bankside Costume Book* by Melicent Stone and lacks the rigidity, neckline, and waistline of the original. (b) is from Albert Racinet's *Historical Encyclopedia of Costumes,* originally published in the 1880s, and has a much longer waistline and longer turnback on the oversleeve, almost hiding the undersleeve.

recognized. No one book can ever give a designer enough information, he or she must draw from a number of sources to get a more rounded viewpoint. It is also true that the quality of the drawings and the accuracy of the information can vary greatly. Even in the best of the costume books the information presented is the author's interpretation of the primary sources, or sources that actually come from the period. Costume history books should be used as a starting point to assist the designer in understanding the period. Primary sources should be consulted as frequently as possible to view the material firsthand and not rely on secondary information. A good line drawing can be useful but a line drawing that wrongly interprets the source or imposes the period feeling of the time of the author back on the period being presented could seriously mislead the viewer (Figure 3.28). The designer who is thoroughly familiar with the primary sources should be able to recognize these inconsistencies.

The best primary sources vary with the historical period being researched. Good information can be found in statuary, wall paintings, illuminated manuscripts, stained glass windows, tapestries, paintings, fashion plates, etchings, photographs, catalogs, magazines, pictorial histories, medals, dolls; there are as many sources of information as there are visual means of recording human history and culture. A guide to the basic shapes of the fashions predominant in the Western world is provided at the end of this book and includes for each period a list of some of the better sources of research material for the era. This is not intended as a miniature costume history book, however, nor as a source to use when designing a production. It is included because the designer needs a starting point to begin researching a show. It is a guide to the basic shapes of historical periods and provides a groundwork that can be used as the designer moves on to more detailed sources.

◆ Chapter 4
Developing the Line

Preceding page: This figure seems to be held in position by muscle control. Design for a player in *Hamlet* by Cletus Anderson.

The practical groundwork has been laid; the time has come for the designer to start sketching the costume ideas for the show. This step in the design process can be accompanied by conflicting emotions because the designer may be eager to give expression to his or her ideas yet reluctant to make a definite commitment on paper. This reluctance cannot be solved by staring at a blank piece of paper. The best approach is to have an understanding of the physical proportions of the figure and to draw it often. As the pencil moves on the paper and the designer experiments with different figures and lines, the development of the character evolves and costume ideas begin to coalesce.

◆ The Quick Sketch

The first step in drawing the costume is usually the quick sketch. This is just a rough expression of the designer's initial thoughts, something that can be put down rapidly to start ideas flowing. These sketches should be done freely and quickly; they are not born out of agony. If an idea doesn't seem to be working, start again.

One of the most practical ways to start quick sketches is to envision both the physical and psychological attributes of the characters. How do they present themselves to the world? What do their bodies look like? How do they stand? Are they introspective or extroverted? Are they beginning to sag or bulge or bend? Move the pencil on the paper until an awareness of the body of a particular character begins to develop. An excellent exercise that will help establish the desired figure is to draw the entire figure without lifting the pencil from the paper. Explore the mass, outline, and movement of the character as the pencil goes from one area to another (Figure 4.1). Once an awareness of the character's figure evolves, the designer will start to understand the lines that will best express the characters in the sketches. Take, for example, Lady Bracknell in Oscar Wilde's *The Importance of Being Earnest*. Lady Bracknell is a very secure, forthright, outspoken woman. As the sketch of her figure begins to develop, the head is up, the chest is out, the stance is firm, the arms open out, the parasol is firmly planted (Figure 4.2a). Her physical characteristics are established in a few quick strokes. In the next step, the lines that reinforce these characteristics are added (Figure 4.2b). Lady Bracknell's torso would be controlled by a corset, which defines the waist, flares the hips, and thrusts the bosom up and out. The corset also provides an excellent psychological base for Lady Bracknell, for it is very much a symbol of the straitlaced, proper world that is the bulwark of her existence. The designer might wish to reinforce what the authors like to call her "forthrighteousness" by adding ruffles or frills on her bodice. The skirt springs smartly at the hip and falls to make a fairly firm outline. The shoulders should be those of a

Figure 4.1 The figure established quickly with just a few strokes of the pencil.

woman who takes command; consider the effectiveness of a slight kick upward before moving into a fairly full puff. The forearms are fitted to reveal the strength of her gestures. The hat goes upward and out to crown her domineering air. The parasol is fairly tailored. The general aura of Lady Bracknell has been established.

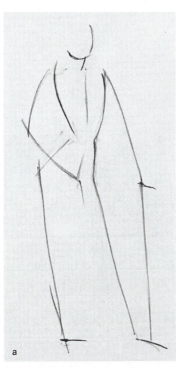

Figure 4.2 Development of a costume for Lady Bracknell.

Reexamining the figure will help the designer clarify the best choices for the character (Figure 4.2c). A high-standing collar adds more rigidity, a suit jacket would give her a tailored, older appearance. There are many decisions still to be made, but the quick impression of the character has been created. The elements should not be chosen at random, however. This Lady Bracknell is being designed for a production set in 1895 and from extensive research the designer would know the lines suitable to the silhouette of that period.

Very early in the designing process the designer should have a good idea of the fabric he or she will use. Lady Bracknell's suit, for example, should not be soft and draping. Her costume should be firm but flowing, with crisp sleeves and made of a somewhat stiff fabric without much shine. A faille would be a logical and workable choice of fabric for this costume.

Figure 4.3 shows the development of another costume idea, this time for Polonius in *Hamlet*. The first sketch shows the stance with just a few strokes—head down, shoulders sloping, belly sagging (Figure 4.3a). The next sketch begins to define specific characteristics: the costume becomes simple and bulky, tending to roundness. The neckline of the robe helps accentuate the droop of Polonius's belly and the slope of his shoulders (Figure 4.3b). In the third sketch ideas begin to clarify (Figure 4.3c). The robe is full, and the fit of the robe and jerkin makes Polonius's head and neck seem smaller and a bit lost. He needs a neck chain because of his social position, but the chain must not be too large or important. The hair tends to be wispy, and might be thin on top. In this case the fabric is soft, heavy, and drapable; a heavy wool with a plush banding that is not too rich would work well.

Figure 4.3   Development of a costume for Polonius.

When working out the quick sketch, jot down thoughts about color or texture or pin appropriate swatches of fabric to the sketch to give added dimension to the costume idea. The more the designer works with costumes and fabrics, the more the texture and drape of the cloth strongly come to mind. Knowledge of different fabrics will guide the pencil and help create the shape and the drape. Fabric and line constantly reinforce each other.

◇ Laying Out the Figure

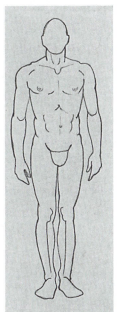

Figure 4.4
The adult male figure.

Whether executing a quick sketch or starting a final rendering, always draw the figure first. The costume is developed using this form as its foundation. It may take but a few lines to place the body on the page, but these will be enough to keep the drawing in proportion. If the body is not plotted out first, the pieces of the costume may not clothe well-proportioned figures.

The basic figure is about eight heads high (Figure 4.4). This is slightly elongated in relation to the norm, but presents a figure that is easy to use. The middle of the figure is the bottom of the torso. The knees come at the midpoint between torso and sole. The head is the top eighth of the body, the area from the shoulders to the waist occupies the next two-eighths, and the area from the waist to the crotch is the final segment of the figure's top half. The pit of the neck is one-third of the way into the second head; the bustline falls at the bottom of this section. The elbow comes to the waist, the wrist to the bottom of the torso, and the hand about one-third of the way to the knee. The male figure has more breadth to the shoulder and chest, about two heads wide, and slimmer hips; the female has narrow shoulders, about one and one-half heads, that are the same width as the pelvic area (Figure 4.5).

As the figure moves, the relationships among body parts stay the same. An arc extending from the waist with the shoulder as the pivot point will keep the elbow in the correct proportion, as will an arc at the knee pivoting from the hip. The figure must be kept in balance. It should have a firm stance and a feeling for the distribution of body weight. The figure's center of gravity drops from the pit of the neck. If the weight is distributed equally, this line of gravity drops to a point between the feet (Figures 4.4 and 4.5). If the body weight shifts, this line falls from the pit of the neck to the support foot (Figure 4.6). When the weight goes to one leg the pelvis shifts, rising over the balance point and dropping the other leg, creating the illusion that the non-weight-bearing leg is longer. As the pelvis shifts, the shoulders may stay square or may counter the move by tilting in the opposite direction. A figure may also be supported by an object such as a cane, table, or stool (Figure 4.7), though supporting objects should be carefully planned if they are used in a costume plate. A figure in action may not have the point of gravity supported in the usual manner, but may seem to be held in position through muscle control (see p. 93).

The Hinge Points

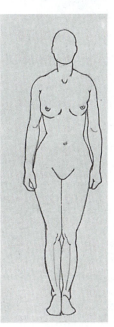

Figure 4.5
The adult female figure.

The natural reference points of the body are the hinge points, those points that give the body its articulation. In designing, the different areas of the costume are scaled in relation to the spaces between these points. The basic layout of the figure must be carefully established in reference to these hinge points, and how the hinges connect one part of the body to the next must be understood. One body area does not just sit on another; it grows out of it.

The following discussion gives a very simplified view of how the body goes together. For more in-depth information on the figure, see Stephen Rogers Peck's *Atlas of Human Anatomy for the Artist, Drawing from Life* by George B. Bridgeman, and *Drawing the Human Form* by William A. Berry.

The Head, Face, Neck, and Shoulders

Viewed from the front the head appears to be an oval, drawn in a ratio of about 6 to 8, with the ears extending out at the sides in the second quarter (Figure 4.8). The neck supports the head from slightly inside the jawline. The contours of the neck are formed by the sternomastoid, the muscle that extends from behind the ear to the collarbone. The back of the neck is joined to the shoulder by the trapezius muscle. Thus, the neck joins the body on two levels: the pit of the neck at the center front is much lower than the connection at the shoulder. From the side, the angle at which the head sits on the neck and the neck on the torso is more evident (Figure 4.9). The side view of the head is based on a square, for the head is about as deep as it is long. The top front of the ear is located at the center of the square.

Figure 4.6 Body weight on the right foot. Costume for *Macbeth*, designed by Cletus Anderson for a production at the Pittsburgh Public Theater, 1980.

Figure 4.7 The staff helps support the figure. Costume for Punch in the film *Knightriders* 1982. Design by Cletus Anderson.

Figure 4.8 The head from the front showing the planes of the face.

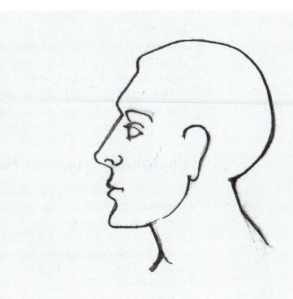

Figure 4.9 The head from the side.

The basic outline of the face goes from the forehead out to the cheekbones, located slightly below the eyes, down and in slightly to the jawbone, a bit below the mouth, then in to the chin. The planes of the face give three-dimensionality to the drawing, though the actual lines would not be used. Figure 4.8 diagrams the face indicating the planes and proportions of the parts. The eyes are placed about the width of one eye apart from each other. Figure 4.10 shows the individual eye.

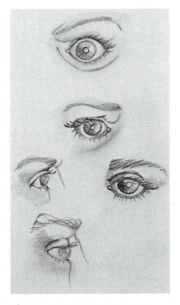

Figure 4.10 The eye.

Figure 4.11 Various styles of indicated faces.

The figure will not seem complete unless a certain amount of detail is included on the face. A blank oval at the top of the neck calls too much attention to itself. The features can be either completely drawn or indicated sketchily (Figure 4.11), depending on the ability of the designer. If the features cannot be drawn to add to the character, then a simple indication that will not distract from the whole should be used. The face may be the first part of the sketch the director notices. It must lead him or her in the right direction to understand the costume for the character.

Shoulder, Arm, and Hand

The arm is connected to the shoulder by the deltoid muscle, which extends from the trapezius to the muscles of the upper arm. The smallest part of the upper arm is just above the elbow, where the upper arm muscles taper into the lower arm muscles. The widest part of the lower arm occurs just below the elbow (Figure 4.12). As the arm bends, the back of the arm from the shoulder to the elbow joint lengthens, and the front of the arm from the shoulder to the bend decreases (Figure 4.13).

The hand joins the wrist at a slight angle that seems to reverse as the hand turns. From the back of the hand the thumb appears to start out higher on the arm. From the palm side, the bulge that leads to the little finger begins first (Figure 4.14). The palm and fingers, which are about equal in length to the span from the tip of the chin to the hairline, seem to be more of a continuation of the arm, with the thumb growing from one side of the palm. From the back of the hand the fingers can make up slightly more than half the length of the hand; from the palm side the fingers are less than half the length. It may be difficult to achieve a well-articulated hand, and often a feeling for the gesture of the hand may be quite sufficient to complete the figure.

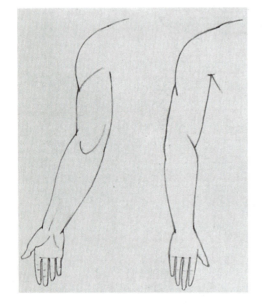

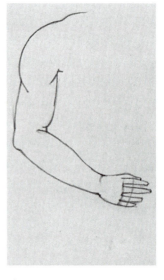

Figure 4.12 The arm, palm out and turned to show the back of the hand.

Figure 4.13 The bent arm.

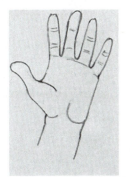

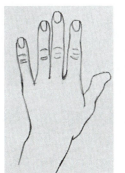

Figure 4.14   The hand.

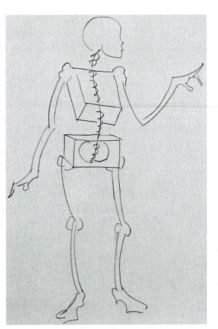

Figure 4.15   Block figure.

The Waist

The torso can be thought of as two blocks connected by a flexible pipe or spine; the top block is the ribcage, the bottom is the pelvis (Figure 4.15). The greater the span between the blocks, the better the possibility to reshape the waistline with some form of corseting. The female waistline curves in, then springs out to the hip; the male waistline is less indented and the hips are narrower (Figures 4.4 and 4.5).

The Hip, Leg, Knee, and Foot

The leg sets into the torso at an angle, forming the hip. This angle is repeated down the leg by the opposing muscles and the indentations of the knee until the ankle bones reverse the direction (Figure 4.16). The curve of a woman's upper thigh is more prominent than a man's; other muscle masses are more obvious in the man's leg. As the knee bends it appears to lengthen the upper leg. From the side the back curve of the buttock goes to the bottom of the torso. The curve of the front thigh muscle starts higher and seems to swing right to the curve of the back calf muscle.

The foot hinges onto the ankle and forms the foundation for the stance. It grows wider from ankle to toes and the weight of the leg sits slightly to the inside so the midpoint of the ankle lines up with the second toe, which is usually the longest one (Figure 4.17). The foot is longer than one head and articulates in three parts: the heel, the arch, and the toes.

Age and Body Shape

The age of a character can definitely be reflected by his or her body. At birth the body is only about four heads high, with the center near the

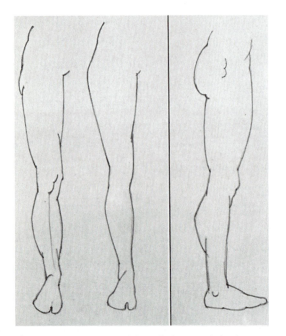

Figure 4.16   Male and female legs and the leg from the side.

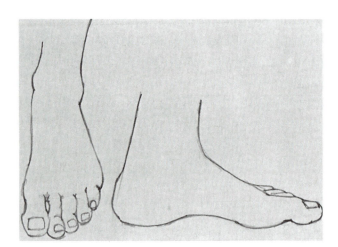

Figure 4.17   The foot.

navel. By age two the body is about four and a half heads high; by eight, about six and a half heads; at puberty or fourteen years, about seven heads; and by eighteen, a full seven and a half to eight heads tall. In old age the body tends to sag and shrink though the head remains the same size, so the figure may again be seven to seven and a half heads tall (Figure 4.18). With

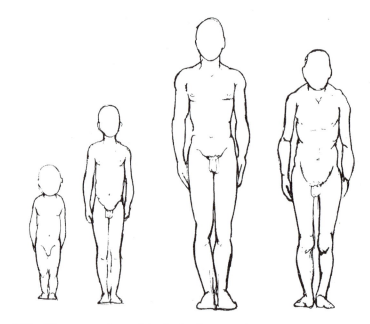

Figure 4.18   The proportions of the body change as it ages.
Young child   Boy   Young man   Old man

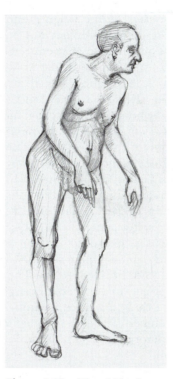

Figure 4.19 The old body.

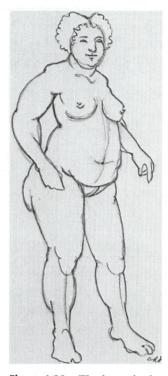

Figure 4.20 The heavy body.

old age, the body begins to succumb to the force of gravity it has withstood for so many years. The head sags forward, the spine curves, the shoulders droop, the stomach muscles give out, and the whole body is pulled downward (Figure 4.19). Extra weight can also bring a curve to the back as the body tries to compensate for the bulk in front, although a young heavy person often is able to carry the excess weight rather than let it pull the body down (Figure 4.20).

◈ Finding the Best Medium for Sketching

Many types of pencils and paper are available for sketching. As the designer develops a style and undertakes different projects, he or she should experiment with different pencils and paper to see how they work. Basically, the paper should not be too smooth. It needs to have some tooth (surface texture) so it can interact with the pencil. Similarly, the pencil should not be too hard. It must be soft enough to allow variation in line. These are not absolute rules. So much can vary in the way each individual likes to draw and the effect that is desired for a particular project. Judgment and creativity are equally important, but an understanding of the basic tools is a prerequisite.

A hard pencil can give a uniform line that stays quite crisp and distinct, but this type of line is often monotonous and does not convey much movement or help create a three-dimensional quality. A softer pencil can easily express a variety of line weights, enhance the three-dimensional quality, and add a sense of movement and vitality to the figure. Figure 4.21 shows the types of line that can be produced by pencils of various degrees of hardness and softness. A pencil that works well for a particular designer does not need to be a "drawing" pencil; an ordinary good-quality writing pencil can be quite effective. An inexpensive pencil, however, can have inconsistencies in the graphite that make it more difficult to use.

Just as a soft pencil interacts more with the paper, a paper surface that has some tooth lends itself to the drawing process. Very slick paper offers little resistance to the pencil, and paper that has quite a bit of tooth can impose its surface on the drawing style. Figures 4.22 and 4.23 illustrate how different papers and pencils affect the quality of the line. The first is done on smooth paper with a hard pencil and the second on paper with some tooth and a softer pencil.

Inexpensive newsprint is often used for quick sketches in the early stages of a design. It is quite rough and not very sturdy, so it may not be suitable for a more finished sketch. The type of paper and pencils can vary from one project to the next. Ideas for heavy costumes with little detail may come more easily if worked up using a soft pencil on a paper with more tooth. Costumes that will be refined, elegant, and highly detailed may develop with more facility on a smoother paper using a pencil with slightly harder lead.

◆ The Importance of Line Quality

Line used to reveal the costume should be reminiscent or descriptive of the fabric, giving a sense of its quality and weight, the way it hangs on the frame, and how it falls or flows. Line can portray both silhouette and movement. A line showing chiffon is not the same as a line used to depict a heavy wool. The motion of a crisp taffeta is not presented in the same way as the

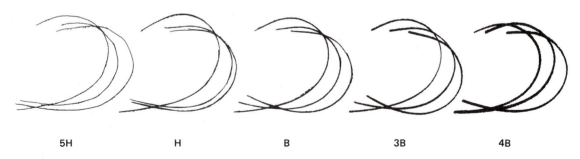

| 5H | H | B | 3B | 4B |

Figure 4.21   Types of lines produced by hard and softer pencils.

Figure 4.22   Figure on smooth paper with a hard pencil.

Figure 4.23   Figure on rough paper with a soft pencil.

drape of a jersey. In Figure 4.24 the dancer is costumed in a light, flowing chiffon that catches the air. The line is light and loose and does not completely surround the area it defines, but suggests it. The contour of the figure is still visible through the fabric. The pencil catches the page, then lifts and floats. In Figure 4.25 the fabric is a wool jersey that falls softly into folds. The line flows smoothly as the fabric would; it is continuous from top to bottom without a great deal of variation. Figure 4.26 shows a woman of 1835 in a taffeta ball gown. The fabric is crisp and light, and the line is shorter and varies in intensity to show the movement that would be present in this type of costume. The man in Figure 4.27 is clothed in a heavy wool robe and hood. The line is correspondingly heavy, feeling its way around the thick folds.

Drawing is a skill designers must master. It is a motor skill that improves the more it is exercised, but drawing must also be combined with intellect and the power of observation. Drawing is a language for designers. By developing the ability to arrange marks and symbols, designers develop means to record and clarify their thoughts and ideas and to communicate them to others. Sketching combines exploration and investigation. Ideas flow from head to hand to paper. The result should look effortless (though, of course, it may not be), not tortured and labored. Designers who do not work to develop this facility do themselves a disservice for they must spend time on simple drawing problems that could be better used to refine the

Figure 4.24 A chiffon costume.

Figure 4.25 A costume of smoothly flowing fabric.

design idea. Even experienced designers strive to better their drawing skills. Draw whenever possible, attend life-drawing classes if they are available, and study anatomy books. Keep a sketchbook handy and draw anything that catches the eye. Control of the arm and pencil comes from constant practice. And the more designers draw, the more they are able to think visually and explore, record, and interpret the world.

◆ The Elements of Design

A knowledge of the basic terminology of design is one more useful tool for the costume designer. The same elements and principles that are used effectively in any form of design can be controlled to produce a desired result in costume design. The following discussion is brief but provides a general understanding of the elements designers use.

The basic elements of design can be considered as line, shape, form, color, texture, and light. The means of controlling the elements that create a design order or composition would be balance, harmony, contrast, sequence, repetition, scale, proportion, gradation, variation, pattern, and focus. Design can be thought of as a means of creating an order, one that is easily recognized or one that is seemingly random.

Figure 4.26 A ball gown of crisp, light taffeta.

Figure 4.27 A robe of heavy wool.

Line, Shape, and Form

Line is a path of action that expresses the character of the force that created it. A line may have a variety of widths or weights and imply direction and movement. It may be fragmented, actual line, or implied line. It may be measured and calculated or free-form. Measured line is man's invention, the beauty of the measured line is implicit in its precision and logic. The free-form line is more spontaneous and seems to be an emotional response to the subject. When it encloses itself it becomes an outline, expresses shape, and defines the silhouette. In a costume drawing this may be actual or implied. A line may clearly define the edges of a shape or the shape may be visible even when every segment of the line is not present. The viewer will complete the picture that is implied by the lines that are drawn (Figure 4.28). Surface contour lines and outer contour lines combine to convey a three-dimensional idea on a two-dimensional surface, thus defining form.

Costume design ideas are usually explained or developed in a two-dimensional drawing, whereas the actual costume will be a three-dimensional, sculptural form moving in light and interacting, moment to moment, with the various other forms of the costumes, props, and scenery. When putting costume ideas on paper, a combination of lines is used to express form. These lines may or may not be present or have the same impact in the actual costume. Lines that indicate edges of fabric or folds of cloth will not be as evident on the three-dimensional figure as those that indicate bands of trim.

A line attracts attention according to the degree of contrast to the ground on which it is drawn. In a costume sketch a line may appear quite

Figure 4.28 The outline of a figure may be clearly defined or implied.

strong because the dark gray line of the pencil is seen against the light background of the paper. If the line depicts a linear trim that will not be in high contrast with its background in the finished costume, this should influence the way the sketch is drawn or painted.

The direction of the line can elicit certain reactions in an audience. Vertical lines emphasize height and can produce a feeling of uprightness and grandeur. The vertical follows the line of growth, which lends itself naturally to the body (Figure 4.29). The horizontal line is not as fundamentally suited to the human figure because it goes across the natural line. The horizontal feeling tends to be more inactive and solid and adds bulk to the figure (Figure 4.30). The diagonal line may give the costume more activity and flow, for it implies action and dynamic movement (Figure 4.31).

Color, Texture, and Light

Color is a powerful stimulant in its own right. Technically it is the chemical treatment of a surface, which absorbs certain wavelengths of light waves and reflects back to the eye selected others which we see as color. Color in the theater can also be modified by colored light (see Chapter 5). Texture is the quality of the surface of the fabric or objects that appeals to the sense of touch. Every surface has a texture; it may be smooth, rough, soft, polished, and so on. Light is an integral element of design that reveals and transforms the interaction of the texture and color of fabric.

Figure 4.29   Line direction can influence the audience. Above: the dominant vertical line.

Figure 4.30   The dominant horizontal line.

Figure 4.31   The dominant diagonal line.

◈ Controlling the Elements

Repetition and Harmony

Repetition is the simplest form of order. A particular shape may be repeated and bring a certain sense of order to an arrangement even if the size (measure), tone, and attitude vary. The harmony is considered perfect if all the elements repeat; that is, shape, measure, tone, attitude, and interval (the space between shapes).

Harmony is produced by repetition. To create a harmony at least one element must occur two or more times. The greater the number of repetitions and the more strongly they are felt, the greater the harmony. Wide intervals between elements or a strong contrast that will catch the eye may break the flow of the repetition and weaken the strength of the harmony it produces.

If harmony brings order into a composition, then variety might be said to bring disorder. But it is through the control of variety that interest and focus can be added to the design. A close harmony can make a boring costume (Figure 4.32). Variety must be present to add interest and focus. However, while a great deal of variety can create interest, it can also be confusing and muddle the figure.

Harmony can be established in measure by the repetition or recurrence of a certain size and in shape by the repetition or recurrence of a certain shape. Harmony of tone can be created three ways: first, by value harmony, in which the values or amount of lightness or darkness in the tones all occur near the level of the one value that is to predominate; second, by having little contrast between colors or hues and producing harmony of color; and third, by keeping the amount of neutralization in each

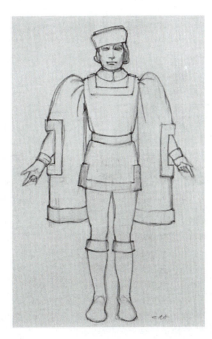

Figure 4.32 A close harmony can make a boring costume.

color about the same to create harmony of intensity. Any of these harmonies may be used together or separately.

Progression and Gradation

A line that creates a shape and repeats it produces a linear progression. The repetitions make up a harmony of shape. If the repetitions are exactly the same, there is a harmony of measure and shape in the progression (Figure 4.33). If the size of the shapes varies, then there exists a harmony of shape without a harmony of measure (Figure 4.34) A progression in which the size of the shapes increases or decreases in a regular sequence creates a gradation, which is also illustrated in Figure 4.34. A gradation is not perceived unless there are at least three shapes that progress in regular steps, moving the eye along. If the intervals between the shapes are too great, the gradation will be imperceptible.

The types of lines and harmonies used can greatly change the effect of a costume. Figures 4.35 and 4.36 show two costumes based on the same simple shape: one is executed in curved harmonies, the other in straight-line and angle harmonies. In each there are harmonies based on a certain type of line with variations in measure and gradation. Two very different types of character grow out of the same basic garments by emphasizing a different type of harmony. The actual use of linear harmonies is seldom this blatant, but exercises in excess often help clarify an idea that can then be incorporated with a bit more finesse.

Sequence

The order of sequence in design becomes apparent when the eye is drawn from one element to another in a systematic way. Like harmony, sequences can be perceived in positions, measures, shapes, attitudes, intervals, and any of the components of tone: hue, value, and intensity.

The three types of sequence are sequence of continuation or repetition, sequence of alternation, and sequence of graduation or progression.

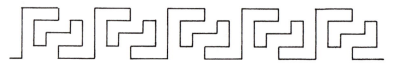

Figure 4.33   A progression with harmony of measure and shape.

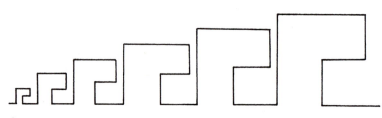

Figure 4.34   A gradation.

Figure 4.35 A costume with curved harmonies.

Figure 4.36 A costume with straight-line and angle harmonies.

The simplest form of the sequence of continuation or repetition is the line, which the eye can follow easily from beginning to end. In Figure 4.37a the sequence of the line is easily followed. In Figure 4.37b the line is broken, but the sequence is still perceptible, for the eye is able to connect one segment to the next. In Figure 4.37c the feeling of the sequence is broken, for the interval is large and the eye may not be able to make the connection easily. A row of buttons down the front of a costume creates a sequence

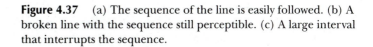

a

b

c

Figure 4.37 (a) The sequence of the line is easily followed. (b) A broken line with the sequence still perceptible. (c) A large interval that interrupts the sequence.

of shapes and tones. If the buttons are too far apart, the feeling of sequence is broken and the buttons become isolated spots.

The sequence of alternation occurs when any sequence is broken repeatedly and at regular intervals. This continuation of regularly recurring breaks or accents creates a feeling of rhythm. The rhythm can be produced by the regular alternation of any of the elements mentioned before: position, tone, shape, measure, or attitude, or by the alternation of any combination of these elements. Figure 4.38 shows a costume in which a sequence of repetition and a sequence of alternation are used for the trim. The repetition moves continuously around the figure. The alternation also moves but does so in a more interesting fashion, which establishes a rhythm.

In design the sequence of progression takes the form of a gradation of one tone, position, measure, shape, or attitude to another, always by degrees. The change that occurs is both gradual and uniform. A smooth wash from white to black through the range of grays is a gradation of value. Figure 4.39 shows a costume that uses a number of gradations. There is a gradation of the size of the bows on the hat and up the bodice of the gown. The ribbons hanging down the front become both longer and wider. There is also a gradation in the spaces between the bands of trim on the skirt.

Balance

There are four different types of balance: symmetrical, asymmetrical, crystallographic, and radial. The simplest form of balance is symmetrical balance, in which the shapes or lines on one side of a vertical axis are mirrored on the opposite side. Since the human body is relatively symmetrical,

Figure 4.38 A costume with a sequence of repetition and a sequence of alternation used as trim.

Figure 4.39 A costume using a number of gradations.

Figure 4.40 A symmetrical costume that balances but has misplaced focus. The eye is drawn to the middle of the figure.

Figure 4.41 Good symmetrical balance. Claudius from *Hamlet*. Watercolor design by Cletus Anderson.

a symmetrical balance is often the starting point for a costume. But symmetry alone does not guarantee an effective design, for misplaced focus is still a possibility (Figure 4.40). Figure 4.41 shows a costume with symmetrical balance; the elements are controlled and well focused.

In asymmetrical balance the elements are not an exact inversion on the vertical axis. Balance is achieved by a form of opposing or contrasting elements that combine to bring a sense of equilibrium to the composition. Assymetrical balance is based on the scale and placement of various elements and their relationship to the axis or fulcrum. A large shape would be placed closer to the axis, while the smaller one would be placed at a greater distance to achieve a sense of balance. The designer's eye is of utmost importance. He or she must be able to see the balance, which cannot be as simply calculated as a symmetrical design. Figure 4.42 is an example of asymmetrical balance on a costumed figure.

Crystallographic balance has equal emphasis over the entire area, an overall pattern that has no particular beginning or end such as might be found in fabric or wallpaper. In radial balance all the elements radiate from a central point. An example might be a medallion or a piece of jewelry.

Two more design elements have a very strong effect on a costume: color and texture. Texture is considered in more detail later in this chapter; color is discussed in Chapter 5. Control of the line and the shape can be considered separately as an exercise on the way to a design but they combine with color and texture to produce the final result. The designer must always be aware of the ultimate contribution of all the design elements to the finished work.

The control of the design elements enables the designer to create a point of resolution, a focal point that leads the eye to the important areas of an effective costume. Focus can be created through placement or contrast.

Figure 4.42 An asymmetrical costume. Dancer in the *Carousel* ballet. Watercolor design by Robert Perdziola, 1982.

Frequently the focus of an actor is the neck and head area. The expression and information is communicated from there. A misplaced focus can distract the audience and cause them to miss important moments.

◆ Developing the Costume Line for the Production

Part of creating the style for a production is deciding upon the period in which it will be set. This could mean England in the 1780s, medieval Scotland, the Belle Époque, a world centuries in the future—practically anything. But whatever it is, the time period in which the action takes place dictates a certain silhouette, a basic line that defines the period. The period should be selected because its silhouette enhances the production, delineates the characters, and helps the audience better understand the ideas being presented. A piece presented in the period for which it was intended, either because it was written during that era or because that was the specific historical time the author selected for the action, usually settles itself into the given silhouette quite easily. When the period is changed, problems can develop because the silhouette may run contrary to the characters and situations. A good, hardy farce like *The Menaechmi* by Plautus may not work well in a period that stresses a long, elegant line. A sophisticated drama such as Ibsen's *Hedda Gabler* may not be effective in a period based on quick, short lines like those of the 1920s. As the designer works out the silhouette of the costume, further discussions with the director may be needed to clarify what each wants the effect to be.

A costume can be defined by the shape it makes in space. It is a form that must be understood from the front, side, and back. This understanding begins with an in-depth investigation of the period decided on for the production. An understanding of the foundation under the costumes, the shapes that are used for the different body areas, and the type of seaming that constructs those shapes is indispensable. The designer explores the forms of the clothing, their social significance, and the ideals that created them. The details of history should not be slavishly reproduced but adapted as needed for particular requirements without losing the flavor, sense, or integrity of the period.

The Silhouette and Its Relation to the Hinge Points

The silhouette to be used for a production must be specifically defined in its relationship to the hinge points, or articulation points, which are the body's major reference areas. The silhouette is established by the way it relates to these points. It is not helpful to say that women's sleeves during a certain period were 10 inches long. What is important to know is how the sleeves of that period related to the elbow and shoulder. Consider each area to clarify the way the line should be placed.

Neck.   The necklines of period costumes can vary greatly. Sometimes the neckline relates more to the shoulder treatment; sometimes it confines the neck tightly and restricts movement. Some periods have one style that is most typical; others incorporate many styles, several of which may be equally right for the same character. A proper Victorian woman may wear a bodice with a high, tight-fitting boned collar for afternoon tea and a ball gown with an extremely low neckline that evening.

Shoulders.   The manner in which the sleeve joins the body will often determine the type of shoulder emphasis the figure will have. The amount of fullness on the top of the sleeve and the manner in which it is controlled are both important to the line, for the shoulder gives a different appearance if the fabric kicks up, extends out, or droops. Added elements can also visually broaden the shoulders.

Bust.   The one major reference area on the body that is not a hinge point, the location of the bust relates closely to the neckline treatment and to seam and trim placement on the front of the bodice.

Elbow and Wrist.   The articulation points of the arm determine both the length of the sleeve and the proportion of the sleeve elements. Many long sleeves are broken up or trimmed in relation to the elbow.

Waist.   The waistline of a garment can vary anywhere from just below the bust to the hipline. It can be a straight line around the body or may point downward at the center front, which appears to lengthen the upper torso. It can be actually delineated by a seam if the top and skirt are cut separately, by a belt that creates a definite line, or by separately constructed garments such as a skirt and blouse. The waistline might be simply implied by the way the garment fits and falls in fullness when vertical seams go from shoulder to hem.

Hip, Knee, and Ankle.   These hinge points most often relate to the length of the body garments or to the manner in which the main trim areas break up the garments. The latter is particularly true with women's clothes, for in proper society a woman's legs were kept hidden by her clothes until this century.

The relationship of the costume to the body, beginning with corsets or padding that may reshape the form and continuing through all the outer layers of clothing that are seen by the audience, helps create the style of the production. Determining the proper proportions for a costume is not a simple matter; each era has its own idea of beauty and fashion. Thoroughly researching a period will help the designer understand how the different elements were used at a particular time. This will in turn help the designer to determine how those elements should best be interpreted for a specific production. Appendix B of this text gives the designer a means to approach research and includes lists of sources for further exploration.

◆ Individual Costume Characterization and Costume Detail

While the basic line gives structure to a production, costume details greatly contribute to character interpretation and add flavor, zest, and a feeling of completeness. A costume detail is any addition to the primary structure. It can be extremely simple, such as a small piping to reinforce the construction lines, or a narrow edging to accent a collar or cuff; or as complex as a textural surface, perhaps of lace overlays, braid, or jewels. Details also include costume accessories such as hairstyles and ornaments, shoes, handkerchiefs, purses, canes, etc.—anything needed to complete the picture. Good costume design is based on character interpretation and much can be communicated about a character through the costume details. The ability to use detail effectively is an essential design skill. Small additions can make a significant difference in a costume. At first glance the gentleman in

Figure 4.43a appears to be properly dressed, but he somehow does not seem complete. Compare him with Figure 4.43b. While essentially the same costume, the added details create the impression of a gentleman who is unquestionably all put together.

Details are very important in developing a costume for Mrs. Malaprop in Richard Brinsley Sheridan's *The Rivals*. She is a woman a bit past her prime, although she would never admit it. Mrs. Malaprop is self-indulgent, pretentious, rich, and fashion-conscious, but her idea of what is fashionable does not coincide with the opinion of the world in general. Although she is a very foolish woman, Mrs. Malaprop is an endearing character. Deep inside she might well look like Figure 4.44, a forthright but rather matronly woman. If she is to be dressed in the styles of 1775 her silhouette would adjust to the fashionable look of the day, as in Figure 4.45. In this sketch, the corset binds Mrs. Malaprop and serves to pull her together tightly. Although not small, her waist is precisely confined, and her skirt springs out in a full silhouette. Her bosom blossoms up and out of the top of the corset (those excess pounds have to go somewhere). Costumes of this period often are soft, with ruffles at the neckline and the sleeves, and Mrs. Malaprop would certainly want to incorporate this into her outfit to enhance what she would consider her youthful qualities. Hairstyles of the period were high and the lady would of course be delighted to follow suit. The skirt could be closed in front, but given a choice of showing two skirts or one, Mrs. Malaprop would probably opt for two. Her basic period silhouette is established. Now the details that will help fill out her character can be added. In Mrs. Malaprop's case this can be a great deal of fun, for given a lady prone to such extravagance in language, it is hard to imagine she would try to contain herself in her dress. The result might be similar to the costume shown in Figure 4.46. In the same play the initial ideas for Julia's

Figure 4.43   (a) A lack of finishing details makes a sketch seem incomplete. (b) With all the elements included, the suit seems much more finished.

Figure 4.44 The basic Mrs. Mala-prop.

Figure 4.45 Mrs. Malaprop as she as-sumes the silhouette of the period.

costume would be quite different, though based on the same silhouette. This character has youth, beauty, simplicity, and taste. Figure 4.47 shows an approach to her silhouette.

Consider the character of Hamlet as he might be costumed in two different periods. He is a young man of royal birth mourning the death of his

Figure 4.46 Mrs. Malaprop with the ex-travagant details that would please her.

Figure 4.47 The simpler Julia.

father and confronted with the probability that his uncle is a murderer and his mother an accomplice. Surrounded by the opulent court, he is alone in his internal and external search for truth and justice. One design approach might include the use of rich fabrics in a simple, youthful, and somber line. Figure 4.48 gives this basic feeling in a late-fifteenth-century costume. The jerkin is slightly V-pleated to emphasize the wide chest and narrow waist, the sleeves are full to stress broad shoulders. The simple short skirt accentuates the long leg. The total effect is attractive, masculine, and subdued. Figure 4.49 is an Elizabethan costume, which can be much more complex than a costume from the fifteenth century. Here elements that will stress the same effect are chosen—broad shoulders, wide chest, narrow waist, and long legs. The padding that could have been used in the pumpkin hose and peascod belly (see page 291 in Appendix A for clarification) is minimized. The effect is quite similar, though the period feeling is totally different.

It is the designer's responsibility to set the style of the show and the manner in which the costumes are detailed is a primary part of that style. When planning detail the designer should begin with the historical period, then translate elements found in the research into details that best delineate the production and its characters. The silhouette should be understood first, then the detail examined to see how it affects the overall feeling of the period and how it relates to the various areas of the costume.

Detailing can vary greatly from period to period. The early medieval period relied mostly on line, with an occasional belt, border treatment, or brooch (Figure 4.50). The Elizabethans, however, used a great deal of decorative detail; their fabrics might have been covered with braid, jewels, and

Figure 4.48   Hamlet in the late fifteenth century.

Figure 4.49   An Elizabethan Hamlet.

Figure 4.50 The early medieval costume relied more on line than on detail. What may seem decorative elements are the artist's way of indicating folds and fur lining. From a medieval illuminated manuscript of Pliny's *Natural History.* Laurentian Library, Florence.

puffs of cloth (Figure 4.51). A gentleman of the early eighteenth century felt properly dressed with elaborate embroideries banding his coat front, pocket flaps, cuffs, and vest, all of which were accented by very decorative buttons (Figure 4.52). By the end of the eighteenth century a proper gentleman wore well-tailored wools with subtle detailing. The highlight of his

Figure 4.51 Elizabethans used a great deal of decorative detail. Queen Elizabeth I, the "Armada" portrait. Collection of the Duke of Bedford.

Figure 4.52 The early-eighteenth-century gentleman enjoyed elaborate embroideries. Etching of the Count Struense, physician to the King of Denmark.

costume was concentrated around the collars and scarves worn at the upper chest and neck (Figure 4.53). In the same time period the silhouette may be similar from country to country, but the type of detail more clearly defines the geographic area of the costume. Figures 4.54 and 4.55 show two women painted just one year apart. Jane Seymour's details show the rigid, enclosed

Figure 4.53 The late-eighteenth-century gentleman approved of subtle detailing. Etching of Goya's portrait of Don Manuel Garcia de la Prada.

Figure 4.54 Titian's portrait of Isabella of Portugal, wife of Carlos V of Spain, about 1535, reveals a southern approach to costume detail. Prado, Madrid.

Figure 4.55 Jane Seymour's costume is rigid and enclosed, typical of the northern countries. Portrait by Hans Holbein, 1536. Vienna, Kunsthistorisches Museum.

feeling of sixteenth-century England, a treatment more typical of the northern European countries. The portrait of Isabella of Portugal reveals the same line, but the hair is looser, the sleeves more open, and soft gathering is used in her dress; this painting evinces a more southern approach to costume detail. The historical guide in Appendix A describes the type of detailing found in each period and the general way in which it can be used.

The designer clarifies the character costume by selecting those elements that best present the period, mood, and spirit desired for a particular production, elements that will be effective artistically, balanced in line and shape, and expressive in color and texture.

◈ Costume Focus

The primary focus of a costume is usually around the shoulder and head area. The choice of details is one of the principal means the designer has to control the focus of the costume. If the detail draws the attention of the audience to the foot or left thigh, there must be a good reason for it. Given a simple costume, the eye tends to go to the face as the most animated and expressive part of the body.

As trim is added it needs to balance so the eye will still move to the top of the figure (Figure 4.56). A great deal of detail can be used without creating a lack of focus on the figure, but it must be carefully controlled. The costume can have many interesting elements for the eye to look at as long as the eye finally focuses where it should (Figure 4.57).

Detail on a costume must relate to the body area it adorns. There are no absolute rules on how to do this, for much depends on the period used as a source and the degree of realism or stylization set for the production.

Figure 4.56 Trim must balance so the eye will move to the top of the figure. Chorus ladies from *Un Ballo in Maschera*. Designs by Brian Hemesath.

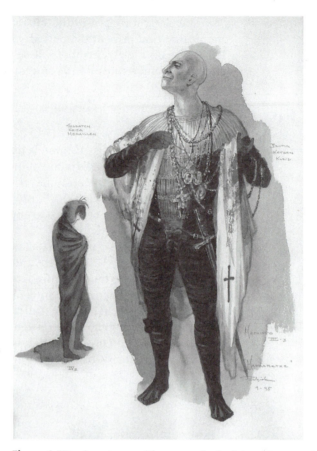

Figure 4.57   A costume with a great deal of visual interest, but the eye still goes to the face. Mephisto in *Margarethe* designed by Robert Perdziola for a 1995 production in Germany.

Perhaps some examples of details that do *not* work well will make it easier to understand the way detail relates to an area. These examples come from primary sources. Just because something was actually used in a period does not necessarily mean it was artistically wonderful. Bad design has existed as long as clothes have.

Figure 4.58 shows a lady of the 1880s in a light gray gown with pleated trim. The activity and contrast of the banding keep the eye on the thickened waist and broad skirt and away from the demure face. The detail in Figure 4.59 almost swallows up the French miss out for a stroll. The hat overwhelms her head and the ruffles on her arms and bodice defy anyone to concentrate on her face. The woman in Figure 4.60 may not be happy with her reception at the ball. The trim on her skirt will attract and hold the eye more than any other part of her costume.

Figure 4.58 Woman in American day dress with pleated trim, 1863.

Costume detail can be either a readily evident addition or a subtle reinforcement of the line of the costume. The direction it takes will be an important aspect of the style of the show. The detail may be quite austere, perhaps only used to emphasize the silhouette. Piping and buttons in the same color as the costume will give a sense of finish but will not impose a decorative element (Figure 4.61a and b). These same items done in a

Figure 4.59 A "merveilleuse" of about 1798. Engraving by Horace Vernet. Cooper-Hewitt Museum, New York.

Figure 4.60 1824 ball dress.

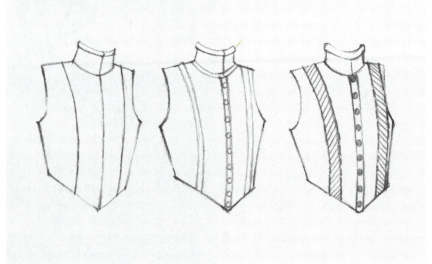

Figure 4.61   (a) Plain bodice. (b) Piped bodice. (c) Bodice with contrasting trim.

contrasting color make a much stronger statement (Figure 4.61c). If the scale of the detail is increased it may become more important than the silhouette and make the first impression on the audience. In Figure 4.62a the trim on the coat accents the shape of the period. In Figure 4.62b the overscaled trim takes the focus and makes the shape of the garment secondary.

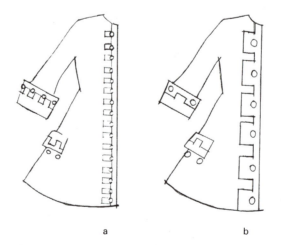

a   b

Figure 4.62   (a) Trim that accents the shape of the period. (b) Overscaled trim that takes focus.

Figures 4.63 through 4.65 illustrate various ways period detail might be used. The fashion plate in Figure 4.63 might be fine for a high comedy just as it is. Figure 4.64 takes the source and adapts it so it seems more appropriate for a serious play; the trim is somewhat simplified and the line is more dominant. In Figure 4.65 the effect is broader and more suitable for a farce or musical. The decorative elements have been emphasized to make a strong statement. The decisions made here are arbitrary and stereotypical because there is no written character to delineate, but the tone of the costume clearly has been changed by the use of accents and trims.

The basic costume line of the show may be quite similar for many of the roles in it, so it is through the use of detail that each becomes differentiated. The designer who knows the psychology and motivation of the characters will know how to approach the costume details. Labels should be included on a group of sketches, but even if the drawings are not named, the director should be able to recognize the characters because of the details the designer has selected.

In *The Importance of Being Earnest*, there should be no doubt who is Lady Bracknell and who is Gwendolyn, though both have the same social background. Lady Bracknell is forthright and commandeering; she expects to be obeyed. Gwendolyn will be very much like her mother when she gets older, for she is a female who knows her own mind, but for the time being she enjoys playing the role of the young coquette. Lady Bracknell's details might present the straightforward dominance of the more matronly figure. Gwendolyn's details will tend more toward youth and frivolity but with a hint of the iron maiden underneath. When Gwendolyn travels to the country she comes face to face with Cecily. Here are two young women of quite different backgrounds, who, beneath it all, are really very similar. The details for Cecily should present her as more of a country girl, but with the finish and strong-mindedness to match Gwendolyn tit for tat. Gwendolyn, of course, would make sure she was "London perfect" before venturing off to the hinterlands.

The designer thinks not only about the clothes, but also how they should be worn. The dressing of the garments, or the way they are arranged on the body, is important to the characterization and should be carefully considered. A white shirt buttoned at the neck with necktie precisely in place suggests a much different attitude than a shirt with the top button undone and the tie slightly loosened. The sketch will present the costume at one particular moment. It may remain this way during the entire performance. But characters' situations could change: they might get more tired, or drunker, or receive some unexpected guests. The designer should provide a guideline to the transitions that might take place and know what impact the variations in detail will have on the total costume.

◆ Movement and the Costume

The actor or actress needs to be able to move in the costume and the designer must make sure that the action required by the piece is possible in the clothes of the characters. In varying degrees, all costumes must

Figure 4.63   Historical source that might be suitable for a high comedy. An early-twentieth-century illustration from *L'Art de la Mode,* New York.

Figure 4.64   The source adapted for a serious play.

Figure 4.65   The source as it might appear in a musical or a farce.

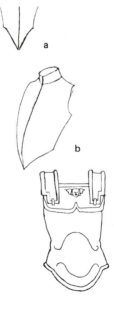

Figure 4.66   (a) The extended point of the bodice would greatly restrict the mobility of the wearer. (b) The padding of the peascod belly can limit a man's ability to bend. (c) Metal body armor can be extremely confining.

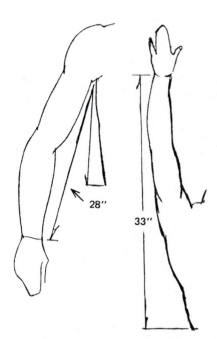

Figure 4.67 The distance from waist to wrist is much longer when the arm is raised than when it hangs at the side.

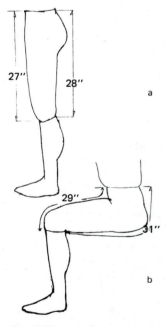

Figure 4.68 Both front and back measurements of waist to below knee are longer on the seated figure.

accommodate movement, and some periods are particularly restricting. The modern actor often needs a mobility that just doesn't exist in certain period costumes. The mobility is directly related to the manner in which the costume fits or restricts the hinge points.

The Waist. Any type of bending is restricted by corseting or padding. Strong boning that extends past the waistline will begin to immobilize the torso. A very long point in front can make bending and even sitting difficult, for the point can poke into the thigh (Figure 4.66a). The Elizabethan man's peascod belly does not confine the waist like a corset, but still keeps the actor from bending forward (Figure 4.66b). Most metal body armor is extremely confining. The Roman molded cuirass (Figure 4.66c) extending from chest to thigh made the Roman officer look quite impressive but was not too practical. He could stand around and give orders, but it was up to his less encumbered underlings to carry on the real business of battle.

The Shoulder and Arm. Actors must be free to move their arms when performing; the costumes of many periods, however, constrict arm movement severely. A tight sleeve attached to a tight bodice may well keep the actor from reaching very far up or forward. The constriction is caused because the length of the arm seems to change as it rotates in its socket. (Figure 4.67a and Figure 4.67b). If the sleeve is tight and can't ride down the arm, and the bodice is tight and can't ride up the body, the arm cannot be fully extended. In addition, if the armseye or armhole of the bodice is cut low, both the bodice underarm and the inside sleeve are shorter, restricting movement even more. A sleeve that fits the arm tightly can restrict bending if the sleeve is not cut to allow more space for the bent elbow. Possible solutions for these problems are discussed in Chapter 9. Even with a fuller sleeve the armseye that extends past the shoulder restricts movement for this seam and in effect ties the arm down to the body. If the armseye is placed at the end of the shoulder, just above the arm joint or slightly inside it, the actor should be able to raise his or her arms easily.

The Legs. Problems can also arise with leg movement. Trousers that are cut high in the crotch will allow for more extension of the leg. Knee breeches, which fasten under the knee, must have extra length in front and back for sitting and bending, for both areas get longer as the leg bends (Figure 4.68). The full-length skirt should present few obstacles to regular movement if care is taken with the cut and fit (see chapters 8 and 9).

The Neck. A high, tight, stiffened collar can definitely immobilize the neck and head. This rigidity can be quite appropriate to some characters and some periods, but the actors must understand the restrictions. If the feeling of the high collar is desirable but more movement is necessary, sloping the collar so that it is lower in front allows the chin to drop without losing the line.

These are just the most common movement problems. Should the actor need to do a somersault or scale a fence, even more careful attention should be paid to the design.

◆ The Quick Change

There is one more practical area to consider—the quick change. Miraculous transformations can take place in less than a minute if carefully conceived, but a quick change not thoughtfully planned can be a nightmare for all involved. It is irresponsible for a designer to create a costume change that is physically difficult and mentally straining and forces the actor to expend more energy backstage than onstage.

All possible quick changes are noted from the beginning of the work on a production and recorded in the costume list and scene breakdown. These change requirements should be in the back of the designer's mind as he or she creates a costume that is right for the character and that also can be changed quickly.

Keep three primary points in mind when planning a quick change.

1. *As much of the costume should come off and go on as a unit as possible.* For example, a shirt, vest, and coat can be preset to be put on as one unit. A skirt, bodice, and petticoats can be tacked together so they can be stepped into as one garment. (And stepping into a costume may be faster and easier on the hairstyle than slipping it over the head.)
2. *Fastenings should be simple and easy to find.* A long row of buttons or hooks and eyes are not quickly negotiated. Velcro is excellent for getting *out* of a garment quickly, although it is not as satisfactory for getting *into* one, for it can be difficult to line up properly and needs firm pressure to make it stay securely. If a zipper is used it should be heavy-duty because it will receive a lot of wear and tear. Buttons or hooks on cuffs can be set on a small piece of elastic that will stretch to allow the hand or foot to slip through without undoing the fastenings.
3. *The actor should have to do as little as possible.* The most efficient changes happen when the actor can come off and stand in the wings, moving his or her hands and feet when necessary to get in and out of the garments as the changers take care of all the fastening and unfastening. Actors tend to get anxious, and if they grab something upside down or backward a tightly timed change may not succeed at all.

An example of quick-change costumes done for a Haydn comic opera is shown in Figures 4.69, 4.70, and 4.71. The actor began one scene as a village gossip (Figure 4.69), had 45 seconds to become a lord (Figure 4.70), and a short time later had to turn into an old hag within 30 seconds (Figure 4.71). Two dressers were used for the changes. The actor started the scene wearing the shoes, hose, and breeches for the second costume under the first. All the pieces of the village-gossip dress were sewn together as a unit. The little shawl was tacked to the dress as far as the back opening, then snapped in place as it continued to wrap around the body. As the actor came offstage, dresser A unsnapped the shawl, then took off the hat and glasses as dresser B unzipped the dress. Dresser A pulled the sleeves over the hands and dropped the dress down. The actor turned while stepping out of the dress and put his arms in the shirt that

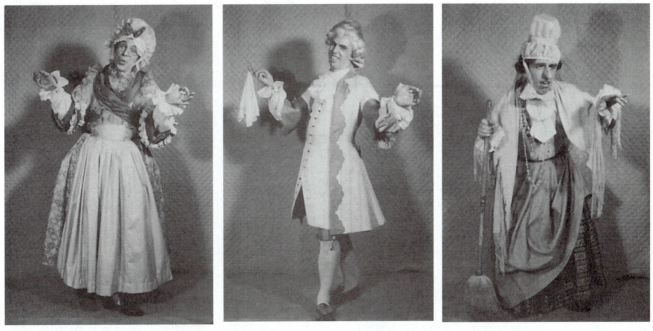

Figure 4.69 Hanswurst as the Gossip in *House Afire*. Presented at Yale University, 1963. Design by Barbara Anderson.

Figure 4.70 Hanswurst as Leander.

Figure 4.71 Hanswurst as the Old Hag.

Dresser B was holding. Dresser A fastened the shirt at the neck with one large hook, dresser B grabbed the coat and vest (preset together), and the actor made sure he was holding the shirt ruffles in each hand so the sleeves would stay down. Dresser B helped the actor into the coat and vest; dresser A pulled the vest together in front, carefully lined up the closing, and pressed the Velcro together. (The vest was fastened with Velcro because the actor had to get out of it even faster than he had to get into it.) Meanwhile, dresser B got the wig positioned on the actor's head, checking to make sure it covered his hairline. Dresser A handed him his handkerchief and he was ready.

The change to Figure 4.71 was done in a similar fashion. Dresser A opened the vest. Dresser B took off the coat and vest while A took off the wig. Dresser A unhooked the shirt; B pulled it off from the front. Dresser A held the dress as the actor stepped into it; B pulled it into position from the back and zipped it up as A put on the wig, which had the hat already pinned to it. Dresser A checked the position of the wig and hooked the hat tie on the side as B stuck on the nose, which had been prepared with double-sided adhesive. The breeches, shoes, and hose stayed on under the costume. And again the actor was ready to go with very little effort on his part, though the crew needed a rest. Actually, it takes good discipline on the part of the actor to stand in the right place, do those moves that are necessary, and try not to help, which would only confuse things.

Figure 4.72 The type of fabrics and textures that will be right for the costume should be known by the time the sketch is completed. The fabrics for this 1996 Ringling Bros. and Barnum & Bailey Clown College costume by Howard Kaplan reinforce the humor in the sketch.

Figure 4.73 The fabric for Merlin's robe was an unknown quantity until a bolt of blue-violet velvet shot with silver was spied during a shopping trip. Design by Barbara Anderson for *A Connecticut Yankee in King Arthur's Court* for the Once Upon a Classic series. ©Metropolitan Pittsburgh Public Broadcasting, Inc., 1977.

◆ Fabric, Texture, and the Basic Design

The effect of the fabric chosen for a costume must always be a part of the overall design idea because the texture of the material is an important component of the total effect. Designers must be familiar with a great variety of textiles. Chapter 8 discusses most of the fabrics available, but words are not adequate when exploring this field. Designers must feel their way through fabric stores and racks of clothes and costume storage areas. They must actually accumulate boxes of fabric swatches and mentally store away images of plush and nubby and shiny and sheer, for the weight, movement, and surface texture are extremely important. When sketching they may not realize that a costume specifically calls for silk moiré taffeta, but they should realize the fabric must be light, crisp, and shiny with a water-marked shimmer.

Ideas for the materials do not necessarily follow after the line has been established; the texture and the flow or movement of the fabrics may be the first impressions that occur to the designer. On reading *Macbeth*, for example, the images might be those of something heavy, thick, and rough, maybe even furred. The fairies in *A Midsummer Night's Dream* might evoke thoughts of shimmery sheers. Lady Sneerwell's social set in Sheridan's *The School for Scandal* could seem ideally suited to shiny, slick surfaces. A piece of fabric suddenly discovered may present a solution to an elusive costume problem.

The costume designer who doesn't find delight in fabric is perhaps in the wrong business, though the allure of these materials can be dangerous. Designers who really like what they do soon discover one of the most serious drawbacks in this business: they quickly acquire drawers and trunks full of pieces of cloth they just couldn't resist.

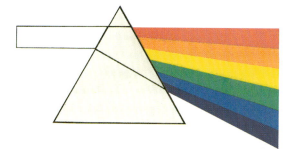

Figure 5.1 White light sent through a prism is dispersed into bands of different wavelengths.

Figure 5.2 The 12-part color wheel. From Johannes Itten, *The Elements of Color* (New York: Van Nostrand Reinhold, 1970)

Figure 5.3 The additive color wheel.

Figure 5.4 Blue and orange and their degrees of neutralization.

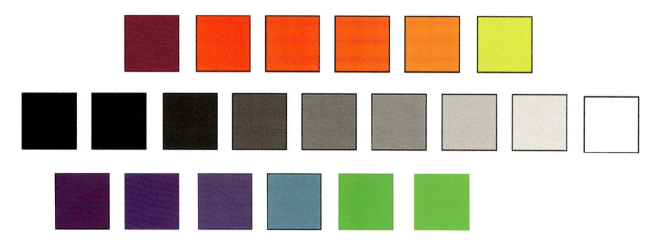

Figure 5.5 The value chart.

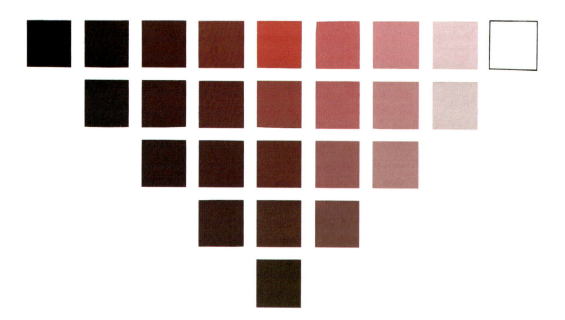

Figure 5.6 The value and intensity chart, hue red.

Figure 5.7   The two halves of the color sphere. From Itten, *The Elements of Color.*

Figure 5.8   The sphere seen as if bisected by a plane at the equator. From Itten, *The Elements of Color.*

Figure 5.9   The sphere bisected by a plane through the poles. From Itten, *The Elements of Color.*

Figure 5.10 The contrast of the three primary hues is more intense than that of the secondary hues.

Figure 5.11 A color grouping with all tones at the value of yellow.

Figure 5.12 Red-orange and blue-green are the two poles of warm-cold contrast.

Figure 5.13   The three primary and
three secondary hues with gray.

Figure 5.14   Blue-green diluted by
white, red-orange (its complement),
and black.

Figure 5.15   The color wheel showing the
harmonious relative areas of the hues.
From Itten, *The Elements of Color.*

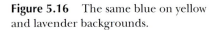

Figure 5.16 The same blue on yellow and lavender backgrounds.

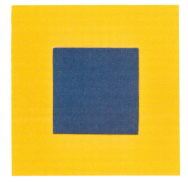

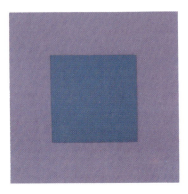

Figure 5.17 The same green appears darker with light tones and lighter with dark ones.

Figure 5.18 Red-violet seems cooler with orange tones, warmer with cool ones.

Figure 5.19 The same green on a colorful and more neutralized background.

Figure 5.20 The use of textures and fabric carefully mottled with paint makes this costume for Pan, god of the shepherds, in the Santa Fe Opera's production of *La Calisto* exciting and theatrical even though the color value and intensity are held in close range. Watercolor design by Robert Perdziola.

Figure 5.21 A wonderful feeling of whimsy is evident in this presentation of a costume for Lady India in Jean Anouilh's *Ring Around the Moon*. The watercolor rendering by Forest Rogers effectively represents the sheer fabric with peacock trim. (Above right)

Figure 5.22 The stronger colors at neckline and hair pull the focus of these costumes to the face. Designs by Ainslie Bruneau for guests in bathing suits in *The Merry Widow*.

Figure 5.23 A technique often associated with fashion illustration was used by Eduardo Castro in this sketch for a modern, stylish costume in the film *Sugar Hill*. Design done in markers. (Above left)

Figure 5.24 This costume rendering clearly reflects the designer's knowledge of the style of the performer. Costume for David Copperfield in *The Magic of David Copperfield*, designed by Daniel Orlandi. Sketch done in watercolor on charcoal paper. (Above right)

Figure 5.25 Malvolio cuts a foolish figure as he dons his dressy outfit in a 1996 production of Shakespeare's *Twelfth Night* at Carnegie Mellon University. The dark tones were built up of a number of washes with some of the lighter color allowed to show through to give interest and texture. Design by Brian Hemesath.

Chapter 5

Designing the Costume:
Color Control

Preceding page: The rendering for Chauncey in *Dracula, A Musical Nightmare* dramatically portrays a costume done predominately in black and white. Designer Susan Tsu added effective color accents in the tie, vest, and spats in the 1993 production at the Alley Theatre in Houston.

Color is a very powerful component of costume design; it makes the strongest initial visual impact and registers on the audience before the other visual elements of shape or detail. Careful color control provides a strong influence that will lead the audience toward a desired emotional response. Ideas about color begin to grow with the preliminary reading of the project, and the color concept is often one of the very first areas the designer and director explore together.

◆ What Is Color?

Colors result from light waves, which are a particular kind of electromagnetic energy. Visible light is a very small part of the electromagnetic spectrum, which travels through space in the form of waves measured from crest to crest. All traveling at the same speed, radio waves are the longest, several thousand feet across; gamma and cosmic waves are at the short-wave end of the spectrum. Light waves fall somewhere in the middle range, between infrared and ultraviolet rays. White light includes all the colors of the visible wavelengths. If a beam of white light is sent through a prism, the light is dispersed or broken into bands of different wavelengths, which produce the colors of the spectrum (Figure 5.1). If the rays of light that make up the spectrum are gathered by a converging lens, white light will once again be produced.

Subtractive Color Mixing: The Pigment Color Wheel

What we know as color is a phenomenon that actually happens within the eye itself. Certain wavelengths of light are perceived as certain hues. We recognize a specific color in an object because of the wavelength of light reflected from the object to the eye. As a ray of white light hits something that appears red, all the colors of the spectrum but red are absorbed and the red light is reflected. The colors that result from this absorption are known as *subtractive colors*. If the wavelength is not present in the light source, the color that is produced by that wavelength cannot be reflected and, thus, perceived. When a green light is directed on a red object the object will appear black, for there is no red light. A white object, while it absorbs some light, reflects all colors equally. A black object absorbs all light rays, subtracting all colors.

Pigment refers to the color agent or colorant in objects. The three primary pigments in the subtractive color wheel are red, yellow, and blue. These three colors, when mixed, will absorb all the light rays projected on them, with a dark, neutral tone as the result. The 12-part subtractive color wheel (Figure 5.2) is a helpful tool that utilizes combinations of the primary pigments to show 12 distinct easily identifiable hues that can be used as a basis for any of the infinite color variations possible. A combination of two primary colors produces a secondary color, which is located halfway between each primary.

Red + yellow = orange

Yellow + blue = green

Blue + red = violet

A combination of a primary and its adjoining secondary results in a tertiary color.

Red + orange = red-orange   Green + blue = blue-green

Orange + yellow = yellow-orange   Blue + violet = blue-violet

Yellow + green = yellow-green   Violet + red = red-violet

The red-violet or purple tones might be considered artificial, for they do not appear in the spectrum (which is a linear band running from red to violet), but they are certainly present in the color wheel and complete the circle. The 12-tone color wheel is standard, but it can be expanded by combining adjoining colors. The step between red and orange could go from red to red-orange-red to red-orange to orange-red-orange to orange and so on.

Additive Color Mixing: The Light Color Wheel

Adding colored light differs from mixing colored pigments. The three primary colors of light are red, green, and blue. When mixed equally these colors produce white light. In combinations of varying proportions, the primary colors can produce all other colors of light. The most common example of this is found in the color television set, which has only red, blue, and green screens yet shows the viewer an entire range of colored images. Since colored light rays are added to each other on the same surface, this is called *additive mixing*. Figure 5.3 shows the light color wheel created by additive mixing. Red and green produce the yellow tones, red and blue the violet tones, and blue and green the blue-green or cyan tones. Any two complementary light colors (those that are opposite on the color wheel) combine to produce white light, since all three primaries are then present: red and blue-green, blue and yellow (red and green), and green and violet (blue and red).

Basic Color Vocabulary

While the use of color and its interpretations can be very subjective, a designer should be familiar with basic color theory and vocabulary. The exact terms may vary slightly with different color systems, but the designer who understands the underlying concepts should be able to adjust to variations.

The term *color* is a general classification that often refers to a number of qualities of the perceived tone. Color is more specifically defined by its three primary qualities—hue, value, and intensity—which are explained in the following paragraphs.

Hue. The term *hue* specifically defines the unmodified colors in the spectrum. Figure 5.2 shows the 12-hue color wheel. The hues opposite each other on the wheel are known as complementary hues. They are considered complementary because their combination is a mixture of the three primary hues. For example, blue and orange are complements. Orange is made of yellow and red; when blue is added, the primary triad is present. Blue-green and red-orange might be thought of as blue (blue + yellow) and red (red + yellow). The primary triad is complete. This completion can be thought of as a *color chord.* The diagram below shows the color wheel with a group of chords, all of which contain the three primaries. Color chords result from complementary pairs, triads from equilateral and isosceles triangles, and tetrads formed from squares and rectangles. Color schemes can be developed based on the hues contained in color chords. In subtractive color, any of these combinations that make up the chords when mixed together will form a dark neutral tone because the light is absorbed and no specific hue is reflected back to the eye.

Some combinations of hues do not combine to incorporate all the primary colors but instead relate to only one section of the color wheel. The hues adjacent to each other on the wheel are known as *analogous hues.* Yellow, yellow-orange, and orange are analogous, as are red, red-violet, and violet.

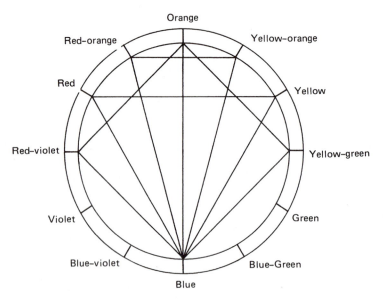

Color chords.

Color Intensity or Chroma. The color wheel presents the hues at their full *intensity* or *chroma*. They are the pure hues, uncontaminated by combination with other hues, black, or white. As a hue is mixed with its complement the purity of the colors, or the intensity, lessens. The hue becomes neutralized. As equal parts of the complementary hues are mixed, the result is a gray tone. Figure 5.4 shows the combinations of the complements blue and orange. The blue moves from full intensity to one-quarter neutralized to one-half neutralized to three-quarters neutralized to the neutral gray that is midway between the blue and orange. On the other half of the chart the orange tones take over as they move from three-quarters neutralized to one-half neutralized to one-quarter neutralized to the pure hue. The formulas below the chart give an idea of how the mixing is achieved, though when actually working with paints it is never quite so easy to accomplish.

Color Value. The scale that indicates the light-to-dark relativity of the tones between white and black is called the *value scale*. The value scale is often considered in nine steps from white to high light, light, low light, medium, high dark, dark, low dark, and black. The hues fall at various levels on this scale. Yellow is a bit below high light, violet is about at low dark and red-orange and blue-green just below medium (Figure 5.5). While each hue has its own level, it can be moved up or down the scale by adding white or black. Tones produced by adding white are called *tints;* those that result from adding black are called *shades.* There are relatively few tints of yellow, for it begins close to white on the scale, but there are many shades of yellow as it moves toward black. Similarly, only a few shades take blue down to near the level of black, but many tints of blue are available.

Tonal Variations and the Color Sphere

While there is only one true hue of any color, its variations in terms of intensity and value are myriad (Figure 5.6). Except for red-orange and blue-green, which are complements at the same value, mixing to neutralize a color will change the value as the darker and lighter hues are combined. But no matter what the intensity, the value can change; and no matter what the value, the intensity can change. Noted colorist Johannes Itten, in his book *The Elements of Color,* presents the color sphere, which is based on the work of Philipp Otto Runge. This is fascinating to study, for in one geometric figure he encompasses the idea of all the color variations. The north pole is white, the south is black, and the central core consists of the achromatic or gray scale. The perimeter at the equator is divided into 12 equal sections, presenting the hues of the color wheel. On the surface of the sphere, tints of the hues move toward the white pole and shades move toward the black. Figure 5.7 shows the two halves of the color sphere. A plane bisecting the sphere at the equator displays the hues as they are neutralized toward gray (Figure 5.8). A plane bisecting the sphere through the poles reveals two complements on each side of the gray core and the tints, shades, and neutralized tones of both hues (Figure 5.9). Using the sphere one can easily visualize the three most common ways of defining colors: by hue, value, and intensity.

Color Contrast

Color does not make a statement in itself. The interaction of colors must always be considered. Itten refers to seven different types of color contrast, which are interesting to consider because they can increase color awareness. His seven contrasts are:

1. Contrast of hue
2. Contrast of value, or light–dark contrast
3. Cold–warm contrast
4. Complementary contrast
5. Simultaneous contrast
6. Contrast of intensity or saturation
7. Contrast of extension

By understanding these contrasts the designer can begin to see the effects of color use in a production. Control of these variables is another means to create an effective design.

Contrast of Hue. The most intense contrast of hue employs the three primaries—red, yellow, and blue, a combination that produces a vigorous effect. The intensity of the contrast of hues diminishes as the hues are removed from the three primaries (Figure 5.10). Orange, green, and violet are not as vibrant a combination, and yellow, yellow-green, and green are even less so. A red dress with green trim could be visually too active because the contrast of hue is too strong. Yellow or violet trim would possibly be much more suitable.

Value or Light–Dark Contrast. Value contrast deals with those variations displayed in the value scale. The ultimate contrast is white and black, with a vast number of grays possible between them limited only by the eye's ability to perceive the variations. Light–dark contrasts can also be present with all the hues, but the pure hue hits only one place on the value scale. A dark yellow is no longer truly yellow because it has been combined with a tone of a lower value. Pure yellow can only appear at high light on the value scale. A color grouping in which all tones are at the level of yellow will present quite a brilliant yellow, while other tones will be more washed out, for no other color is at the value of yellow unless some white has been added to it (Figure 5.11). Value contrast is often particularly strong in the light shirts and dark suits of men's costumes.

Cold–Warm Contrast. The two poles of the cold–warm contrast are blue-green and red-orange (Figure 5.12). Experiments have shown that people definitely associate warmth and activity with the red-orange side of the spectrum and coolness and quietness with the blue-green.

Complementary Contrast. Complementary colors have been discussed earlier in this chapter. Complementary pairs have interesting properties. Put side by side, they incite each other to maximum vividness; mixed together, they neutralize each other to gray-black. The mixing of complements to form the grayed tones can produce many more interesting variations than would be possible when just adding black or white to the hues. Pointillists, who created their paintings by placing thousands of tiny dots of color on the canvas, found grays much more vibrant when dots of the complements were placed side by side and the mixing was done in the eye. This same effect is sometimes found in fabric. If thin blue and orange threads are closely woven together, the fabric will appear gray at a distance, but a vibrant gray with both blue and orange overtones.

Simultaneous Contrast. Simultaneous contrast occurs in the eye, for when a color is perceived the eye requires the complementary color and will generate it simultaneously if it is not present. To perform an experiment that clearly shows this phenomenon take sheets of the six pure hues and placing on each a gray square of the same value as the hue (Figure 5.13). The gray on the yellow will have a violet cast; on the violet it will seem yellowish. The gray on the orange hue will tend toward blue; on the blue it will tend toward orange. The gray on the red will take on a green feeling, while the gray on the green will go more toward red. If a strip of the same gray is placed near each color but is slightly separate and surrounded by white, it will not appear to be the same tone as the gray in the squares, for the eye will not alter it.

A similar phenomenon is called successive contrast. When the eye stares at a colored square, such as red, and then closes or looks away, an afterimage of the complement (green in this case) appears. In both cases the eye is completing the spectrum and providing the hues that are missing. Brightly lit intense hues in costumes can cause the eye to distort the color or detect an afterimage when the costume moves.

Contrast of Intensity or Saturation. As explained earlier, intensity relates to the degree of purity of a color. The contrast of intensity or saturation is the contrast between the pure, uncontaminated hue and its diluted variations (Figure 5.14). Colors can be diluted in four ways:

1. *By adding white* to produce a tint
2. *By adding black* to darken and deaden the color
3. *By adding gray* to move the color to a more neutral tone
4. *By adding the complement* to neutralize the color, usually in a more interesting fashion than when gray is added

A costume can easily jump out of a group because it seems intense and pure compared to the grayed or diluted shades around it. A red dress will take focus when surrounded by tones of pink.

Contrast of Extension. Contrast of extension deals with the relative areas of two color patches or the contrast between a larger area and a smaller one. Certain proportions of one color to another seem to put the hues in balance. Hues that are higher on the value scale seem to have more brilliance and require less area to balance with hues of a darker value. Ratios developed by Goethe, better known for his literary endeavors, and used by Itten indicate how the hues relate to each other. If values are given to the primary and secondary colors as follows:

Yellow	Orange	Red	Green	Blue	Violet
3	4	6	6	8	9

it is easy to see that yellow balances with orange in a 3 : 4 ratio, with red in a 3 : 6 (1 : 2) ratio, and so on. The proportion of yellow to red to blue would be 3 : 6 : 8, and for orange, green, and violet 4 : 6 : 9. Other ratios can be discovered on the same basis. A color wheel that shows the harmonious relative areas of the hues can be constructed. With a total of 36 units assigned to the six hues and the wheel made up of 360 degrees, 10 degrees of the arc can be allotted for each unit. The wheel would have 30° yellow, 40° orange, 60° red, 60° green, 80° blue, and 90° violet (Figure 5.15). The proportions given relate only to the balance of the pure hues. As the color changes in intensity and value, its relationships to other colors also change.

Color Relationships

One fact is absolutely certain about color: it is never absolute. Color perception varies with circumstances, which can involve the surrounding objects, the available light, the type of color surface, or the frame of reference of the viewer.

Variations in color relationships occur in all the different ways color is perceived. The six basic spectrum hues easily bring to mind specific colors. Yet these six hues present a decidedly different color feeling when seen before a white, medium gray, or black background. A blue square on a yellow ground has a vibrancy that will not be present if the same square is placed on violet (Figure 5.16). The same yellow that may seem lifeless against beige could be too active when paired with a bright green.

The value of either hues or gray tones is relative. Green might appear quite dark in a grouping of yellows and oranges, but quite light if the other tones are blue-violets and violets (Figure 5.17). Medium gray is very dark when surrounded by white and light gray, and quite light in the midst of black and dark gray. A red gown in the midst of pinks and maroons is one thing, surrounded by only black it makes an entirely different statement.

As with value contrast, cold–warm contrast can vary depending on the tones that are used. Blue-green and red-orange are always cold and warm, respectively, but the other colors can take on different meanings. A red-violet may seem quite cool when grouped with orange hues and very warm when shown with cool ones (Figure 5.18).

The effect of changing the intensity of a color is again relative. The same color can appear dull when placed next to a more vivid tone, and vivid if paired with a duller one. Green at half intensity will seem quite subdued next to pure green, but very colorful if combined with a green that has been almost completely neutralized to gray (Figure 5.19).

The designer must have a well-founded understanding of color and what it does under various circumstances. The best way to achieve this understanding is to experiment with color combinations to increase awareness of what is possible. The most effective way to explore color is with paintbox and brush in hand. Making up color charts that vary hue, value, and intensity can be a bit tedious, but the experience is invaluable.

Work with colored papers can also help the designer develop an awareness of color relationships; the papers can be mixed and matched easily and quickly to create interactions among tones. Color-Aid papers come in a 2″ × 4 1/2″ set of more than 300 tones with black, white, and grays, and Pantone Color Paper Selector, Uncoated provides more than 1,000 tones in a 2″ by 4″ format. These are an effective starting point but may prove both limiting and unwieldy. Besides, while basic relationships can be explored, often the right tone for a costume is nowhere to be found.

Color computers offer another extreme. A computer is able to show millions of different tones. Many available programs allow the designer to explore an infinite number of color combinations.

When working on color exercises, pick a neutral shape to use for the examples. A square or rectangle works quite well and is easy to produce. Varying the shapes can give connotations to the color that makes appreciation of the single element of tone more difficult. Colored fabrics can also be very useful for exploring color combinations, though they add the element of texture to the color feeling. They therefore provide a less accurate exploration of color theory, but do show colors more as the costume designer usually sees them.

Color Symbolism

Thus far colors have been judged on their physical properties. Color, however, causes definite subjective reactions in the beholder. The subjective response is not easily specified, for the psychological reaction to color can be a very personal thing, conditioned by experience and environment. Some color responses, however, are generally accepted as relating to a majority of people, and these should be taken into consideration.

Nature is a constant that influences everyone's color sensibilities. The tones of the outside world are always there, familiar and therefore comfortable, and anything that falls within these guidelines is readily accepted by the audience. Grass is green. If it is red it is unnatural. Mashed potatoes are white. If they are blue they are unpalatable. The seasons of the year are known by the colors they present. Spring gives the yellow-greens and pastels of new growth; summer is full of deep green foliage against bright blue skies; autumn brings rusts, reds, and oranges; and winter closes the year with its whites, grays, and gray-blues. Variations to the colors of nature may startle the audience. This technique can of course be very effective in certain instances. No one will believe an ingenue with a pale green face, but if she has just returned from the grave this odd complexion may be just perfect.

Nature and conditioning provide colors with meanings that may hold true for a number of people. The following emotional responses to the six basic colors are not absolute, but they should be considered because they represent typical reactions that may be found in the audience:

> **Red**   Warmth, activity, power, passion, strength. Red variations can run quite a gamut, from satanic, bloody, warlike deep tones to cherubic pinks.

Orange   Festivity, active energy, earthy vibrancy. Variations to orange can go from warm, restful beiges to dull, withered browns.

Yellow   Brightness, knowledge, youth, radiance. Pure yellows tend toward truth and understanding while neutralized yellows move more to distrust and decay.

Green   Fruitfulness, lush nature, contentment. Greens reflect the growth in the world, but when grayed can become sinister or when mixed with blue take on a colder, more aggressive tone.

Blue   Coldness, passivity, spiritualism, faith, introversion. Light blue has a transparent quality. Blue becomes more vibrant as it moves to black, and grayed tones seem suitable for superstition and the supernatural.

Violet   Piety, mastery, menace, chaos, solitude, royalty, terror. Violet variations can cover a great range from the lilac of lovely spring flowers to the terrifying purples that may inhabit a nightmare.

Color Symbols.   In any society certain color symbols are used so often they are readily accepted as the way things ought to be. A variety of conditioned responses may be triggered in the audience when a certain tone is presented. Red is associated with fire trucks, flashing alarms, stop signs, and the garments of high church officials. Yellow is the color on caution signs; a lighter association is implied by the slogan "Blondes have more fun." Green means go, and a shade of green is used for "Mr. Yuk" on poison labels. The Virgin Mary typically wears blue, as do police officers. Brides wear white; priests, nuns, and mourners wear black. The color of the military uniforms of a country can evoke a response. Certain colors are expected in certain situations. If they are not used, the reason should be clear. Color symbolism can be quite helpful, but if it is not used carefully it can get in the way of the story line, for it could tell too much or move in a direction that goes against the plot. For example, a vibrant red is often associated with a lady of ill repute and in some situations could be used quite effectively as such. If, however, the audience isn't to know immediately about the lady's moral shortcomings it would be better not to clothe her in such a blatant symbol. If a character seems about to lose touch with reality, misty blues and lavenders might seem ideal. As a general rule it is wise to avoid the temptation to make the costumes of lovers match. In many cases color symbolism can be helpful, but the colors must hold effectively within the scene even if the symbol is not read by the audience.

◆ Color Approach to a Production

Scripted Color Needs

A piece may have specific color needs written into the script and these should be noted by the designer. It is important to decide if a color mentioned in the script is essential to the production or if it can be exchanged for another equally appropriate color. For example, Cyrano du Bergerac refers to his white plume, and that symbolic plume is quite central to the play. George Bernard Shaw was very fond of specifying the settings and costumes of his plays in great detail; in *Candida* he describes Marchbanks as wearing "an old blue serge jacket, unbuttoned, over a woolen lawn tennis shirt, with a silk handkerchief for a cravat, trousers matching the jacket, and brown canvas shoes." From this the designer can get a good idea of how Shaw saw the character, but there is no reason that Shaw's stipulations should be followed to the letter. However, in *The Devil's Disciple* the Presbyterian minister, Anderson, must have a black coat as Shaw suggests, for a black coat is an easily recognized symbol for a minister; by donning Anderson's coat Dick Dudgeon assumes the other's identity to fool the arresting officer.

Sometimes a production may require costumes that automatically make a strong statement in the color scheme. A formal ball usually involves men in black and white. If the British are invading the American colonies, the Redcoats will make a definite color impact. Uniforms, church costumes, and formal wear produce a strong color direction and the color helps produce an expected emotional response in the audience.

In the same vein, the setting of the piece may point to the use of certain colors and establish color limits for the costumes. A scene in a forest could provide an environment of dominant green tones, just as one in a castle may tend to stone gray. Black velour curtains or a blue cyclorama are stage elements often used for either practical or artistic reasons, and either sets a strong color direction.

Color Ideas from the Director

Just as a guide to the color scheme can come from the script, so can it come from the director who may want a certain color feeling in a certain scene. It is then important for the designer to make sure the colors of the rest of the production revolve around that scene properly. For example, if the final scene of Shakespeare's *A Midsummer Night's Dream* were to be designed as a sumptuous masque, with the wedding party and courtiers all in golds and whites, the designer would not want to use those tones in the earlier scenes but would save them for the visual impact at the end.

It is possible for a director to have some color ideas that the designer does not agree with and vice versa. When this happens it is usually more efficient to work up color ideas around both suggestions and see which seems best for the production. In most cases, satisfactory solutions can be found through intelligent discussion; very seldom is there only one color solution to any problem.

Color for Character Identification

Color can be a valuable tool to help the audience keep track of character relationships, particularly in productions with large casts where individuals may not be clearly defined but group identity is important. In Shakespeare's *Romeo and Juliet* the Montagues must be different from the Capulets. In *Richard III,* Richard's supporters must be distinguished from Richmond's. Good color control helps the audience identify any opposing forces, whether armies, cheerleaders, or good and evil.

◆ Planning the Color

Color should be discussed with color samples or a color layout at hand that all can view and comment on. The designer may have a well-developed sense of color, but it may not be at all like that of the director.

The first color indications may come from a photograph, painting, or collage that says something about the show to either the designer or the director. It need not be exact or complete, but it is a conversation starter for preliminary discussions. Given this, the designer can work on a more specific color presentation, one that carefully applies itself to the emotional color of the show. This presentation could take the form of a preexisting photograph or painting, or a color collage made specifically to portray the colors that will be seen.

Any color guide the costume designer uses is a tool that helps develop the color scheme and should incorporate enough variety to suggest all the costumes. It should also contain some of the colors that will be used in the scenery, for this provides the setting in which the costumes will be seen. A layout for Shakespeare's *As You Like It* is incomplete if it concentrates only on woodsy, pastoral tones and ignores the beginning court scene, which should have a very different color impact.

While a color layout presents the hues, values, and intensities that will be emotionally right for the show, color should not be considered completely divorced from texture. A photograph or painting may be chosen because it contains implied textures that are right for the desired effect. A photograph of a decaying or weathered piece of wood might contain the same shades of browns and grays as a photo of a modern office building. If the costumes were to be done with textured, painted, aged fabrics the former would be more appropriate; if they were to be clean, crisp, stylish clothes, the latter would be better.

A costume collage can give the designer a wonderful opportunity to express both color feeling and texture of the show, for almost anything can be incorporated, fabric swatches, metallic bits, pieces of beading, old sticks, torn-up doilies, spatters of paint, a leaf or flower—anything that opens up possibilities and sparks the imagination to use color.

Setting Color Limitations

Color control can be used to produce a unified visual effect in a production, one that is appropriate to the emotional content as a whole and to the individual characters. Various types of color schemes can be set up based on the three main properties of color. The hues that are to be used could be limited. In *As You Like It,* maroons, blues, and purples could be designated for the court scene, with browns, oranges, greens, and yellows reserved for the forest. The tonal values to be used could be defined. In Sheridan's *The Rivals* the color tones could all range from medium to white, giving a bright, airy, pastel feeling. Lowering the intensity of colors can help bring a unified quality to the picture. Brecht's somber *Mother Courage* could well be done with the colors one-half to three-quarters neutralized.

Never think that limitations have to produce a dull theatrical picture. A production done only in shades of brown could be quite breathtaking and give a very colorful effect, for there are light browns, dark browns, warm browns, cool browns, intense browns, grayed browns . . . a whole color riot of browns alone. In addition to the variations possible within the most limited palette there are also variations provided by the textures of the fabrics. Even a production done only in black with white accents could be fascinating and have a great deal of variety. The only true black will be a velvet with the pile running up. All others will appear a degree or so lighter, depending upon the textures of the fabrics used.

Color Progression

A color progression easily can be established for some productions. The colors used in a staging of *Mother Courage* could become less intense as the war continues and drains the life and color from the landscape and its inhabitants. The townspeople in Dürrenmatt's *The Visit* might be quite drab as the play starts, then gain in color as they draw nearer and nearer to accepting the bribe offered them. Ibsen's *Peer Gynt* might be defined effectively by the colors Peer encounters on his odyssey.

Color Coordination of Scenery and Costumes

No costume color scheme can be completely successful on its own. The costumes are always seen in relation to the surrounding space, which is usually scenery or a location. The designers should know how the elements will go together and what effect they will produce. If the ingenue is to stand out like a jewel she might be costumed in a bright, crisp yellow. But if the set is yellow, perhaps she should appear in a white dress. Once the color progression is established for the show, the steps it makes and where they occur should be clear to both the scenic and the costume designers. Tones that are very similar should retain a degree of differentiation. Colored stage light can make some hues blend together. It is always discomfiting to design a costume that looks as if it were made from the fabric left over after covering the sofa.

Friendly cooperation should be the keystone of the relationship between the scene designer and the costume designer. There are no rules about whose ideas are more important and which area should get first consideration. The scheme should develop because all involved are exchanging ideas and trying to find the best possible presentation. Thorough discussion allows both designers to work on their color ideas separately and come up with schemes that will work together. As mentioned earlier, certain color requirements may be specifically stipulated in the script. It is likely that the Forest of Arden in *As You Like It* will be done in green tones; the costume designer should consider this from the beginning. It is equally probable that a scene in a nunnery will require many black costumes; the scene designer should always keep this in mind.

◆ Realism and Stylization in the Color Scheme

Costumes that must give a strongly realistic effect need a color scheme drawn from colors that were popular and commonly used in the period and locale in which the piece is set, or at least those generally accepted as the ones most prevalent in that particular time and place. For more recent periods, colored photographs are good reference materials; for earlier times, paintings give the flavor of an era, though it may well be idealized by the artist. From paintings it becomes quite apparent that the tonality of an Elizabethan tragedy is quite different from that of an eighteenth-century pastoral play. The former seems more often depicted in deeper, richer colors; the latter in lighter, frothier ones.

A production can take on a very stylized look if the designer uses historically nontraditional color. A Molière piece done in black, white, and gray immediately lets the audience know that this presentation takes an unconventional point of view. However, color stylization does not have to be so blatant. Subtle variations can be used to create an effect that gives a slight twist that adds interest without calling attention to itself.

◆ The Individual Costume Within the Color Scheme

The color scheme provides the plan for the entire production. From this major scheme the designer selects the tones that will be used in each individual scene; after that he or she may choose those tones that will give the main thrust to each costume.

A scene breakdown color plot can be quite useful in laying out the show. With it the designer can project how each scene will look and judge the effectiveness of the color control. This color breakdown can be laid out in the same form as the scene breakdown in Chapter 2, or it could be done as illustrated in the chart on the next page. The format here is perhaps easier to read for this purpose since the colors in each scene go across the page. Only the predominant costume colors need be included, in approximately the same proportion that they will be seen in the costumes. For example, with a red costume trimmed in black, a much larger area of red than of black is represented graphically.

The computer can be a valuable tool for this step. Not only can it create the color blocks for the costumes, it can also add the background color and provide a means to explore basic blocking layouts.

As a designer looks at the colors that will be used in a scene, he or she must carefully consider the action of that scene. The colors must reinforce the dramatic focus. For example, if the scene is a coronation, there can be little doubt that the colors worn by the king should be emphasized and highlighted over all other costumes. As Hamlet watches the play within a play the stage will be filled with many courtiers, plus the players, yet Hamlet must retain the dramatic focus of the scene.

A Word of Warning. Many costume shops are equipped with fluorescent lights, most of which illuminate with a limited spectrum; the red areas are particularly bad. A fabric that seems to be a pleasant maroon in the shop might appear closer to fire-engine red in daylight. It is very important to have varied light sources available. The warning must go one step further, for many fabric departments are also illuminated by fluorescent lighting. When shopping, particularly for red tones, use either an incandescent

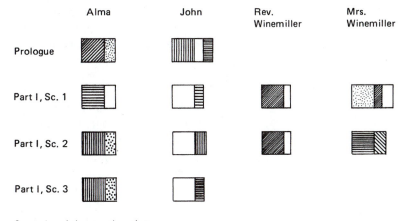

Scene breakdown color plot
for *Summer and Smoke*

Scene breakdown color plot for *Summer and Smoke.*

light or daylight from an untinted window to check the color of a fabric before making a commitment.

Color Within the Individual Costume

Abstract discussion about the proper way to set up the color schemes for the individual costumes can be a bit difficult, but when the designer is in the midst of a project, actually deciding which colors are best for which characters will not seem such an elusive task. Equipped with a clear idea of basic color theory, a knowledge of the script, an understanding of the characters, and a thoughtful consideration of the overall color scheme, the designer's task is far less formidable.

Color harmonies are created in a costume through the control of hue, value, and intensity, but total harmony can become total monotony. Every costume needs focus, and, as mentioned earlier, the focus is usually aimed toward the speaking part of the body. The arrangement of color as well as of line can lead the eye to the face (Figure 5.21). For a simple peasant frock, the design may need only one tone, and the color accent will be the face and hair. As more tones enter the picture more care must be taken so the attention of the audience will not be misplaced. If a man wears a black suit with a white shirt and a blue-striped tie, the shirt and tie will help focus attention to the top of his body. If he wears yellow shoes they had better be important to the scene, because that's where the audience will be looking.

In Sheridan's *The Rivals,* Mrs. Malaprop is much too outrageous to clothe herself in a quiet color scheme, while the more demure Julia would probably not have nearly as much contrast in her ensemble. In Molière's *Le Bourgeois Gentilhomme,* Monsieur Jourdain is terribly eager to join the world of the elite and embarks on this mission with full force and no noticeable taste; his colors would reflect this approach to life. Cleante, the young suitor for Jourdain's daughter, is much more straightforward and honest, traits that can be reinforced by the colors of his clothes.

Ideas about colors should never really be separated from ideas about textures. The types of fabric used greatly influence how the color will be perceived. Kelly-green cotton, satin, and velvet can produce three completely different color feelings. Texture variations could provide the variety and focus needed for an effective costume. Traditionally a bride is dressed only in white, but a bridal outfit usually does not seem monotonous, for contrast and focus are provided by veils, laces, and trims; a variety of textures.

Certain color combinations make some tones seem to advance and others recede, just as some tones will seem of lighter weight and others heavier. These effects rely very much upon the way the tones are put together; the designer must be able to judge the effect against the intent. As a general rule, lighter tones advance from a dark background while darker tones recede into it; darker shades advance from a light background while light ones recede. Warm tones advance while cool ones retreat. Lighter tones seem to have less weight than darker ones. All this is nevertheless quite relative, depending on the types of tones used and the way they interrelate.

The spatial qualities of color can be useful when the designer wishes to minimize some figure problems. For (as the ad agencies put it) a full-figured woman, a lighter panel for the front of the gown and darker shades to the side will help achieve a slimming effect. As lighter, brighter tones tend to advance they may not work well for slacks on a fuller figure.

The swatches or color chips used to do the color layouts for the individual costumes should always be arranged in the proportions seen in the costume, relative to the way they will appear on the body. This makes them more helpful to the designer and director, who can begin to visualize how the completed costume will look.

◆ The Effect of Colored Light on Fabric

Costumes and scenery are revealed and modified by the lighting used. Film and television use predominately white light; the stage employs color mediums to help mold the picture, add interest to the composition, and heighten the emotional impact of the scene. The color mediums in the light can greatly influence the color effect of the costumes and scenery.

For the stage the costume designer and lighting designer can discuss the basic color approach early in the design process. Once the costume designer has selected most of the fabrics that will be used in the production, a practical session with the lighting designer can be arranged to view the fabrics in the main colors that will be used. The costume designer may need to adjust the tonal values of some of the fabrics, which can often be done with dyes; the lighting designer can see if the colors he or she wishes to use will best enhance the fabric or if another combination will more effectively produce the desired result.

Many of the effects of colored light on fabric can be anticipated by merely thinking through how selective reflection works. Red fabric in blue light will not seem red. It will be a nondescript dark tone, for the blue light has no red rays to be reflected. Orange fabric in red light will appear red. The orange fabric reflects red and yellow rays, but the red light provides only red rays. If green light is added, the orange fabric will appear orange, for the green light with the red mixes to create yellow. Color theory is easy to understand, but color elements, whether dye, paint, fabric, light mediums, or the like, are rarely pure, and unforeseen variations always pop up.

The stage is seldom illuminated with only one color, therefore a deficiency in one tone can be compensated for by another. So many variations are available that it is difficult to say what a specific color will do on a specific fabric. Scenes that need strongly colored lighting effects should be given particular attention when thinking through costume colors.

Color is the first scenic element to affect the audience and the one that is the most difficult to control because so many factors can influence the way it is perceived. An A-line skirt is always an A-line skirt, but a yellow skirt can be changed in a number of directions. Good color control requires a great many decisions and a keen sense of judgment.

◆ Chapter 6

Costume Presentation: Rendering or Final Sketch

Preceding page: The fantasy costume can be a real challenge for a designer. Costume design by Susan Tsu for The Queen of the Netherlands in *And the Sea Shall Give Up Its Dead,* produced by WHA-TV for PBS. Colored pencil and graphite on drawing paper. A 14″ figure on an 11.75″ × 18″ sheet of drawing paper.

The aim of the costume rendering or final sketch is to present a clear design that helps convey and support the character (Figure 6.20). The costume design is developed with careful thought to the overall approach to the production; the lines, colors, and textures are selected because they best delineate the character within the guidelines of this overall approach. The ideas must now be expressed in final form. For many designers this can be traumatic, perhaps because it seems like the ultimate commitment.

The costume rendering or final sketch is important, but it should be considered a means and not an end in itself. The costume, not the drawing, is the final product, but the drawing is the vehicle that communicates the designer's ideas to everyone involved in the production (Figure 6.4). In fact, it provides a means for designers to communicate with themselves. A carefully executed sketch brings the costume impressions from the imagination to the paper, where designers can examine their ideas, judge the effect, and make specific decisions to clarify their choices. This is the last private moment to organize thoughts. Once the rendering gets to the shop there will be many demands, often simultaneous, on the designer. He or she should know what is required beforehand so that well-considered judgment will take the place of spur-of-the-moment decisions.

Effective costume renderings or final sketches serve multiple purposes as the designer presents the work to others (Figure 6.6). They certainly help convey ideas to the director and inspire the actors by showing them how they will look and by pointing out character nuances within each costume. The sketches can interest the crew members and get them excited about building the show and making the costumes that will look just like the drawings.

◆ The Costume Design Presentation

The costume design presentation is not necessarily a work of art; it is a clear indication of what the costume will be, easily read and understood by those involved. If everything cannot be seen on the main figure, supplemental sketches should be added (Figure 6.1). If possible, it should include swatches of the actual materials and trims to be used, or perhaps texture indications, so the designer can present as much information as is needed to clarify his or her ideas (Figure 6.19). The completed rendering must contain all the elements of the costume, including the hair, headdress, accessories, and footwear (Figures 6.18 and 6.22). A sketch should be an honest representation of the costume, something that can actually be built to give the same effect when worn in the production.

A certain amount of idealization can be included if it will give the flavor of the production. For a period piece, the costume plates might tend toward the illustration style used at that time (Figure 6.13). If the style of a farce is to have a broad, comic-book feeling, the plates could reflect this. A piece that incorporates a lot of movement might have renderings that show this activity. But if a costume will not be seen with three wind machines always blowing at it, it should not be illustrated as such. It is very poetic to think of the costume sketch as showing "five yards of emotion," but a shop cannot build this, nor can an actor maintain the fever pitch of intensity and action needed to duplicate the impression created by the sketch.

No matter how clear and accurate the costume sketch is, it may not be properly understood by someone viewing it. The sketch must be as complete as possible, but it is up to the designer to discuss each sketch, point out the various elements, note how the articles work, what comes off, what has pockets, and so forth. Many people cannot conceptualize a drawing and do not really understand what they are seeing until they have a three-dimensional object before them. Some of these people are directors and it is not uncommon for them to say "I didn't know it would look like that," even though the costume was completed exactly as it was presented on the sketch.

◆ Establishing the Figure

The figure in the costume sketch should emphasize physical qualities that are important to establish the character. Should the role call for a heroic and elegant personage, some elongation might be used (Figure 6.15). All the figures need not be ideally proportioned; the costume sketches should reflect physical differences between characters.

The detail of the costume can be seen more easily on a figure that opens out. The set of the body and the positioning of the limbs should not hide important details (Figure 6.11). A woman wearing an intricately tucked, pleated, and trimmed blouse will hide significant information from the viewer if she is drawn with her arms folded over her chest. If she is wearing a plain sweater, the position of the arms is far less important. Some costumes cannot be completely seen on one figure, no matter how it is posed. An 1885 bustle gown has as much going on in back as it does in front, and both sides may not be the same. Additional sketches will undoubtedly be needed (Figure 6.1). If an actress stays curled up in a ball the entire time she is seen, perhaps the costume plate should show this as the main view. (A supplementary sketch will still be necessary; it's too difficult for the shop to build a curled-up ball.)

Vitality can add a great deal of interest to the sketch. The figure need not be engaged in violent action but should have a sense of movement, a physical attitude to the body that makes it seem alive (Figure 6.5). A figure flattened out on the page as if plastered there by a steamroller does little to sell a costume idea. Hand props can often be used effectively to add a bit of spark to the presentation (Figure 6.22). These props can also be important because they help clarify characters by showing them with objects they will actually use. The Gravedigger in *Hamlet,* for example, looks like just another peasant until a skull or spade is placed in his hand to define his occupation. Sir Toby Belch in *Twelfth Night* could well be depicted raising a tankard of ale, for it certainly would be in character.

Two different approaches can be used to draw the final figure. The design can be drawn directly on the paper or board. This may give a more spontaneous and vital feeling, but the surface could get messy if much redrawing is needed. The beginning designer may feel more comfortable developing the figure on a less expensive drawing surface, then transferring it to the good paper or board. If the presentation paper is not too heavy, this could be done on a copy machine, perhaps even using a colored toner. Should this method not be available the figure could be transferred with a graphite sheet. If medium- to lightweight watercolor paper is used, transferring could be done on a light table: the drawing is overlaid with the watercolor paper and secured on a piece of glass that is illuminated from below by a bright light. The line thus appears through the heavier paper.

◆ Media

There is a great variety of color media, boards, and papers to use for costume renderings. No one type is better than any other. The effectiveness of any material depends upon what it is being used for and who is using it. It is quite important for the beginning designer to try a number of media to understand how the different materials work and to discover those that are most effective. Materials should vary depending upon the type of sketch that is to be produced.

A costume plate is often a colored drawing rather than a painting, though the materials used to produce either could be the same. For costume work the very finest equipment is not always needed to create an acceptable representation of the design, although it is important to have good tools since they make the work easier and the results better. Materials, whether color media, papers, or brushes, come in student's grade and artist's grade. The former is more suitable while experimenting and learning; the latter will be more satisfactory to the skilled designer. Fighting inferior materials can make producing the costume sketch much more difficult.

Papers and Boards

The papers and boards that can be used for a costume rendering come in a great variety of surface textures, thicknesses, fiber contents, and colors. Some are best suited for particular paints; others are more versatile and can adapt to many different techniques.

Watercolor paper, which comes in white or off-white, makes an excellent ground for many types of costume plates. Handmade papers are by far the best because they have a higher linen rag content. The paper is made of a felted mass of interlaced fibers; this is very important because these fibers give the paper the ability to catch and hold the paint. High linen rag content produces an excellent working surface, one that is flexible and takes paint easily. It can be worked on without destroying the surface because the paint can be blended, blotted, or picked up with a sponge or brush without dissolving the paper. Cotton fibers are not as good, although many cotton-fiber papers are quite usable. Wood-pulp papers produce neither a particularly pleasant surface to work on nor one that can be worked over without some disintegration. Quality papers are watermarked. The watermark is legible on the side of the paper that is most suitable for watercolor techniques, and can be seen by holding the paper up to a light. The surface of handmade paper is much more interesting than paper made by machine, which tends to have a monotonous grain. As might be expected, it is also much more expensive. Good handmade papers are manufactured by Arches, Fabriano, J. B. Green, James Watman and Son, and T. H. Saunders. Usable but less expensive papers are Bockingford (a cellulose-fiber paper) and Strathmore 500 (a cotton-fiber paper).

The finish on the paper can greatly influence the look of the final drawing. The primary finishes applied to papers are cold-pressed (CP), not-pressed (NP), rough, and hot-pressed (HP). Cold-pressed and not-pressed finishes provide an open or coarse texture. Rough delivers an even coarser grain. These are all suited to transparent color media, but rough is more difficult to control because of the very high surface texture, or tooth, though it can give an interesting textural feeling when used for a broad style of presentation. A medium tooth can be effectively employed either for a wash or for fine detail and is serviceable for much costume work. Hot-pressed paper has a smoother surface and is thus better suited to line-and-wash work or opaque paints than to transparent watercolors.

Thickness is also an important factor in the behavior of the paper. Watercolor papers are graded by the weight of a ream (variously 472, 480, 500, or 516 sheets). Thin is 72 pounds per ream, intermediate is 90 pounds, and fairly heavy 140 pounds. Very heavy sheets, which are more like boards, can be as heavy as 250 or 400 pounds per ream. Seventy-two-pound paper is quite thin and may corkle, or wrinkle, when worked; 90-pound paper is a good working weight; and 140-pound paper can be used to provide an even sturdier background—though, of course, it is expensive. If thin paper is to be used it can be prestretched to minimize any corkling. To do this the paper is completely saturated, then fastened down with paper tape to a sturdy flat surface to dry. It may wrinkle a bit in use, but will flatten out again when the moisture evaporates. Some of the better papers come in blocks that have a gummed surface around all the edges, holding the sheets together as a solid mass. The top sheet can be used while it is held in tension, then removed from the block after it is dry. Premounted watercolor papers are already adhered to a board and provide a very sturdy working surface. These are expensive and get quite heavy if a number are needed.

Illustration or art boards can provide an adequate working surface for the costume designer and are sturdier and heavier than watercolor paper. The sturdiness is an advantage, but the heaviness is not. A show with 50 costume plates done on board can be a real strain on the back. Boards provide an interesting surface, however, for some projects.

Boards come in hot-pressed and cold-pressed finishes, although the cold-pressed surface usually has less texture than most watercolor paper. Boards also come in different plies or thicknesses. The thicker board stands up better if a lot of paint is to be used, but for a costume rendering the thinner board is quite satisfactory. Good-quality white boards are manufactured by Crescent, Bainbridge, and Bristol.

A colored background can be provided by using mat boards and papers, Ingres-type papers, or pastel papers such as Krash and Canson Mi-Tientes. The surface varies from fairly smooth to moderately textured and is soft enough to allow the paint to sink in and not blend or move on the paper. These are therefore more suitable for opaque techniques or pastels. Although the surface quality of these boards and papers is not ideal for a watercolor technique, they are usable and come in a range of colors that can lend a specific mood to the presentation. A shade should be selected that reinforces the color scheme but does not intrude on the costume sketch. Lighter tints are usually most satisfactory, though a darker, fairly neutral shade can be used effectively. Hot pink or purple may be a bit hard to take and is certainly not easy to work on for any length of time.

As mentioned previously, the rendering is a colored drawing and the surface used should be a pleasant one on which to draw. In addition, if a transparent color medium is used, allowing the paper to show through the paint or leaving holidays (blank spaces), the paper should provide some luminosity and vitality to the painting. With an opaque technique the paper merely needs to hold the paint, for its qualities are concealed by the medium.

Color Media

Watercolor. Watercolors are transparent glazes made from finely ground pigments combined with gum arabic. They come in dry cakes, semimoist pans, and tubes. Quality watercolors provide both clarity of color and density of pigment. Among the more reliable manufacturers of watercolor paints are Windsor and Newton, Grumbacher, Pelikan, Rowney, and Reeves.

A watercolor rendering uses the white of the paper for the white and pale tints of the presentation. Because of this, the quality of the paper plays an important part in the final result. An appropriate surface adds clarity, sparkle, and luminosity to the work.

Watercolor can be applied with either a dry or a wet technique. The transparent wash is the basis for the wet technique. To achieve a smooth wash the desired color should be mixed in sufficient quantity, then applied in slightly overlapping horizontal strokes with a fully loaded brush. The paper should be at a slight angle and the pigment remixed each time the brush is dipped in to keep the color uniform. The brush should go across the area, then back again, then be reloaded for the next stroke. Blotting paper can pick up any excess pigment at the bottom of the wash. To avoid streakiness, some papers should be dampened before the wash is applied. Washes may be overlaid to deepen the color or change the tone, though the first color should be allowed to dry before the second is applied unless a loose, wet effect is desired. More than three layers can give a muddy, unattractive result. It is important to remember that watercolors should not be used so thickly that they fill up or clot the grain.

A slightly drier technique uses a fully loaded brush to create a stroke that follows the folds of the fabric, leaving occasional holidays and white lines to accent the dimensional qualities of the costume. Dry brushing is a third technique that can be used to add detail and interest. The brush is

Figure 6.1 This sketch for Praskova Ossipovna, a hysterical and uppity Russian housewife in *The Nose*, produced at the Santa Fe Opera in 1987, includes three views of a very complex skirt as well as a detail of the hairstyle. A large format was used so the designer could accommodate all he wanted to say about the design without crowding the presentation. Design by Robert Perdziola, watercolor on an 18″ × 24″ sheet, figure 15$\frac{1}{2}$″.

Figure 6.2 An exceptionally striking costume was created by Robert Perdziola for the vengeful housewife Juno in *La Calisto*, performed in 1989 at the Santa Fe Opera. The overall impression is a grand one, the focus right where it needs to be, on the face. The 18″ figure is done in watercolor sketch on 18″ × 24″ paper.

Figure 6.3 The draping quality of the fabric for these chorus ladies of Walpurgisnacht in the opera *Faust* is very evident in this rendering by Robert Perdziola. The 1995 German production was called *Margarethe* in that country. Presentation is in watercolor on 18″ × 24″ paper, the figures 15″ tall.

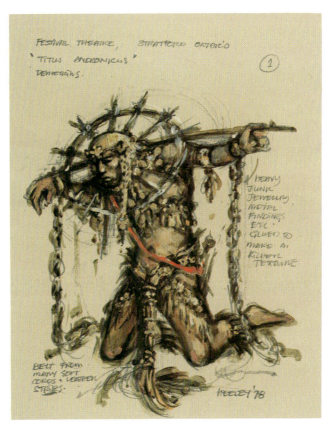

Figure 6.4 The costume sketch is the way the designer communicates ideas. Costume designed by Cletus Anderson for Bluebeard in *Bluebeard's Castle,* produced at Carnegie Mellon University. Watercolor and charcoal on gray Crescent Charko-board. Figure is 17″ high on a 16″ × 20″ board. (Above left)

Figure 6.5 The figure should have a physical attitude to the body that makes it seem alive. Costume design by Frank Bevan for Egeus in *A Midsummer Night's Dream,* produced at Yale University. Casein on beige Bainbridge Board, Rough. The figure is $14\frac{1}{2}$″ high on a 14″ × 20″ board. (Above right)

Figure 6.6 A costume sketch can be an inspiration as well as a description of the costume to be built. Designed in 1978 by Desmond Healey for Demetrius in *Titus Andronicus,* produced at the Festival Theatre, Stratford, Ontario. Acrylic on tan paper. Figure is $10\frac{1}{2}$″ high on an 11″ × 14″ sheet.

Figure 6.7a–6.7d These designs were for Shakespeare's *The Tempest,* performed at the Oregon Shakespeare Festival in 1994. Susan Tsu's sketches for Stephano and Trinculo use a watercolor technique that allows holidays, or intervals, in the paint to define the costume with the white of the paper. The colors used for Prospero's magic robe are glazed to reflect a shinier quality of the fabric; his gown underneath is left with the flat finish. Two sketches were necessary to show the complex appliqués for the robe. The watercolor designs were done on 11″ × 14″ paper. Trinculo is 13″, Stephano 12″, and Prospero 13″, back view 10″.

Figure 6.8   This costume for Mimi in the opera *La Bohème,* designed by Molly Maginnis, uses heightened reality to present a shop girl of the middle of the nineteenth century. The fabrics have a homespun quality and a hoop is used to created the silhouette of the period. The opera was presented at the Texas Opera Theatre in Houston. Watercolor on an 11″ × 14″ sheet, 12″ figure. (Above left)

Figure 6.9   Molly Maginnis designed this gown for Mary Steenburgen for the 1989 film *Miss Firecracker Contest.* The costume, for a beauty pageant winner in 1973, was a taffeta with a silk overlay woven in alternating stripes of red sheer and sheen. Watercolor sketch on 11″ × 14″ paper, figure 13″. (Above right)

Figure 6.10   A number of chorus costumes can be presented on one plate to give the same type of group effect that will be seen onstage. Design by William P. Brewer for *See Saw.* Watercolor, pencil, and marker on cold-press paper. Figures are 11½″ high on an 18″ × 24″ sheet.

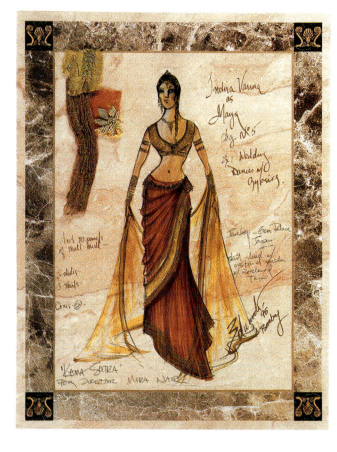

Figure 6.11 Design for Indira Varina as Maya in the feature film *Kama Sutra* directed by Mira Nair. The design by Eduardo Castro was done on an 14″ × 10½″ marbleized paper and featured bright gold paint for the trim. The figure is 10″ tall. Notes indicate the number of garments to be made, lining to be used, and the location of the store for the jewelry. The project involved designing hundreds of costumes in a very short time. (Above left)

Figure 6.12 The costume idea for Halle Berry in Warren Beatty's 1998 film *Bullworth* was easily presented by designer Eduardo Castro using markers. The figure is 12″ tall. (Above right)

Figure 6.13 A certain amount of elongation may be used very effectively in some costume plates. Costume design by Carrie F. Robbins for the Bride in *Frankenstein*, produced at the Palace Theatre, New York, 1981. Mixed media.

Figure 6.14 Different nonrealistic versions of Hitler were required for the film, *The Empty Mirror,* designed by Melinda Eshelman. This version shows The Big Suit. The Translucent Suit and the Virtual Reality Hitler can be seen in Chapter 7. (20″ watercolor figure on 18″ × 24″ sheets)

Figure 6.15 This design for the Queen of the Lake Puppet in *Prince Free of Sorrow,* produced at the Asolo Center for the Performing Arts in 1991, is an excellent example of utilizing key elements to create a stylized characterization on a puppet shape. The 7 foot figure, designed by Howard Kaplan, was controlled by actors onstage with it. Sketch is a $15\frac{1}{2}$″ figure done with markers on 11″ × 17″ paper. (Below left)

Figure 6.16 Grumpy Face, a Gnome/Goblin designed by Howard Tsvi Kaplan for the *Fantasia de la Primavera* at the Parque Espana, Tokyo, presents many interesting challenges for the construction crew. The designer has included a number of notes to guide those who will build the costume and planned how the actor inside the creation will be able to see. "Eyeholes in hat" indicates that the face of the goblin is actually below the face of the actor. Done with markers. Figure 13″ high on 11″ × 17″ paper. (Below right)

Figure 6.17 A costume plate should have life, and humor if appropriate. Costume design by Michael Olich for Dolly in *You Never Can Tell*, produced at the Alley Theatre, Houston. Designer color and pencil on mat board. Figure 12″ high on an 11″ × 16″ board.

Figure 6.18 The design for Argan in Molière's *The Imaginary Invalid* is based on a period noted for its excessive detail. This interpretation expands on the frivolity to create humorous attire for the self-indulgent hypochondriac. Watercolor rendering by S. Scott Welborn on 11″ × 14″ paper, figure 11″. (Above right)

Figure 6.19 Swatches and notes may be necessary to give a clear guide to the shop of the way the costume should be constructed. Design by John Conklin for a Gypsy Woman in Rossini's *The Turk in Italy,* produced by the New York City Opera, director Tito Capobianco. Acrylic and colored pencil on a smooth sketch paper. Figure 11$\frac{1}{2}$″ on a 13″ × 18″ sheet.

Figure 6.20 Figure, helmet detail, and swatches arranged to balance the plate. Costume designed by Cletus Anderson for Sir William in the film *Knightriders*. Charcoal pencil and oil wash on Fabriani watercolor paper. Figure is 16″ high on a 13″ × 19″ sheet.

Figure 6.21 The completed rendering must contain all the elements of the costume. Costume design by Kevin Rupnik for Julie in *Miss Julie*. Windsor Newton watercolors, Prismacolor, and pencil on watercolor paper. Figure is 10″ high on an 11″ × 15″ sheet. (Above right)

Figure 6.22 Judith Bliss is every inch the actress tending her garden as she makes her initial entrance in this costume for Noel Coward's *Hay Fever*. Garments, accessories, and props are designed to make an immediate impact on the audience. Costume by Cletus Anderson for a 1983 production at the Pittsburgh Public Theater. Figure is 12″ done in watercolor on 15½″ by 12½″ paper.

dipped in the dissolved pigment, then wiped on an extra piece of paper so the paint is applied with little water in the brush.

Watercolors are very difficult to change, although some corrections can be made if good paper or board is used, for the paint can be picked up with a wet brush or sponge. This procedure may alter the surface texture, however. Highlights can also be recaptured in this fashion. They could also be preplanned and a masking agent, such as Copydex, painted on before the color is applied. The masking agent is then rolled off the paper when the rendering is completely dry, revealing the white paper. A practical book on watercolor is *The Encyclopedia of Watercolor Techniques* by Hazel Harrison.

Gouache.   Gouache or designer's colors are opaque watercolors, which means that the colors have white incorporated in them. When applied, gouache forms a solid body of color and creates a thicker layer of paint than watercolor. Unlike watercolor, which is more like a stain, gouache does not rely on the paper to appear through the color. It can be worked from dark shades to light as well as from light to dark. Tinted backgrounds can be used quite successfully with this medium. Because white is contained in every color but black, the dried tones are lighter than the wet color and have a mat, slightly chalky appearance. Gouache can be used with any of the boards and papers mentioned earlier, though the very smooth or very rough are not ideal for most projects.

Designer's colors, which commonly come in tubes, are made by Pelikan, Windsor and Newton, and Grumbacher, among other manufacturers. To apply a wash the paint should be thinned with water to the consistency of very thin cream and either applied from the top downward, like the watercolor wash, or flooded into the areas in pools of color. This medium works better on a level surface than on a tilted one. A second coat can be applied after the first has been allowed to dry thoroughly. The washes can be overlaid and modeled with a finer brush. The dried paint surface is rather absorbent, so a fairly wet brush should be used if a smooth effect is desired. The dry surface is also easily marked; blotting paper can be placed over previously painted areas to allow freedom to work without fear of spoiling what has already been done. If alterations are necessary, the gouache can be picked up from the paper by soaking the area with a sponge, then blotting it, brushing more water onto the area, and blotting it again until enough paint has come off. Paint can be reapplied to this section. Gouache may be thinned to give a watercolor effect, but the resulting tones will not be as brilliant as with watercolor.

Tempera.   Tempera paint is a medium that contains oils in emulsion and can be used with water. Available in tubes from such companies as Rowney, Grumbacher, and Windsor and Newton, it is extremely durable and characterized by a brilliant, luminous crispness. It dries rapidly, becomes quite insoluble, and cannot be softened for blending. Because of this inflexibility its mastery requires practice and its use in a costume rendering calls for serious consideration.

Though poster and show-card colors are sometimes labeled tempera, technically they are not. Their use in costume renderings is not advised because they produce thick, chalky color that is not easily blended.

Acrylics.   Acrylics, actually acrylic polymers, are synthetic resins in which pigment is dispersed in an acrylic emulsion. Acrylics can be thinned with water but they dry to a tough, flexible film that is impervious to water. They can be used on a wider variety of surfaces than any other medium. Only an oil-primed surface is unsuitable for use with acrylics. An excellent surface can even be created by using any type of mounting cardboard coated with acrylic primer or emulsion paint that has the brush marks left to give bite to the surface.

Rowney, Liquitex, and Grumbacher all manufacture fine acrylic paints. Acrylics come in tubes or plastic containers and can be worked like watercolor and gouache, but they dry more quickly. Glycerine can be added to slow down the drying time. Acrylic washes, which dry quickly and have a hard edge, are not as brilliant as those done in watercolor, but a number of layers can be applied without producing a muddy effect. Two thin washes are often more effective than one thicker layer.

Acrylics are also suitable for impasto, which is thick, heavy painting done with bristle brushes or a palette knife and more commonly associated with oil paints.

Because the acrylic is insoluble, changes or corrections can be made by painting over the area when it is dry with white acrylic, emulsion paint, or gesso and starting the work again. Regular acrylics dry to a semigloss finish, but a polymer medium added to the wet pigment will produce either a mat or gloss finish. These media can be added to watercolor or gouache to give them an insoluble finish that can be worked over when dry. Mat medium is also often used with watercolors to speed the drying time and extend the pigment.

Casein.   Casein actually refers to pigments bound with milk curd and is available in commercially prepared tubes. It is coarser and less sensitive than gouache, though it can produce a gouachelike effect. It can also be diluted and used like watercolor, though it has much less brilliance.

Oils.   Oils are a fascinating medium, but not easily used for costume renderings as they are most commonly applied to a stretched canvas and can be very slow drying.

Pastels.   Pastels can produce strong true colors because not much medium is mixed with the pigment to create the crayons, but the variety of colors available is more limited since they cannot be combined like paint to create new shades. It is also true that the results may not bear up well under wear and tear for the color can smudge and smear. Soft pastels, such as those made by Rowney or Grumbacher, combine the qualities of drawing and painting and work well on almost any type of soft drawing paper with a rough surface that will file off and retain particles of the pastel crayon. Papers most commonly used with pastels are fibrous and include drawing and watercolor papers; pastel papers with soft, fine, sandpaperlike coatings; and flocked papers with velvety finishes. Pastels are best applied with firm strokes using plenty of crayon. If the grain of the paper becomes overloaded with the pastels, subsequent layers will clog and become smeary. The pastels can be manipulated with paper stumps, stiff bristle brushes, and fingers. Pastels can produce wonderfully wispy, soft effects. Because the result is so fragile, the rendering must be sprayed with a clear fixative. This must be done with a carefully applied light mist, for oversaturating the picture causes the color to lose its brilliance and darkens the tone. Excess fixative can also run and cause ridges in the drawing.

In a costume rendering, pastels can be used most effectively to highlight and accent a painted sketch. Pastel pencils, such as those made by Carb-Othello, are especially suited to this use. Oil pastels and crayons, both the artist's grade and the regular children's type, are much sturdier and more resistant to smudging and smearing. They can be blended on the surface of the paper.

Pencils and Markers. Colored pencils and felt- and fiber-tipped markers are excellent for exploring quick color ideas or bringing out details and highlights in a painted rendering. Pencils are available in both waterproof and water-soluble styles and with either thick or thin leads. Felt-tipped markers give a much broader line than the fiber-tips, and have a shorter life. The ink in both is spirit based and tends to evaporate quickly, especially if the cap is left off.

Brushes

Good brushes are extremely important. Those made by hand from fine materials by skilled craftspeople, can be expensive. However, buying and using cheap brushes can be a false economy. With proper care a good brush will last longer and improve the quality of the work.

Since most costume renderings are done with water-based media, watercolor brushes are the first type the designer will need. The best brushes are made of red sable in a style called round, which has a good point, smoothly shapes out to fullness, and comes back in slightly to the handle. There should be no concave droop to the point. These brushes have good resilience and durability. They can be examined by wetting the brush, shaking out the extra water, then molding it gently with the fingers to make sure it forms a good point. The point of the paintbrush is made of the ends of the hair carefully placed to create the brush's shape. It should never be cut or trimmed.

Some less-expensive red sable brushes that also work well are made with shorter hair or a blend of sable and oxhair. Next in quality are the Russian fitch sables and the brown and black sables. Camel's hair brushes are not made of camel's hair at all, but a variety of other types of hair, mostly squirrel. These are usually too soft and do not have good elasticity or longevity. They tend to be rather floppy and moplike. Oxhair brushes are more rigid and do not work well with watercolor.

Brushes are sized by numbers; a higher number indicates a larger brush. Always use the largest brush possible; don't try to fill in a big area with a little brush. Sizes 2, 4, 8, and 12 will form a good beginning brush collection.

Brushes should be cleaned immediately after each use. Those used in water-based media should be washed with soap and water, preferably mild dish soap; thoroughly rinsed; gently shaped; and stored upright.

Acrylics can be more destructive to brushes than other media because they may begin to dry in the head while the brush is still being used—paint accumulates even if the brush is kept submerged in water. If paint begins to build up it can be removed with methylated spirits or commercial brush cleaners. In addition to watercolor brushes special polymer or acrylic brushes made with nylon bristles can be used, for they are less expensive and easier to clean. They come in the various shapes already mentioned and also in stiffer and wider versions often used with oils.

Collage

A collage technique is another method of presenting costume plates. In a collage a combination of fabrics, papers, trims, laces—anything the designer feels expresses his or her ideas—is glued to a board and combined with paint or other color media to create the costume effect. It is sometimes difficult to find materials that stay in the right scale for the size of the figure, but a collage can produce a fascinating presentation and give a real feeling for the textures of the completed costume.

◆ The Layout of the Costume Plate

Just as the costume needs to be well designed, the costume plate should be laid out with an eye toward composition. When placed properly in the space the figure will not crowd the sides, seem to float out the top, or fall off the bottom. A certain distance from the lower edge of the paper can be established as the floor line for the series so that when the plates are lined up all the figures appear on the same plane. A child should not be the same size as his father, but he can stand on the same floor. If detail sketches and fabric swatches are to be displayed, the figure should be placed so the other elements can be included and still present a well-balanced plate. Figures 6.9, 6.20, and 6.7, show three different layouts that might be used to incorporate the different elements to be presented. Figure 6.9 shows the placement of a single figure and swatches to balance the figure. In Figure 6.20 the figure, detail, and swatches are all arranged attractively, with the focus on the figure. Figure 6.7 shows a fairly symmetrical single figure well placed on the page.

Fabric swatches should be grouped in proportion to the way they will be seen on the costume, attached so the fabric can be felt but does not steal the focus from the figure. Swatches might also be placed on a separate card.

The optimum size of a costume plate is tied directly to the size of the figure the designer wishes to use. The paper should contain the figure easily, not crowd it in or be so large that the amount of space diminishes the costume. As the designer explores different methods of presenting the work, he or she should try different sizes of figure. Some projects might work best in a small area; for others a large plate may be more effective. The actual size of each plate reproduced in this chapter is indicated to show the variety that can be used and to help the designer visualize how a figure looks on different types of mounting.

The title of the production, the name of the character, and an identification of the costume are shown on each plate. The lettering should be executed neatly and in a consistent style. Lettering that is so extensive or elaborate that it upstages the drawing can be quite pretentious, for the design is the important element being presented and time and space should not be wasted on fancy labeling. The signature of the designer should be included, along with the date, though it need not be tremendously prominent. Some costume sketches have two signatures, the designer's and the sketch artist's.

Sometimes a designer gets the urge to use an elaborate background in the plates. This urge should usually be suppressed. Unless they are well executed, backgrounds can be distracting and diminish the impact of the presentation. Even if well done they may disturb the focus. A simple wash or tone behind the figure could add interest and a sense of depth to the sketch, but it is not wise to add unnecessary detail. The effort should go into the costume design, not into a glossy presentation style that can mislead the viewer. The costume plate is meant to present costume ideas, not become a campaign ad or a poster.

In the same vein, mats or elaborate mountings of various types are also unnecessary and add both time and weight to the work. Costume plates can be mounted for a formal exhibition but not as part of the work in progress. When the sketches are given to the shop they may be covered with acetate to help preserve them through the wear and tear of the building process. Photocopies are also very useful at this time for those constructing the costumes to keep handy for easy reference and notes.

A set of plates should be considered as a group with a number of constants that will present a uniform impression when shown together. The same type board and color medium should be used throughout. The size of the figures should remain consistent, as should the type of lettering and the way the fabric swatches are arranged, though the placement of the last two items may vary because of the placement of the figure on the plate. Occasionally the sizes of the plates vary. This could happen if a costume is so big it just won't fit on the standard size being used, or if a number of costumes are to be presented on one plate, which might be desirable with groups of minor characters (Figure 6.10). Minor characters and chorus costumes are sometimes done in a slightly smaller format, which is quite acceptable if done consistently. A well-organized set of plates could use 10″ × 14″ paper vertically for the principal players and horizontally for the groups of smaller figures.

The costume plate should be an honest presentation of ideas that are clearly arranged and neatly executed. It is intended to present the design of the costume and the quality of workmanship of the designer. A brilliant idea on a messy plate may not be accepted because the director is too distracted by the smudges and paint blobs, or because he or she questions the craftsmanship the designer will use when actually producing the costume. On the other hand, a flashy plate that has little actual substance may sell a badly designed costume the first time a designer works for a director. The designer may never get the chance to try again.

❖ The Costume Portfolio

Establishing and organizing a portfolio is important for young designers who are planning to become professionals. Sketches, photographs, and costume plates provide visual evidence of the designer's abilities, taste, and talent. Though the time crunch during the preparation for a production often pushes thoughts of documenting both the process and final product out of mind, a good photographic record of the work is essential. Photographing the work in progress in a well-defined space and the costume on the actor in its dramatic setting is most often the best way to capture an effective image. Poor photos with distorted colors or photos of the work in the midst of extraneous clutter usually are more detrimental than useful. A decent camera and the ability to use it effectively can be of significant value to the designer.

In preparing the portfolio, present the work in a chronological order beginning with the most recently completed projects. Costume plates arranged with photographs can demonstrate both intent and result. Label all sketches and photographs with the name and date of the production, character, producing organization, and director. Some original work should be included, but reduced color photocopies can also be quite effective and space efficient. Organize each page for clarity of information. The focus should be on the costume design work, not on an overly embellished graphic display. Double mats in various colors could be distracting and perhaps pretentious, and add unnecessary pounds to the portfolio. Résumés printed on one $8\frac{1}{2}'' \times 11''$ single sheet should be available during the interview. It is not uncommon for the design work in the portfolio to be protected by a layer of clear acetate. The glare created by this can be annoying and distracting. If the work is in a decent portfolio it may not need this additional protection.

The portfolio should be easily manageable and small enough in size to be carried on board an airplane. Two small or one medium-size portfolio, between $16'' \times 19''$ and $20'' \times 24''$, could accommodate the work, while a portfolio $24'' \times 32''$ or larger can be quite cumbersome and heavy when loaded with photographs and costume plates.

A portfolio of work should be updated at regular intervals. In addition the material selected to display should address the type of position the designer is going for. When applying to be an assistant or for a craft position choose examples of work that demonstrate talents in those areas.

Chapter 7

Designing for Film and Television

EMMA SAMMS
TIBETIAN PRINCESS

THE MAGIC OF DAVID COPPERFIELD

Preceding page: This costume for Emma Samms as the Tibetan Princess in *The Magic of David Copperfield* was presented effectively and simply with pencil, a bit of watercolor, gold paint, and some white crayon to give texture to the gown. Design by Daniel Orlandi.

Designing for film and television is not really very different from designing for other forms of production, a character is a character no matter what the milieu. In this arena the details may be quite telling or completely lost, for the camera can bring the actor right to the audience or separate them to such a degree that only a general effect is perceived. This medium is very expensive and organization is extremely important. Technical crews, equipment, and studio space, not to mention the talent, producers, and directing team, come at a premium and time is never in the designer's favor. It is important to be prepared and have the insight to anticipate possible problems.

In film and much of television, as opposed to live presentation, the scenes are not necessarily taped or filmed in the order of the script, the end may be shot before the beginning and there is never a final product until months after the wardrobe work is finished. It is therefore more important than ever for the designer to have the concept of the production well

Figure 7.1 Developing a costume for Isabella Rossellini in the film *The Funeral* was no different than creating and sketching a costume idea in any other form of production. Design by Melinda Eshelman.

TOOTHLESS

KIRSTIE ALLEY
AS
THE TOOTHFAIRY

Figure 7.2 The opportunity to create fantasy and period costumes is not too common in film or television. This one was for Kirstie Alley as the Toothfairy in *Toothless*, designed by Molly Maginnis in 1997 for the Wonderful World of Disney on ABC Television.

established and a timeline created even though the sequence is not particularly apparent during the shooting of the film.

As in most types of production, the work starts with conferences with the director and perhaps the producer(s). In episodic television or situation comedies each episode may have a different director so the communication is with the producer or writer/producer. At this time a draft of the script might be available, or an outline, or possibly just a statement of the situation with a list of the characters. Chances are excellent the script will change continuously during production, particularly in film. This is a field where the designer must be quite specific, and at the same time very flexible. It is extremely important for the designer to be familiar with the characters and the situations so if a change occurs he or she will know what choices are effective and appropriate.

It is essential that an exchange of ideas occurs with the other members of the creative team. In television this can be the art director and lighting designer; in film the art director or, often now, the production designer and the director of photography or cinematographer. In both mediums close coordination with the hair and makeup departments is also necessary.

The main thrust of this chapter will deal with work that applies to feature films, television films, and those series that are shot like films. A television show taped in a studio, perhaps before an audience, can be approached in much the same way as a theater piece. This will be discussed later in this section.

◆ The Scene and Costume Breakdown

The designer will need a complete listing of the scenes, which characters are in them, and what they might be wearing. Of particular note are situations in which something might happen to the costumes. It could be something simple—a note in the script that says "suddenly it starts to rain," —or more complex—a note that reads "his arm is shot off at the elbow." Since it is entirely possible that a scene will be filmed more than once and from different angles,

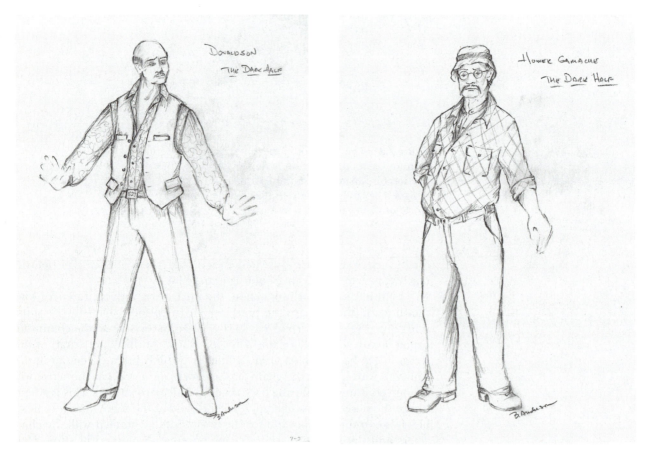

Figure 7.3   These line drawings were created to establish the character feeling for two men about to be done in by the villain in *The Dark Half,* a feature film released in 1993. Small photocopies were made and painted, then taken along on shopping trips to find the actual garments. Designs by Barbara Anderson.

it is necessary to have enough costumes to cover the possibilities. In the case of the rainstorm, two or three sets of clothes and a hairdryer may be sufficient for a number of takes. If the arm is shot off the damage to the costume may be so extensive with the preplanned tearing and staining that a new shirt, coat, or whatever must be available for each time it happens. So the costume list includes not only what the actor will be wearing, but how many versions of it might be needed and might also include a notation to check to see if a stunt double will be required. A double will need a costume identical to that of the actor. SAG (Screen Actor's Guild) rules prohibit the use of the same costume on different actors unless it has been properly cleaned. It is also entirely possible that the double will not be exactly the same size as the actor, and he or she may be wearing padding or some other sort of protective garment underneath. A stand-in, used for preblocking and setting light levels, must be in something similar in shape and color, referred to as "camera color," but the clothes do not have to be exactly the same.

When creating the basic costume list the designer must know the time span of the script. Sometimes this is quite obvious; the action could all take place in one day or the activities clearly suggest a change in time, such as getting up, going to bed, celebrating Thanksgiving in one scene and Christmas in the next. Sometimes there is just a sense of time passing but the actual breakdown of the days may not be clear. The actor could get up, go to work, have a meeting, tour a factory, take his wife to dinner. This could all be one day, or it could be a number of days and imply a whole workweek. If a span of time is to be suggested, then a change of clothes will help convey this to the audience. So the time span of the script must be established, which could be done by the directing team, particularly the script supervisor. This person may not start working until a week or so before shooting commences. Since the costume designer needs the information much earlier he or she may tentatively set the days, discuss them with the director, and exchange information with the script supervisor when he or she begins. If one scene is designated Day One and the next Day Two, this indicates the time break but does not necessarily mean that Day One is Wednesday and Day Two is Thursday. They are different days with the time span between not specified.

The following are examples of the types of lists that may be useful.

◆ BIG MOVIE Scenery/Costume Breakdown

Scene		Setting	
		Scenery	**Costumes**
1	**Ext**	**Day**	**College Building Rotunda**
Day	1	Ceremony preparation for service honoring graduating class. Dais and 40 chairs. Rain and thunder.	Big Male Star in academic robes (Gets wet?) Big Female Star in something nice (Gets wet?) Sweet Young Thing, coming down with a headache. She faints. (Gets wet and dirty?) The Maid, dusts the chairs and leaves Milling Parents

2	Int	Day		Professor's Office Inside Building
Day	1	Chic office with desk, computer table, day bed, bar, small refrigerator, clothes tree.		Big Male Star in suit, jacket off. Wet robes hanging on clothes tree. Sweet Young Thing resting, clothes loosened, ice pack on head.

◆ **BIG MOVIE Costume List**

Principles and Day Players	
Character	**Costume**
BIG MALE STAR	**1.** Academic robes, suit underdressed (Day 1, Scene 1) (duplicates for rain) **1A.** Scholarly suit, robe off (Day 1, Scenes 2, 4, 5) **2.** Jogging outfit (Day 2, Scenes 11, 12, 15, 16) (Gets shot) **3.** Hospital gown (Day 2, Scenes 22, 23) **4.** Tuxedo (Day 3, Scenes 32–40, 43) (punch spilled on shirt)
BIG FEMALE STAR	**1.** Silk day dress (Day 1, Scene 1) (duplicates for rain) **2.** Hunting outfit (Day 2, Scenes 12, 16) **3.** Prison Garb (Day 3, Scene 29)
SWEET YOUNG THING	**1.** Youthful, sexy day dress (Day 1, Scenes 1, 2) (duplicates for rain and fainting) **2.** Jogging shorts and halter (Day 2, Scenes 11, 12, 15) (gets blood splattered) **3.** Bridal gown (Day 3, Scenes 34–40)

◆ **BIG MOVIE Detailed Costume List**

Character	Costume	Piece Cost	Costume Cost	Character Cost
BIG MALE STAR				
1.	Academic Outfit			
1A.	Robe (3 for rain)	450		
	Mortar board (3 for rain)	75		
	Tweedy gray 3 piece scholarly suit	500		
	Shirt and tie	60		
	Shoes and socks	120		
	Jewelry—watch, ring	150	1,355	
2.	Jogging Outfit			
	Gray T-shirt (5 for shoulder shot)	200		
	Dark gray sweat pants	80		
	Running shoes	200		
	Socks	10		
	Towel around neck (5 duplicates)	50	540	

Character	Costume	Piece Cost	Costume Cost	Character Cost
3.	Hospital gown			
	Gown	40		
	Shoulder bandage	30	70	
4.	Tuxedo			
	Tuxedo	500		
	Formal shirt (3 for punch spill)	180		
	Bow tie	30		
	Studs and cuff links	90		
	Formal shoes and socks	150		
	Watch and ring as before		950	
				2,915

The **Scenery/Costume Breakdown** could be the result of the second read-through of the script. Here is a record of the visual information; where the scenes are happening, when they are happening, and who is involved. It also includes suggestions and questions that need consideration. Though not all of this is necessary for the costume designer it is much better to be armed with as much information as possible. The work on film can be so fragmented that anything that can help keep in mind the overall goals is very useful. Though the colors of the rooms and furniture may not be known when this list is first created, conferences with the production designer might fill in useful information that could in turn be added to the breakdown.

The **Costume List** breaks out the wardrobe needs of each of the actors. The general type of outfit should be indicated, the script day and the scenes in which it will be worn. By this time the designer may know how some of the scenes will be shot and what duplicate costumes may be necessary.

The **Detailed Costume List** is an expansion of the one before, now including all the elements of the costume. In this the designer will itemize everything that needs to be provided and will let the wardrobe crew know all the pieces that must be there for the actor when the scene is shot. For budgeting purposes a cost estimate is sometimes included.

The shooting schedule, which gives the actual order in which the scenes are to be filmed, will be provided by the directing team, usually the first assistant director. This schedule is dependent on many things and very often does not follow the time line of the script. Availability of locations, actors, sets, time of day, traffic conditions, season, weather, special effects—any number of things can determine what might be shot when, and any number of factors can cause a schedule change. The schedule lists each shooting day, its date, the scenes that will be done (identified by a one-liner, a brief description of the action), which principals and day players are in them, and how many pages long they are. From this the designer can better determine what duplicate costumes may be needed and also create a list for the wardrobe team that lets them know when each costume will be used. The following examples may help explain this phase:

Principals and Day Players

1. Big Male Star
2. Big Female Star
3. Sweet Young Thing
4. Doctor Fixit
5. Nurse Caring
6. Maid
7. Mother
8. Mother-in-Law
9. Detective Snooper

◆ **BIG MOVIE Oneline Schedule**

Shoot Day #1		**Monday, June 15, 2001**		
Scene 1	Ext	**College Building Rotunda** Sweet Young Thing gets sunstroke	**Day** 1, 2, 3, 6, 7	3/8 pgs
Scene 3	Ext	**College Building Rotunda** Big Female Star goes off in huff	**Day** 2, 6	1/8 pgs
Scene 6	Ext	**College Parking Lot** Big Female Star peels rubber	**Day** 2	1/8 pgs
End Day #1				**Total Pages: 5/8**
Shoot Day #2		**Tuesday, June 16, 2001**		
Scene 12	Ext	**Lane Near Pond** Happy couple hears strange noise	**Evening** 1, 3	1/8 pgs
Scene 15	Ext	**Lane Near Pond** BMS gets shot in shoulder	**Evening** 1, 3	3/8 pgs
Scene 11	Ext	**Lane Through Wooded Park** BMS and SYT on cozy jog	**Evening** 1, 3	2/8 pgs
End Day #2				**Total Pages 6/8**
Shoot Day #3		**Wednesday, June 17, 2001**		
Scene 2	Int	**Professor's Office** Big Male Star makes a pass	**Day** 1, 3	1 1/8 pgs
Scene 7	Int	**College Hallway** Maid takes a peek	**Day** 6	1/8 pgs
End Day #3				**Total Pages 1 2/8**

With this information the designer can now rearrange the original list into a document that can tell those in the costume area what scenes are being shot, who is in them, what costume they are wearing, and if this is the first time the costume is seen. It is wise to highlight the new costumes with a bright, showy color. On this chart they will be underlined.

◆ **Costume Ready List**

Day 1			**Monday, June 15**	
Scene 1	**Ext**	**Day**	**College Rotunda**	Big Male Star 1
	Day 1		Quick rain storm	Big Female Star 1
				Sweet Young Thing 1
				Maid 1
				Milling parents
Scene 3	**Ext**	**Day**	**College Rotunda**	Big Female Star 1
				Maid 1
				A few parents
Scene 6			**College Parking Lot**	Big Female Star 1
				A few parents
				College students
Day 2			**Tuesday, June 16**	
Scene 12	**Ext**	**Evening**	**Lane Near Pond**	Big Male Star 2
				Sweet Young Thing 2
Scene 15	**Ext**	**Evening**	**Lane Near Pond**	Big Male Star 2
				(double shirts and towels for shooting)
				Sweet Young Thing 2
Scene 11	**Ext**	**Evening**	**Lane Through Wooded Park**	Big Male Star 2
				Sweet Young Thing 2
				4 Joggers
Day 3			**Wednesday, June 12**	
Scene 2	**Int**	**Day**	**Professor's Office**	Big Male Star 1A (robe on set damp)
				Sweet Young Thing (ice pack)
Scene 7	**Int**	**Day**	**College Hallway**	Maid 1

The Costume Ready List provides valuable information, for no film is completely finished during preproduction before the shooting starts. While many things may be acquired and organized during those few weeks, much may also be in process to be finalized as necessary. This list tells the crew what must be ready today, what must be organized for tomorrow, and what should be almost finished now if it is to be ready for the day after.

In the Costume Ready List notice that there are some characters who have not been mentioned before. These are the extras who may be in the scenes but have no lines. A separate Extras Schedule is created and is of particular interest to both the extras casting person and the costume department; these two entities need to be in constant communication. Extras may be asked to bring their own clothes; the parents, college students, and joggers above may well have things that would be appropriate. Extras can be told the types and colors of clothes to bring, usually two or three choices, and the designer or assistant can look over the possibilities and make selections. The wise wardrobe department will always have other choices on hand should nothing be suitable. Perhaps one of the joggers brings in three outfits—one bright pink, one Day-Glo yellow, and the third screaming orange. A forest green ensemble found in the wardrobe trailer may help keep the focus of the scene on the Big Male Star where it belongs.

Some extras will need to be costumed, especially those who will be wearing uniforms. Usually the uniforms need to be acquired before the extras are cast. In this case the casting person will need to know what size can be accommodated, such as two 40s and three 42s. For a period film all of the extras will need to be costumed, so if it is at all possible prefittings should be done. Only too often the wardrobe department is faced with hundreds of bodies that must be completely transformed within a very short time.

◆ Continuity

The primary task of the costume designer is to design and provide the costumes for the film, the next is to make sure that those clothes look the same from shot to shot. Since the designer is not always on the set but may be preparing for the next day, the task of actually recording the way the costume is being worn is usually given to the on-set wardrobe person who uses what is called a continuity sheet. There should be a clear understanding of the information that must be on the continuity sheet. Everyone has seen instances, for example, where the blouse is buttoned to the neck in the master shot, the wide shot that includes everyone in the scene, and the two top buttons are undone for the close-up. This can be easy to explain. The actress ate lunch between takes and took off the blouse to make sure it didn't get dirty. A scene may have two minutes screen time, but the shooting of it may be the better part of a day. The continuity sheet needs to have lists, notes, and pictures on it to make sure the look can be exactly re-created, and should be referenced often. The information needed includes:

- Actor and character
- Costume number and a detailed list of all the pieces, which should include color, size, maker, and particulars that could help reconstruct the exact look should reshoots be necessary at a later time
- Scene number, shooting day, script day, location
- Diagrams and notes on dressing (sleeves rolled, buttons, etc.)
- Polaroid shots of actor, including hands and feet. A number of shots may be necessary for good documentation.

The amount of Polaroid film needed can be quite impressive, but it is a necessary expense. Sometimes lapses in continuity happen that are completely out of the control of the wardrobe department; long after filming is over the director and editor may decide that the order of certain scenes must be changed to help the story. But careless mistakes do not have to occur while shooting.

The costume designer may have time to discuss the costume approach and have fittings with the leading players. They could be available a few days or perhaps a week or so early for rehearsals and they often wish to have significant input to the wardrobe decisions. It is also possible that a major cast member can be signed at the last minute. Film actors are often cast because of the persona they present on screen. This must be given major consideration when establishing the wardrobe for them, so character development may take a sudden change in direction very close to the time the character will go on camera. Day players may also require last-minute decisions. Sometimes only a phone conversation is possible until the day player arrives, which is often the day before, or perhaps even the morning of, shooting. Since the measurements have been acquired by phone and

Figure 7.4 Flexibility is essential when working on films. Only a few days before shooting began on *The Dark Half* the character of Rawlie DeLesseps changed from a man to a woman when Julie Harris was cast in the part. The costumes were redesigned, retaining the eccentricities of the original, which were not changed in the script. Designs by Barbara Anderson.

the time to get the person ready for filming is short, it is often wise to have a number of possibilities available.

In theater the designer is usually able to observe the costumes in action during several dress rehearsals and refine the ideas. This is not the situation in film. The fitting takes place, the costume is finalized, the actor is dressed, the scene is shot. A day or two later the designer can see how it looked on film; and of course, it is then too late to change anything.

When shooting exteriors the weather can greatly influence the schedule and have a direct impact on the costumes. Except in Los Angeles where the norm is sunny skies, the directing team will have certain scenes in mind for rain cover. If, at the last minute, an outdoor scene can't be shot, an interior scene will replace it so that time will not be lost. Rain cover is usually determined by the availability of a location, and the wardrobe for that scene must be ready as well as the clothes for the originally scheduled scenes. Should this be impossible, the designer must let the directing team know at once so the schedule can be rearranged before the crisis arises.

◆ Paperwork and Hours

One of the prime differences between working in the theater and working on a film is the amount of paperwork involved. The lists are essential to keep all the elements under control, and they will change often. In the beginning the script and shooting schedule are on white paper; as each new revision comes out the inserts are printed on different colored sheets. Before filming is completed both may look like a rainbow. The most efficient way to keep up

Figure 7.5   The nonrealistic film, *The Empty Mirror,* gave Melinda Eshelman an opportunity to create different versions of Hitler. These are the Translucent Suit and the Virtual Reality Hitler. The Big Suit is shown in Figure 6.14.

with the changes is to have the lists on the computer so information can be added, subtracted, and moved easily. The particular program is not important, but the ease with which it can be used is. Some film and television companies prefer to use a program that ties directly in to all the other organizational aspects of the production. This can be a good limited solution, but it may not give the designer the necessary flexibility and scope.

No discussion of film work would be complete without a few words about the hours. They are very long and often quite stressful, for deadlines must be met continuously. The members of the wardrobe department are some of the first to be called to greet the actors, or talent, when they arrive for costumes and makeup. They are among the last to leave after putting away garments that were just used or freshening those that are needed for the next day. Compensation is usually better than it is in theater, and it should be.

◈ Equipment and Budgets

When working in a studio situation or out of a costume rental house the designer has access to areas already set up to store and produce costumes. Many feature or television films are done either totally or partially on location, with

Figure 7.6   Designer Molly Maginnis used an "overly romantic" approach when developing the costume ideas for the 1998 film, *The Mighty Joe Young*. Simple elegance is reflected in this design for Charlize Theron as Jill Young.

the production company created just for that one project. The spaces that are needed will have to be found along with the equipment, which may be rented, purchased, or borrowed. Wardrobe will need rooms that can accommodate workspace, machines, hanging and box storage, cleaning equipment, and fitting area. If the company is traveling to various locations, then a van or trailer that can accommodate all these functions, though usually on a limited basis, should be available.

Equipment especially needed on the road includes an iron and ironing board, a steamer, portable hanging racks, hairdryers for quick drying situations, a basic sewing kit, a sewing machine, if at all possible a small washer and dryer with water hookup, and instant electricity to run all this stuff and provide light in the van so the costumes and accessories can be located. Regular washing and drying facilities are also essential and can perhaps be arranged for at the hotel or motel where the crew is staying. A dry cleaner willing to provide very fast and even late-night service should be located.

The designer may be given the budget by the production company and it may have three components: equipment, staff, and costumes. Create ballpark figures for these areas as soon as possible to see if the work can be done for this amount. If not, find out if more money is available or if the scope of any or all of the areas needs to be scaled back.

The filming staff can consist of the designer, an assistant, the costume supervisor, and the costumer, depending on the size of the production. Even if everything is designed before filming commences, a number of people are needed to do the costume acquiring, fitting, preparing, repairing, and on-set supervising that can happen all at the same time. On days where a large cast is being used additional costumers may need to be hired. If extensive construction or alterations are necessary then a separate shop crew may need to be established.

◆ Television

Designing for a television situation comedy or a soap opera that has a home base at a studio may be much like working for a repertory company. A wardrobe may be established for the regular characters and added to as the scripts require. Guest stars, day players, and extras are dealt with on a week-by-week basis and if the show lasts long enough, a significant stock of costumes may be accumulated. The hours are more regular and the shooting schedule is not at the whim of the weather or location availability. The show may be videotaped or filmed; up to four cameras may be used at the same time. A wide shot, two close-ups, and a medium shot can occur on the same action sequence. Continuity is necessary but not as crucial as with film for there will not be as many setups for a single scene. The scene can be viewed and checked immediately to see if there are any problems that could require another take. The entire time allotted to do a television show from preparation through taping is much shorter than it would be for a film.

The difference between tape and film will affect the costume designer mostly in the way the colors are perceived. When working on tape in television, he or she should ask to observe a camera test to see how the particular equipment registers different tones and if some small patterns will strobe. In film the designer should check with the director of photography to find out the type of film stock being used and how it reacts to different colors.

◆ Flexibility and Stamina

Film can be much more wearing on the designer than work on live productions. The involvement time is longer, the hours are longer, and the gratification of seeing the work completed before an audience is much delayed. Decisions are made and changed continuously. Input into the design decisions can come from all directions and it may have more to do with business than with artistic integrity. The majority of the projects are done in

Figure 7.7   The designer's pen and pencil sketch is included with photos of the actor in garments found to convey the same idea. Designs by Eduardo Castro for the character Goggles in the feature film *Sugar Hill*.

modern dress. The characters still need to be well defined, but the designer may do more clipping and shopping than drawing and patterning; and everyone in the company may consider himself or herself an expert on the era by virtue of the fact that he or she also wears clothes. Schedule changes that may seem quite simple to the directing staff can produce monumental headaches for the wardrobe department.

Film and television are very costly mediums. The number of people working on a project is extensive, a shooting day is an expensive commitment, and delays can cost thousands of dollars. Many times the majority of the people are waiting while a few are engaged in the work, but when it's time to contribute it must be done efficiently and effectively. Reliability and organization are as important as flair and flashes of genius, but the latter are certainly welcome in what can be an industry dominated by the business-minded.

◆ Chapter 8

Costume Construction

Exploring costume ideas, sketching preliminary drawings, and developing those sketches into finished renderings are very rewarding processes for the designer. Taking the costume plates to the shop and presenting them to the technicians who will bring the ideas from paper to reality can also begin an exciting phase of the work. Once again the designer is participating in a give-and-take of ideas. The process of distilling ideas and expressing them graphically provides creative satisfaction, but it is a solitary experience. Many people work in the performing arts because they like the group collaboration, so beginning the actual construction period can be a delight.

Costume designers don't have to be brilliant at construction, although that skill can be invaluable at times, but they must know enough about building costumes to be able to guide those who work with them. In many costume shops the foreman and drapers are extremely talented and experienced, and they will know instantly what must be done to realize the sketches. Talented people with this kind of skill can actually enhance the designs with their expertise and would probably be upset if the designer tried to tell them how to do every little thing.

In many building situations, however, people with extensive knowledge and experience may not be available. It is, therefore, vital that the designer know how to interpret the sketch as a matter of self-preservation, for a good design can be easily lost in poor construction.

◆ The Modern Dress Show

A production set in a time close to the present day must be as carefully planned as one designed for a period, but the costumes may not go through the costume shop except for alterations. The designer should consider carefully the garments that are needed to determine the ideal types of fabrics and colors before going shopping. It is wise for the designer to have small sketches, color indications, measurement sheets, and a tape measure along when faced with a world of clothes, both new and used.

◆ Developing an Approach to Building

The approach to building a show must be the same as the design approach. The entire production is considered and decisions are made about the fabrics, lines, and yardages that will work best to establish the silhouette and movement. Certain lines or shapes must be set to provide a basis for variation. A skirt with a five-yard hem is a full skirt, but the feeling it gives the character will be different if all the other skirts have eight-yard hems, or perhaps only three-yard hems. A robe of corduroy has a certain weight and depth; it can seem rich next to robes made of cotton, or less elegant if other robes are velvets. Edging an area with gold braid may add richness, but the effect is not as strong if another costume is edged with a band of three different golds appliquéd together.

A careful look at the entire production should reveal the basic lines that are to be used for the show. For women, the number of pieces in the bodice and the size and shape of the skirt may be the place to begin. Not all the costumes will be built the same; many may be variations on a theme. The seven-piece bodice is a very good approach to the women's costumes from the beginning of the sixteenth century to the end of the eighteenth century (see Figures 9.17 and 9.18) and can be chosen as the line for the middle and upper classes in a production that takes place within this time period. Once the theme is chosen, there may be many individualized treatments, for the placement of the neckline, the positioning of the seams on the body, the waist treatment, and the type of closing to be used can shift according to the design and the body of the actress (see Figure 8.2).

Nineteenth-century costumes are more intricately tailored. The basic line of the bodice may need more pieces to shape the body. A nine-piece bodice (Figures 9.19 and 9.20) can mold much more easily around the curved bustline to the high neck that is a common feature of nineteenth-century day wear (see Figure 8.1). Vertical darts might be incorporated if a seam line needs to be eliminated, though often the seam line reinforces

Figure 8.1   Nineteenth-century tailoring was used in creating the realistic costume below for a play based on Chekhov's *The Duel,* produced at Yale University in 1961. The silhouette is definitely molded by the corset. Design by Barbara Anderson.

the period feeling. Horizontal darts usually are not suitable for period construction.

The line of the woman's bodice can also reveal the class of the character. Differences in social status can be indicated by the intricacies present in the construction.

The woman's skirt, usually in one or two distinct styles, should be mocked up or developed in muslin and checked with the proper types of petticoats. Once the fall and flow are established in the mockup, variations to accommodate the specific design and actor size can easily be indicated.

When setting the line of the show it is important that the designer mock up enough forms to be sure the period feeling is correct, but time may be wasted if certain similarities are not recognized in preplanning so that patterns are not unnecessarily duplicated. Sleeves may have a great deal of variety, but each does not need to be tackled as an entirely new problem. A certain sleeve design can be solved; then the next can be worked on in terms of what has been learned from the first. For example, sleeve B is similar to sleeve A but needs more kick or flair at the top of the cap and is four to five inches less full. Mockups are most often done in unbleached muslin because it is easy to work with, can be marked on readily, and is inexpensive when purchased in bulk. In some cases, however, the costume itself will be made of a fabric whose qualities are so different from muslin that the mockup will not tell the designer what he or she needs to know. This is particularly true if the real fabric will be very sheer, very drapable, or very heavy. Then a patterning fabric that has more of the qualities that will be present in the actual costume should be used. A shop that has a budget for basic equipment should always keep an eye open for closeouts where bolts of fabric of different weights can be acquired at reasonable prices. Color should make no difference in this type of purchase (though something inoffensive is always preferable), but weave, weight, and texture are of primary importance.

Establishing the line of the men's period costumes before the nineteenth century is very similar to the approach for the women. The bodice generally has no more than three to five pieces. Robe and tunic skirts are seldom shaped to control the fall in the same manner as the women's, so here the question may simply be one of fullness and length.

The line that will keep the men of the nineteenth and twentieth centuries looking like they all live in the same world can be created in very subtle ways since variations are not great from period to period. The fit at the waist, the width of the lapel, the number of buttons on the front of the coat, and the width of the pants are some of the areas where the fashion can be set.

Skirt lengths for either men or women require particular consideration. A skirt that appears to be floor length seldom falls to the floor in front to enable the actor to move without lifting it. The center front may need to be three-quarters of an inch to an inch off, then taper from the side front to hit the floor at about the side seam. In any full-length skirt, particularly if it has a train that is gradually added from the side seams to the center back, the performer must realize that movement is easiest when it begins with a forward motion. A direct step to the side or back may cause the actor or actress to tread on the garment. A small step forward followed by a gradual turn will help the skirt to follow the actor or actress and stay out from underfoot.

The length of a skirt that does not reach to the floor is usually geared to a certain point on the body, such as the anklebone, the bottom of the calf muscle, above the knee, or perhaps the middle of the thigh. In some shows, particularly when characters are grouped together in a line (such as a chorus grouping) the skirt length might be set at a particular distance from the floor rather than geared to the individual (Figure 8.2). Chaos will prevail if 10 women are lined up as a group that should have a unified feeling and each hem is an inch or two different from the one beside it.

In any of these instances, deciding on a line for the show does not mean that everything must conform to a central overview. It is a method of establishing certain guidelines for the look of the production and then filling out the picture in relation to these guidelines. Even in construction there must be a point of reference that can be used as a control.

Figure 8.2 These three chorus dancers for *Kiss Me Kate* in a production at Carnegie Mellon University were different heights but the consistent skirt length helped them look like a well-organized unit. Design by Cletus Anderson.

◆ Translating the Sketch to the Costume

The designer must develop an eye for translating the costume from a two-dimensional sketch to a three-dimensional form, a crucial skill that is not easy to acquire. It involves being able to read the sketch to determine what body areas are involved, then deciding on what portion of that area the costume piece covers. Essentially, the body breaks up at the hinge points: neck, waist, torso, knees, ankles, shoulders, elbows, and wrists; and the costume must relate to these points in order to give flexibility and movement to the form. The hinge points are the references that can be used to block in the basic design lines. An example of how this is done can be seen in Figure 8.3, a costume for Mr. Folair in *Nicholas Nickleby*. The vest is a bit short, stopping about an inch above the waist. The trouser top could stop just at the waist so the shirt can dress down over to show 4 inches between vest and trousers. The shoulder line drops a bit longer than the shirt overhang or 4-1/2 inches. The total stitching width is 1-1/2 inches or one-third of the drop, with 1/2 inch between each row. The cuff and the ruffle are each about 1-1/2 inches, the same width as the total stitching. The bows of the tie are half the length of neck to waist front, 8 inches. The hat crown is one-half of the visible part of the face, or 3-1/2 inches, and the band about one-third of that, or 1-1/4 inches. The height of hats and headpieces should be considered carefully, for there is a general tendency to overstate them. The trim on the vest collar is one-half the hat band or 5/8 inch and the diameter

The Life and Adventures of
Nicholas Nickleby

Mr. Folair
CRA 10-92

Figure 8.3 Costume sketch for Mr. Folair in *The Life and Adventures of Nicholas Nickleby* by Charles Dickens. The production was designed by Cletus Anderson at Carnegie Mellon University in 1992.

of the buttons the same. Thus the actual measurements of the different costume parts are discovered by considering both the size of the performer and the relationship of elements to each other.

Cross-checking some of the measurements to make sure the scaling is consistent must be done regularly. There are three major problems that cause the actual costume to differ from the proportions created in the sketch. First, the dimensions may be wrong and can easily be corrected with a little reassessment. Second, the sketch may create something of an optical illusion so that what seems to be one size at first glance may really be another when carefully considered in relation to the areas around it. The third cause of discrepancy is that the proportions of the sketch do not relate well to those of the actor and must be reinterpreted. If the actor's body and the design are in conflict, the scale may need to change. This may be evident as the pattern is developed, or it may become more obvious as the mockup is fitted and the three-dimensional garment is viewed on the figure.

Consider now the sketch for Pluto in the musical The *Happiest Girl in the World* (Figure 8.4). The costume for Mr. Folair relates closely to the actual physique of the actor. Pluto, however, strives to add stature and create a more monumental presence. Actually designed for a baritone standing about six foot two, the scale of the costume could closely resemble that of the sketch. With the distance from neck to waist about 16 inches, the breastplate starts 1 inch below the pit of the neck and extends 6 inches past the waist. The decorative tab hangs 10 inches longer than that. The shoulder could be about 6-1/2 inches total and the armor would be 4-1/2 inches wide. The arm treatment has two main areas. If the arm is 25 inches long, the top drape appears to be slightly less than half, or 11 inches; the cuff is a bit wider than the

Figure 8.4 Costume design for Pluto from *The Happiest Girl in the World*. Design by Cletus Anderson for the Carnegie Mellon Theatre Company.

shoulder of the armor, or 5 inches, with the top and bottom bands about 1 inch, leaving 3 inches between. When considering the arm, always think of what the bent elbow does to the areas. A deep cuff and a short sleeve both may have problems if they conflict with the bending of the arm.

The skirt ends just below the torso and flares slightly, which would indicate moderate gores with pleats deep enough to hold the fold from the waist to the hem. The cape is extremely full and gored with a five- to six-yard hem, and pleated at the top to give fullness and breadth to the shoulder. A swag is cut into one side to add more significance to the shoulder/ chest area. The helmet is slightly less than the height of the face, 6-3/4 inches with the visor 2-3/4 inches wide. The plumes rise higher than the face size, about 7-1/2 inches.

Converting from sketch to costume accurately is an essential skill for designers, one that can only be developed through experience. Designers who are learning their craft should take every possible opportunity to develop their eye. An excellent exercise to aid this training can take place in the costume workshop. As costumes designed by others are being built, novice designers can pick a sketch and make notes on how they would scale it themselves. They can then go to the rack and find the actual costume, seeing how their notes compare to what is being done.

A general guide to the yardage needed for different costume elements is provided in Chapter 2. If the budget allows and the fabric is available, err slightly on the side of too much rather than too little. A great deal of time can be wasted if it takes hours to lay out a pattern because it won't quite fit the available fabric, or if work must stop because more fabric must be purchased. And if the cloth has been treated in some way—dyed or painted, for instance—it may be impossible, or at best very time-consuming, to match a second piece to it.

◆ Fabric Selection

The importance of selecting the proper fabrics for the costumes cannot be underestimated. Unless a fabric has the right qualities it will never produce the line and movement that can realize the design effectively. The appropriate weave, weight, and texture are actually more important than the color on many occasions because a certain quality of drape must be inherent in the fabric, while the color can be corrected by dyeing or painting. If this is not possible, color relationships might be shifted slightly to accommodate a color variation.

Fabric selection has been complicated in the past few years with the great number of synthetic fiber varieties on the market, plus many blends of synthetic and natural fibers. For some costumes the new fabrics are even more suitable than the originals they are made to imitate. Often they are not appropriate at all, for the draping quality is entirely different. The following discussion introduces fibers, how they are made, and the qualities that they can usually be expected to have. The more common fabrics are discussed in some detail; those less usual are mentioned briefly to at least familiarize readers with the terminology. The list of synthetic fibers is based on their generic names, for each year new variations appear on the market

Figure 8.5 The appropriate weave, weight and texture are vital to a costume and good tailoring can be achieved effectively with wools. Costumes for the John Marshall series sponsored by the U.S. Judicial Commission. Photo by Norris Brock. ©Metropolitan Pittsburgh Public Broadcasting, Inc., 1976. Design by Barbara Anderson.

under new trade names registered by specific textile companies. All fabrics are now carefully marked as to their content, but the quality and specific treatment of the fabric can vary so greatly that this marking does not necessarily tell the designer what the fabric will do. It is always best to pull out one or two yards and see how it falls and drapes and what movement qualities it has. Designers must constantly feel and test fabrics, even though it may not make them the most popular customers in the fabric store.

Natural Fibers

Wool. One of the oldest and most universally used fibers, wool has a protein base and comes from the fleece of sheep (and sometimes goats). It is made into fabrics that are sold as either woolens or worsteds. Woolen yarns tend to be soft and fuzzy. Worsted yarns are smooth and strong and usually have a high twist. Woolens most often have a rough, textured surface; worsteds have a smooth surface that makes the weave more conspicuous. Wool comes in a wide variety of weaves and weights, from the lightweight worsted challis to a heavy woolen broadcloth suitable for a winter coat.

Though most wool has good draping qualities, the fabrics with harder threads and tighter weaves are less supple. Wool can be quite flexible and resilient, wrinkling slightly and dropping the wrinkles easily when hung out. Wool may be attacked by moths unless treated with a mothproofing chemical in the finishing process. Some of the types of fabric available in wool are tweed, broadcloth, flannel, challis, crepe, and jersey. Other hair fibers that produce specialty wool fabrics are angora, cashmere, camel, alpaca, llama, and vicuna. Wool fiber has an affinity for dye, though care must be taken in noncommercial dyeing to keep some types of the fabric from shrinking, felting, and fuzzing. Wool blends are becoming more and more common. The dyeing properties of the synthetic fibers that are combined with wool may not be the same. The synthetic may also be one particular thread of the weave, so part of the fabric may dye readily while another part remains untouched.

One method of judging the quality and usability of wool—or any fabric, for that matter—is referred to as its "hand." Though this may not seem a very scientific term, it is commonly used in reference to fabrics by those who work with them and indicates the quality that can be defined or evaluated by the sense of touch. The more fabrics one handles, the keener his or her perception of the variations.

Silk.   A continuous filament protein fiber, silk may be cultivated either where the silkworm is raised in a carefully controlled atmosphere specifically for the purpose of producing fibers or in the wild, where the silkworm is not controlled but spins a cocoon under natural conditions. Sericulture, or the production of cultivated silk, is a process not so easily automated as some textile manufacturing, and escalating labor costs have made silk fabric quite expensive. Probably partly because of its cost and inaccessibility, silk is thought of as a luxury fiber, but it cannot be denied that it is a delight to the eye and the touch. It drapes easily, is pliable, and has good elasticity and ability to retain its shape. Silk takes dye well and can have a depth of color or jewel-like tone hard to find in any other fabric. It can be washed and ironed if the yarn is not creped, though it should be checked to make sure the dye is colorfast.

The second category of natural fibers is composed of cellulose fibers such as cotton, flax, jute, hemp, and ramie. These are built up naturally during the growth of the plant and come from the seed, stem, or leaves. Rayon is also cellulose but considered man-made because cellulose fibers are not in their natural state; they are regenerated by being dissolved and resolidified. Characteristically, natural cellulose fibers have good absorbency and conduct heat well. They are generally easy to care for as they thrive on soap-and-water washes and are actually stronger when wet than dry. They can withstand high temperatures, so no special precautions are needed during ironing. Fabrics from cellulose fibers do wrinkle easily unless treated with various resin finishes, which may provide benefits such as starchless finish, ease of ironing, crease recovery, and permanent pleating.

Cotton.   The most widely used fiber in the world, cotton comes from the seed of the cotton plant, which blossoms and produces a bole or pod of cotton fiber. Cotton is classified by its staple, or fiber length, and its grade and fiber character. The staple varies from about half an inch to two inches. A longer staple, such as pima, is classified as the finer cotton. Cotton dyes well, but the color may fade and the fabric weaken with long exposure to the sun. The varieties of cotton fabric are legion: light, heavy, smooth, rough, shiny, dull, pile, or flat. Long known as a fabric for work clothes because of its long life and ease of cleaning, new weaves and finishes have established cotton as a fashion leader acceptable for any occasion.

Linen.   Obtained from the stem of the flax plant and the oldest textile fiber known to man, linen fabrics were found in the Swiss lake dwellings of Neolithic man, dating back over 10,000 years. More important in the past than it is today, flax fiber represents only 1 percent of the total world production of fiber. Linen tends to be an expensive fabric because processing flax is extremely laborious. Linen fabric is stronger than cotton and its tensile strength increases when wet, so it is very washable. The long, hard fibers do not soil easily and give up a stain readily. While it may be dyed to a degree, linen does not dye easily due to the hardness and lack of penetrability of the fiber. Natural linen is yellowish-buff to gray and heavy bleaching may weaken the fiber. Dress linens are often treated with crease-resistant chemicals that make them much more usable but less durable. Linen is made into a variety of fabrics in plain and twill weave, as well as the beautiful damasks familiar in table linens.

Less Common Cellulose Fibers

Ramie.   A grass cloth used for several thousand years in China, ramie's fiber is similar to flax, but it is pure white and has a silklike luster. One of the strongest fibers known, it is stiff and has low resiliency, thus wrinkling very easily if not treated. It is made up into fabrics resembling linen and is used for suiting, shirting, and table linen.

Jute.   A stem fiber chiefly exported by India, jute is the cheapest textile fiber. It is used mostly for backings, bagging, and wrapping for it is thick, stiff, and not particularly strong. Jute is naturally a light tan and cannot be bleached. Its most commonly known form is burlap, which can be used as a decorator fabric when dyed in dark colors. Jute deteriorates fairly rapidly under moist conditions, so burlap does not wash or dry-clean successfully.

Hemp.   Another bast or stem fiber made up of long, strong fibers, hemp is difficult to spin into fine counts, so it is more often utilized in the manufacture of canvas, cordage, rope, and fishing line. Sisal is a leaf fiber similar to hemp that is easier to process for cordage and ropes.

Man-made Cellulose Fibers

Rayon and Acetate.   Both rayon and acetate fibers come from the same base and are considered man-made, but they can have different properties and do have a basic difference in construction. Rayon is made from cottonseed or wood pulp linters which are regenerated into a solution and then extruded through spinnerets into fiber, physically changed but chemically the same as cellulose. Acetate is the result of a chemical change, for the cellulose is combined with acetic compounds before being extruded. There are several differences between rayon and acetate: rayon scorches with too much heat while acetate melts; acetate dissolves in acetone but rayon does not; rayon is more absorbent and has less static than acetate; acetate wrinkles less when dry; and rayon is more versatile and can be made into fabrics similar to any of the natural fabrics, while acetate is usually used for silklike garments. Rayon is a very versatile fabric that can be produced at low cost. It is easily dyed, has good creping qualities, and does not pill. Some types are stronger than others. It can have excellent colorfastness. A few of its trademark names are Avril, Avron, Bemberg, Celanese, Cupioni, Enka Rayon, Fortisan, Jetspun, Lirelle, Nupron, and Zantrel.

Acetates have an excellent hand and good draping ability, fair wrinkle resistance, but poor crease retention. They must be ironed at low temperature, are usually low in cost, and have limited strength. Some well-known acetate trade names are Acele, Avisco, Celafil, Celaloft, Chromspun, Estron, and Loftura. Triacetates, a chemical variation of acetates, are less sensitive to heat, have good wash-and-wear properties, wrinkle resistance, pressed-pleat retention, and colorfastness. The best-known triacetate is Arnel. Acetates do not dye easily with household dyes.

Synthetic Fibers

Nylon.   The first truly synthetic fabric, nylon was introduced to consumers in 1939. It is made of air, water, and coal in a melt-spinning process. Nylon is a light fiber and one of the strongest, and its strength does not deteriorate with age. The degree of resilience is high and wrinkles fall out readily. It can drape fairly well if it is soft, sheer, or a medium- to heavy-weight fabric. Many types of nylon will dye well; others will only take a tint. Whites, however, pick up color easily when washed with other fabrics and may become gray. Nylon can be combined with any of the natural or man-made cellulose fibers. Some of the more common nylon trade names are Antron, Cantrece, Capriolan, Crepeset, Nytelle, and Qiana.

Acrylic Fibers.   Acrylics are manufactured much like nylon, but their principal raw materials are coal, air, petroleum, limestone, and natural gases. Acrylics are soft and bulky but lightweight. While commercial colors are quite colorfast, acrylics do not dye well with household dyes. Acrylic holds its shape well, washes easily, dries quickly, and needs little or no ironing. The most common acrylic trade names are Orlon, Acrilan, Creslan, and Zefran II.

Modacrylics.   Modacrylics are modified acrylics, such as Dynel or Verel, that are resistant to flame, water, microorganisms, insects, and sunlight. They have good colorfastness, wash-and-wear properties, and wrinkle resistance. Modacrylics do not dye easily with household dyes and melt unless ironed at low temperatures. They are often used for knitted pile fleece, fur-like fabrics, and wigs.

Polyester Fibers.   Made of a combination of an alcohol obtained from petroleum and an acid, polyester fibers truly require little care. They are wrinkle resistant, stand up fairly well to repeated launderings, do not sag, and can be permanently pleated. Colorfast in commercially produced fabric, they do not dye easily and require special dyes if a significant color change is desired. Polyester comes in many types of fabric, and when it is blended with natural fiber many easy-care qualities are added. It can be ironed at a moderate setting. Well-known trademarks for polyester are Dacron, Avlin, Encron, Fortrel, Kodel, Quintess, and Vycron.

Other generic groups of man-made fibers include anidex, an elastic fiber; azlon, produced from protein found in plants such as peanuts and soya beans; fiberglass, found mostly in draperies; metallics, used as decorative additions for glitter or sheen; nytril, which is furlike; olefin (such as Herculon), popular for seat covers and outdoor furniture; rubber, which has good stretch and recovery and is used for foundation garments and swimwear; Saran, which is tough, flexible, and stiff; spandex (such as Lycra or Vyrene), which is lightweight with good elasticity, and vinal, which is strong and abrasive resistant,

These are all the generic classifications for the man-made fibers set forth in the Textile Fiber Product Identifications Act of 1958; the generic term must be included in all labeling. New variations under different trademarks and improvements of the fibers are developed every year.

Weaves

Many types of weave are used in making fabrics. The threads that run the length of the piece are called the warp and those that run across the fabric are called the fill. The three basic weaves are plain, twill, and satin. The simplest is the plain weave, which has yarns at right angles passing alternately over and under each other (Figure 8.6). A variation of this is the basket weave, in which two or more warp or filling yarns are used as one (Figure 8.7). A rib variation is achieved if either the warp or fill yarns are much heavier than the other, or if the weave is unbalanced with more threads woven closer together in one direction.

Twill is the most durable of weaves and is produced when the filling yarns are interlaced with the warps in such a way that they form diagonal ridges across the fabric. In an even twill the fill passes over the same number of warps it passes under, while in an uneven twill the fill passes over more warps (but not more than four) than it passes under, making a filling-faced twill. In a warp-faced twill the warp threads are the most prominent. Figure 8.8 shows the fill passing over two warps and under one. The most common twill variation is herringbone, where the diagonal runs one direction for a few rows, then reverses and goes in the opposite direction, with a variation at the apex of the V to reverse the wales (Figure 8.9).

Satin and sateen weaves produce a shiny, smooth fabric because more of either the warp or fill are visible on the right side. In satin, made of silk or rayon, more warp threads are exposed on the right side (Figure 8.10), while sateen, made of cotton, has more fill fibers showing (Figure 8.11). The weave is similar to twill except the top thread does not interlace with the thread underneath for four to twelve yarns. The sheen has a definite direction and patterns should be cut accordingly and not turned so that some run the length of the fabric and some the width. This weave produces smooth, lustrous, rich-looking fabric, but the longer the float, the more potential for snagging and

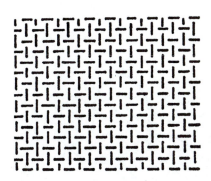

Figure 8.6   Plain weave.

Figure 8.7   Basket weave.

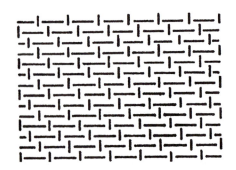

Figure 8.8   Filling-faced twill.

Figure 8.9   Herringbone weave.

Figure 8.10   Four-float warp satin.

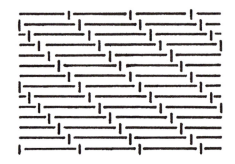

Figure 8.11   Five-float filling sateen.

Figure 8.12   Pile weave done with extra filling yarn.

pulling. A variation is satin crepe, in which a smooth yarn is used for the warp and a duller, tightly twisted or creped yarn is used for fill. This easily draped fabric is reversible, giving two very different surface effects.

Fancier weaves include pile, jacquard, dobby, and leno. The pile weaves, such as velvets, velours, and plushes, have soft, sometimes clipped yarns or pile on the right side; the back is smooth, showing the weave. The pile is produced by weaving an additional warp or filling yarn into the basic

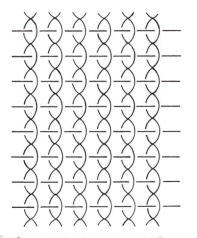

Figure 8.13   Leno weave in figure-8 pattern.

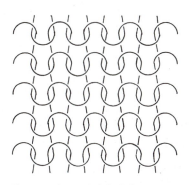

Figure 8.14   Weft knitting.

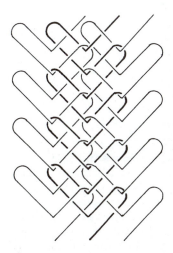

Figure 8.15   Warp knitting.

structure. Velvets, terrys, and plush fabrics are made with an extra warp yarn, while velveteens and corduroy are made with an extra filling yarn (Figure 8.12). Most pile fabrics have a definite direction and must be cut with all pattern pieces lying the same way.

Small patterns are made on a loom with a dobby attachment, which makes designs that are simple, limited in size, and usually geometric in form. The dobby or cam raises or lowers 20 to 40 harnesses that control the warp threads to form the pattern.

More complex patterns are done on the jacquard loom, which has a mechanism that controls thousands of heddles, needlelike wires through which the warp threads pass, and allows them to be lifted independently. Cards are punched to the pattern for each fill line of the design. As the cards progress the warp yarns are raised according to the pattern holes. This is the most expensive form of weaving, and setting up the loom may take several weeks or months.

The leno or gauze weave involves two sets of warp threads and one filling thread. The warp threads seem to twist around each other at the interstice of the fill thread. The weave gives a lacelike effect such as that found in marquisette or casement (Figure 8.13).

Knitted fabrics make up a large portion of textile goods and can be produced faster than woven fabrics. Simply put, knitting is a series of loops dependent on each other. The loops that run the length of the piece corresponding to the warp yarn are called the wale, while a row across similar to the filling yarn or weft is a course. Knitting machines produce either warp or weft knitting. Weft knitting is similar to hand knitting (Figure 8.14). In warp knitting many yarns are fed vertically to an equal number of needles and the individual warp yarns are interlooped into the loop of the adjacent warp yarns (Figure 8.15).

True crepe fabrics are not the result of the weave, which may be plain, but are caused by the yarn, natural fiber or rayon, which is highly twisted. One variation is seersucker, in which the warp yarns are regular while the filling yarns are alternating groups of regular and creped yarns. A crepe effect can be achieved by texturing the polyester yarns or by weaving high-twist yarns in irregular interlacings. A crepe effect can also be added to a fabric with a finish. A chemical can be printed on the woven cloth, causing it to shrink in areas while the untreated fabric crinkles in between.

Nonwoven fabrics come in two categories: felt, whose fibers are interlocked by a combination of chemical action, mechanical work, moisture and heat; and other nonwovens, which use a bonding agent. Felt is made of wool or fur, often blended with other fibers, and comes in a great variety of thicknesses. Wool is the most suitable fiber for felt because the physical properties of the fiber make it snag together and tangle easily. Other nonwovens are made of cellulose fiber and synthetics held together by a bonding agent or the thermoplastic quality of the fibers in the blends. Many new types and uses for the nonwoven fabrics are developed every year.

Leather might not be considered a fabric, but it certainly is a material often used for both garments and accessories. Leather, which comes in a variety of thicknesses, finishes, and colors from many different animals, is sold by the square foot and comes in hides or half hides, which are irregularly shaped. Various leather garments are seen in Figures 8.17, 8.18, and 8.20.

Checking the Hand of the Fabric

With all the blends and synthetics that are on the market today designers must develop a knack for understanding the hand or feel of the goods. They must be able to pull out a length of material to see if it will react properly, then check the contents for any fibers that might fight against the right line. Polyester fabrics often drape beautifully, but their resilience can give the folds an undesired roundness. Cotton-and-dacron combinations can give a soft yet crisp look but may not be acceptable if the garments must look old and slept in (Figure 8.16). Dacron chiffons are very soft and drape well, but they do not hold air and float as well as silk. Linens have a lovely quality, but unless they are treated for wrinkle resistance it may be difficult to maintain a crisp, neat look through an entire energetic act. Synthetic fibers may not tailor well; they will not ease and shrink to take a shape.

When searching for the best fabrics for a show, designers must not limit themselves to dressmaker fabric departments. Some of the most suitable fabrics for period productions are found in the drapery and upholstery sections. There are nevertheless some pitfalls to avoid in this area. Drapery fabrics made of fiberglass should not be purchased unless special construction methods can be used. When cut, fiberglass is extremely uncomfortable

Figure 8.16 Real cottons were used so they would look worn and wrinkled in this costume for *The Leatherstocking Tales.* Photo by Walt Seng. ©Metropolitan Pittsburgh Public Broadcasting Inc., 1979. Design by Barbara Anderson.

against the skin. Fiberglass fabrics are also not particularly durable and pull apart at stress seams. Upholstery fabrics backed with a rubber coating should also be avoided. They are uncomfortable to wear, do not drape or mold well, and if dry-cleaned may become extremely stiff and rigid.

◆ Dyeing the Fabric

While the proper fabric must have the right body and drape, color is certainly another primary factor in the creation of a costume. The search for just the right shade can sometimes be solved in the dye area of the costume shop, but first two important facts should be ascertained: (1) Will the fabric take the dye? and (2) What happens to it during the dyeing process?

There currently are many different dyes on the market; the type of fabric to be colored will determine which dye should be used.

Types of Dye

In general, as discussed previously, natural fibers, rayon, and many nylons will dye readily with household or union dyes such as Rit or Tintex, which can be purchased economically in bulk. These dyes are readily available and contain a blend of many different types of dye, which enables them to color a wide variety of fabrics. To some degree they may even work on acetates and polyesters. These dyes can produce fairly intense colors if used in increased quantities and processed in near-boiling or boiling water, but the colors tend to fade after repeated washing. When dyeing plant fibers, salt is added to the dye bath, though it may be already present in packaged dyes; with animal fibers, vinegar assists the dyeing process. The life of the color will be prolonged if the garment is washed separately in cool water with a mild detergent. Garments that are dry-cleaned maintain their colors quite well. Union dyes are easy to use because they require no special chemicals or procedures.

While union dyes are not especially effective on polyester, acrylics, and some acetates, these fabrics can take a tint, particularly if a mordant such as alum (which makes the fiber more receptive to the dye) is rinsed through the fabric before dyeing, or even added to the dye water itself. The alum may react with the dye, changing the color, so this must be pretested. Alum can also be used with wools to give them a deeper, richer tone. Blends of natural and synthetic fibers may dye to a degree, but will not go to dark shades with union dyes. If a fabric is made up of yarns of different types of fibers, it will not dye uniformly. This can sometimes give a very interesting effect. Patterned fabrics can often be overdyed quite successfully. Cotton drapery fabrics can be very useful for period garments; they are available in period style prints, often on a white or light background that can be dyed down. Of course, the colors of the pattern, particularly the lighter ones, will also be affected by the dye.

Disperse dyes, which are brilliant in color and stay well through both washing and dry-cleaning, were specially created to dye acetates and other synthetics such as polyester and nylon and plastics like buttons and buckles. They will dye silk and wool with slightly less intense results. These dyes work best if a mild detergent is included in the dye bath. The colorfastness depends on high heat during dyeing, almost to the boiling point, and thorough rinsing.

Basic or cationic dyes provide very brilliant colors but tend to fade when washed. They hold up fairly well when dry-cleaned. Basic dyes, which need acetic acid or vinegar added to the dye water, are particularly useful when dyeing silk, wool, and some acrylics. They will dye cotton, linen, and rayon if the fabric has been mordanted. This mordanting is done by dipping the fabric in a tannic acid bath, heating and cooling it, letting it dry, dipping it in a tartar emetic bath for 30 minutes, then dyeing it. This process can be time-consuming, so a quicker means to almost the same brilliance of color is to dye the fabric with the household or union dyes, then to overdye it with the basic dye. In this process, which is called topping, the union dye works as a mordant for the basic.

Direct dyes are relatively inexpensive and easy to use. They work in a fashion similar to the union dyes. The colors are not as brilliant as some of the other types, but they do work quite well on cotton, achieving a more intense color than the union dyes. Their major drawbacks are a tendency to fade when washed (though this can be slowed down with the use of cool water and mild detergent) and an inclination toward streaking. Direct dyes are most effective on cotton, linen, and viscose rayon and sometimes work well on silk, wool, and nylon.

Fiber-reactive dyes produce brilliant, quite permanent colors that take well from lukewarm to cold temperatures. This makes them extremely useful for hand painting, silk-screening, or batik. They work best on cotton, linen, and viscose rayon and can be used on silk and wool, though with less brilliant results. Salt and washing soda are added to the dye water.

Acid dyes work particularly well on silk and wool and may be effective on nylons and Lycra Spandex. Sometimes referred to as aniline dyes, though aniline is no longer used in making them, they need acetic acid or vinegar added to the dye bath. They tend to wash out if care is not taken. Acid dyes do dry-clean quite satisfactorily. Metal complex dyes are fairly new and provide a brilliance of color on the same fabrics as acid dyes. They are much more colorfast.

Dyeing Techniques and Problems

Some fabrics take dye well, but wetting them and/or heating them may change certain characteristics. A drapery fabric called antique satin is a good example of this. The fabric right off the bolt has good body and drapes well. It dyes easily, but after it becomes wet it loses all its body and is extremely limp. In this form it might be just right for certain costumes, but it will never make the sweeping ball gown it was so suitable for previously. Many wools dye well, but soft woolen weaves may shrink and become heavier. Washable wools do not do this, but neither do they dye as readily. Shrinking can be minimized if the fabric is warmed up and cooled gradually during the dyeing process. Wool that might shrink should not be put in a dryer. The surface quality of wool may become rougher during the necessary agitating or stirring to allow the dye to take evenly in the fabric, particularly in the washing machine. Then again, this may be desirable if the goal is to give the fabric a heavier, more rustic quality. Some synthetics tint, but the dye will migrate to the edges of the folds if spun out, producing a streaked effect. And some sheers, most specifically crisp ones, may acquire wrinkles in a hot dye solution, particularly during the spin cycle if done in a washing machine. These wrinkles will be heat-set and will never come out.

All fabrics should be thoroughly wet before dyeing. Some must be washed to remove sizing or chemicals in the fabric that make the yarns resist the color. To effectively reproduce a color the dyer should note the weight of the dry fabric, the amount in weight of dye used, the time in the dye, the temperature of the water, and the chemical assistants used. The quantity of water does not affect the shade achieved, but it may slow down the process and assist in creating an even color. All fabrics should be stirred during the dyeing process to minimize streaking and blotching.

The only safe way to dye fabric is to pretest it. Always check the size of the piece before and after processing it. Some shrinkage may be quite acceptable, but enough fabric must be purchased to allow for it. If the small piece requires boiling to achieve the desired color, a large amount will not dye successfully in the washing machine. It will not take on the proper color without the necessary heat.

After the garment or fabric has been dyed, wash it in mild detergent that does not contain additives for brightening whites and colors. Detergents that contain these additives are fine, however, if the shade needs to be lightened a bit.

An excellent book on this subject is *Fabric Painting and Dyeing for the Theatre* by Deborah M. Dryden (Heineman, 1993). The author, who has had experience in a variety of techniques, provides a clear guide to many types of fabric treatment, materials, and safety practices.

◈ Fabric Painting

Although dyeing is the most practical technique to achieve an overall color change, the color of a fabric also can be changed by painting. Fabric painting can produce unique effects in a costume.

Painting can be used to shade the form of a constructed costume. The sides or folds of a garment can be toned down or sections can be highlighted to add to the costume's three-dimensional quality. A garment that cannot be immersed without losing its shape might be lightly sprayed to change the color tone, though this is difficult to do successfully if the desired effect is to look smooth. Painting can add a textured look to a fabric, create a pattern, or reinforce an already existing pattern.

Various techniques and materials can be used to achieve different effects. General shading and toning can be done with a brush, aerosol spray, or an airbrush. An interesting surface texture can be achieved by spattering, preferably using more than one color. Patterns can be created using a silk-screen process, a simpler stencil technique, batik, or merely by brush painting or airbrushing the shapes on the fabric. An existing pattern can be reinforced by painting in highlights and shadows with a brush or marker. Dimension can be added to the pattern with hot glue and filler

Figure 8.17   Costume for Macbeth painted to give it dimension and age. Overtunic is a suede leather, boots a heavier cowhide. Designed for a National Geographic film by Barbara Anderson. Photo courtesy the National Geographic Society.

Figure 8.18   Armor for Ed Harris in the film *Knightriders* was made of heavy leather and painted for texture and interest. Photo by James Hamilton. Courtesy Laurel-Knights, Inc., New York. Design by Cletus Anderson.

compound. Color can be mixed in with the compound before it is applied or painted on after it has set.

Fabric painting can be done with union dyes, fiber-reactive dyes, dyes dissolved in alcohol and combined with shellac (know as FEV or French enamel varnish), water-base or oil-base textile inks, acrylic paint, metallic paint and bronzing powders, shoe or leather paints and dyes, floral sprays, spray enamels, or permanent markers. The union dyes are better for light shading effects, for though they are dissolved in hot water, when brushed or sprayed on they are relatively cool and deep colors will not take and stay. The fiber-reactive dyes produce an intense color when cool and can be effectively set by steaming. Actually, many of the dyes mentioned earlier can be used to paint costumes if they are combined with a dye paste and steamed to set the color. The FEV can produce deep, transparent tones but

Figure 8.19 This costume for Richard Basehart as King Arthur masquerading as a peasant was both frayed and painted. Designed for *A Connecticut Yankee in King Arthur's Court* in the Once Upon a Classic series by Barbara Anderson. Photo by Mitchell Greenberg. ©Metropolitan Pittsburgh Public Broadcasting, Inc., 1977.

Figure 8.20 Leathers for the Indian costumes in *The Leatherstocking Tales* were dyed and oiled to give them age and wear. Photo by Walt Seng. © Metropolitan Pittsburgh Public Broadcasting, Inc., 1979. Design by Barbara Anderson.

may stiffen the garment if used in any quantity. Textile inks, acrylic and metallic paints, and spray enamels can also stiffen the fabric to a degree, depending on its original texture and body and the amount of medium used. Floral spray is more flexible. Leather dyes and markers can add fairly intense color when used in small areas that can be easily controlled. They do not stiffen the fabric, but the markers are not necessarily permanent and may lose brilliance in either washing or dry-cleaning.

Any spraying, dyeing, or painting done with materials that have potentially toxic fumes should take place in a well-ventilated area; all personnel involved in the process should wear some type of mask or filter. Many materials used by performing arts craftspeople are potentially dangerous if not used properly. The bibliography contains a section on fabrics and construction in which several good references for the safe use of these materials are listed.

◆ Aging the Costume

Most of the techniques mentioned above embellish and enhance the costume. Sometimes the costumer's goal is to break down the fabric and the form to give it a well-worn or lived-in look. Aging garments is an art in itself and should be approached with a definite feeling for the ways clothes would break down and disintegrate on their own if they had been in the circumstances prescribed by the production.

A well-worn garment usually is more soiled and frayed around the stress points: the neck, cuffs, hem, elbows, pockets, knees, and seat. These areas can be sanded down or roughened up with a rasp and edges can be torn and snagged. Inner structures, such as shoulder pads and interfacings, can be removed to encourage sagging, and this can be quickly enhanced by weighting down the areas that should be baggy and droopy, then wetting or heavily steaming the garment and letting it dry with the weights in place. Faded areas can be created by carefully scrubbing in bleach or cleanser. Paint can be lightly sprayed or brushed over a roughened surface to highlight it for a faded, dusty quality. Browns and grays can be worked into areas that should be dirty and grimy. Black is more difficult to use effectively since it may produce a harsh, unrealistic appearance. Figures 8.19 and 8.20 show costumes that have been both worn down and painted down.

A costume that needs to be aged down but must be reclaimed after the production can be treated with colored hair sprays. These are a bit more expensive than the other painting and spraying media but usually clean out quite successfully. Real dirt, which can also be used for a moderately smudgy look, is almost always readily available.

When aging costumes, note which areas of the garment logically show the most wear and work them down in gradual steps. It is very easy to age something a bit more if it doesn't look old and dirty enough, but trying to bring it back if it has gone too far can be very difficult.

Chapter 9

Patterning and Building the Costume

THE BLACKOUT
CLAUDIA SCHIFFER
as
SUSAN
beach finale

Preceding page: In the 1998 film *The Blackout* Claudia Schiffer's final scene was on the beach, and she ended it by walking out into the water. To ensure a costume ready for retakes designer Melinda Eshelman did three copies of this gown.

Developing costume patterns is not difficult, but it does require a familiarity with fabric shapes and how they work on the body, a willingness to explore and try different approaches to discover the best solution, and a sense of neatness and order. The two primary methods used in creating a costume shape are flat patterning and draping. These are not mutually exclusive systems, though each has its advocates. The most sensible solution is to be proficient in both methods and to use whichever will best solve a particular problem. Many times techniques from each approach are needed to construct the costume.

In *flat patterning* the shapes of the pieces are drawn on patterning paper or brown paper, transferred to fabric, cut, then basted together and fitted on the person or dummy. In *draping* the uncut fabric is pinned into shapes directly on the person or dummy, with the pin lines creating the potential seams and excess fabric cut away as the shapes begin to approach the final form. Some garments cannot be flat-patterned and must be formed around the body figure (Figure 9.1). Many costume shapes can be drawn up more

Figure 9.1 This bustle could not be flat-patterned and was first draped in muslin on a form. Costume for the Carnegie Mellon Theatre Company. Design by Barbara Anderson.

Figure 9.2   Most of the patterning for this turn-of-the century gown was done flat, but the center front of the bodice needed to be draped on a dummy. Costume for the Carnegie Mellon Theatre Company. Design by Barbara Anderson.

quickly than draped, then refined when put on the figure (Figure 9.2). This can be an extremely efficient approach, particularly if there is a shortage of dressmaker's dummies, which are expensive and may not be available in small costume shops. Although a live model can be a substitute for a dummy, he or she can't be pinned into and may fidget if required to stand still for a long time.

This chapter deals mainly with flat patterning because it is a concept that can be easily presented on the printed page in a limited space. A good patterning imagination is invaluable. The basic shape should be quickly achieved, tried and adjusted, evaluated, ripped apart if an area doesn't look like it should, and repinned. If a line isn't right, investigate the cause of the problem, consider its remedy, undo the seam, and try it again. When working up a pattern always think about what each line is doing; never copy something automatically. Understanding each length and curve develops an understanding of the changes that will make the pattern more effective.

◆ Pattern Sources

Costume patterns do not have to be completely created in the shop. A number of sources are available to help the process along, although a preexisting pattern seldom matches the sketch exactly. The designer who understands how shapes work can more easily use other patterns as a starting point.

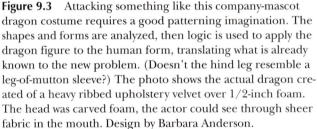

Figure 9.3 Attacking something like this company-mascot dragon costume requires a good patterning imagination. The shapes and forms are analyzed, then logic is used to apply the dragon figure to the human form, translating what is already known to the new problem. (Doesn't the hind leg resemble a leg-of-mutton sleeve?) The photo shows the actual dragon created of a heavy ribbed upholstery velvet over 1/2-inch foam. The head was carved foam, the actor could see through sheer fabric in the mouth. Design by Barbara Anderson.

Historical patterns can be found in some books on the history of clothing and patterning books, including *The Cut of Men's Clothes* and *The Cut of Women's Clothes* by Norah Waugh; five volumes by Herbert Norris titled *Costume and Fashion; A History of Costume* by Carl Kohler; the first edition *of History of Costume* by Blanche Payne; two volumes of *Patterns of Fashion* by Janet Arnold; *The Evolution of Fashion* by Margot Hill and Peter Bucknell; and *The Blue Book of Men's Tailoring* by Frederick Croonberg. Many designers also use nineteenth- and twentieth-century fashion magazines and tailoring guides, a number of which have been reprinted recently by Dover Publications. Some patterns are merely indications of the way a piece of clothing was cut; others have been drafted from actual garments. Either may be a good source of ideas, but often modern cutting methods give better results. For example, the seaming of bodices and jackets in the nineteenth century was often quite interesting and intricate. These patterns will still need to be adapted, however, for the reshaping of the body with corsets and pads was often more extreme than is advisable today, and people were much smaller than they are now.

Commercial patterns can be quite useful when building a fairly contemporary show, but just because the pattern is purchased doesn't mean it is right. The amount of fullness in a skirt might be exaggerated in the drawing. Be sure to check the inches around the hem listed on the back of the pattern packet. Sleeves are sometimes cut with a skimpy cap that may look fine but can really hamper movement. Even though there may be problems, a commercial pattern can save enough time to be valuable if it is carefully checked and adjusted where necessary to match the costume sketch. Historic patterns from the commercial pattern companies are not particularly useful. They present a modern impression of a period garment with seaming and control that is a bit too simple to give a true historic silhouette.

◈ Measurements

Making the design a reality begins with the sketch in one hand and the measurements of the actor in the other. An accurate set of measurements is essential but not necessarily easy to acquire. The human body is flexible and expands and contracts easily, and the measurer has few specific points to go to and from. There is no absolute way to take measurements, but each shop should establish a system to be used and make sure everyone understands what the numbers stand for. Figure 9.4 illustrates a standard measurement chart and Figure 9.5 indicates the hither and yon of many of the areas that are also explained in the guidelines. A tape tied securely around the waist can help locate some of the areas. When measuring someone maintain a pleasant expression and avoid extraneous editorial comments, even when informed by the actor that he or she will lose weight before the costume is needed. Most likely a change in the actor's basic body size and shape will not be a problem that will need to be faced.

> **Height and Weight (1)** Ask the actor for these measurements, but realize they may be inaccurate. Women often underestimate their weight and men tend to overestimate their height.
>
> **Chest or Bust (2)** The relaxed chest around the largest area.
>
> **Waist (3)** Just above the hipbone where the body is pliable and can be condensed.
>
> **Hips (4)** Low on the hip at its fullest point. Always find the maximum that will need to be encompassed, but eliminate wallets and keys in pockets.
>
> **Width of bust (5)** Women only. The point-to-point measurement.
>
> **Shoulder to bust (6)** Women only. Near the neck to the point of the bust. Note whether or not the actress is wearing a bra, for the point of the bust is usually much lower without one.
>
> **Shoulder to waist (7)** Near the neck straight down to the waist. For women, over the bust to the waist.

COSTUME MEASUREMENT SHEET

NAME _____

CHARACTER _____

TELEPHONE NUMBER _____   DATE _____

HEIGHT _____*1*_____		WAIST TO THIGH _____*23*_____	
WEIGHT _____*1*_____		WAIST TO KNEE _____*24*_____	
CHEST OR BUST _____*2*_____		WAIST TO FLOOR _____*25*_____	
WAIST _____*3*_____		INSEAM TO FLOOR _____*26*_____	
HIPS _____*4*_____		CROTCH _____*27*_____	
WIDTH OF BUST _____*5*_____		GIRTH _____*28*_____	
SHOULDER TO BUST _____*6*_____		THIGH _____*29*_____	
SHOULDER TO WAIST _____*7*_____		KNEE ABOVE _____*30*_____	
UNDERBUST _____*8*_____		KNEE BELOW _____*31*_____	
UNDERBUST TO WAIST _____*9*_____		CALF _____*32*_____	
WIDTH OF CHEST—FRONT _____*10*_____		ANKLE _____*33*_____	
BACK _____*10*_____		NECK—BASE _____*34*_____	
SHOULDERS—BOTH _____*11*_____		MID _____*35*_____	
ONE _____*12*_____		HEAD _____*36*_____	
NECK TO WAIST—FRONT _____*13*_____		HAT _____*37*_____	
BACK _____*14*_____		DRESS OR SUIT _____*38*_____	
ARM LENGTH—OUTSIDE _____*15*_____		SHIRT OR BLOUSE _____*39*_____	
TO ELBOW _____*16*_____		TROUSERS—INSEAM _____*40*_____	
INSIDE _____*17*_____		WAIST _____*40*_____	
AROUND BICEP _____*18*_____		GLOVE _____*41*_____	
AROUND FOREARM _____*19*_____		STOCKINGS/TIGHTS _____*42*_____	
AROUND WRIST _____*20*_____		SHOE _____*43*_____	
ARMSEYE _____*21*_____		BALLET SLIPPER _____*44*_____	
UNDERARM TO WAIST _____*22*_____		BRA SIZE _____*45*_____	
		OTHER _____	

Figure 9.4 Costume measurement sheet.

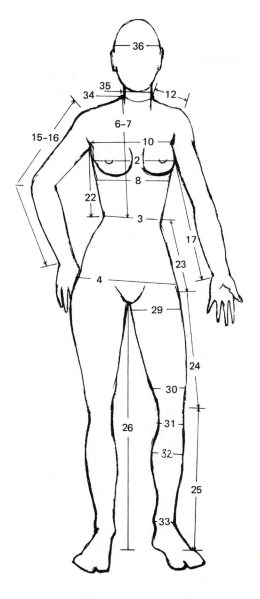

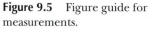

Figure 9.5 Figure guide for measurements.

Underbust (8) Women only. Around the chest right under the bust.

Underbust to waist (9) Right under the bust down to waist.

Width of chest front/back (10) Across the front or back of the chest from the point where the arms join the body. These two measurements do not add up to the chest measurement, for the depth of the body is not included.

Shoulders—Both (11) Across the top back of the shoulders to the ends of the shoulder bone. **One (12)** Side of the neck to the end of the shoulder bone. One shoulder is less than half the shoulder measurement because the width of the neck is not included.

Neck to waist—Front (13) Top of the collarbone to the waist. **Back (14)** Last large vertebra to the waist. The neck joins the body on an angle and neck-to-waist back is almost always two to three inches longer than the front.

Arm length—Outside (15) Shoulder bone to the wrist over the elbow on a slightly bent arm. **To elbow (16)** Pick this up on the way to the full arm measurement. **Inside (17)** The point where the arm joins the body to the wrist.

Around bicep (18) The relaxed muscle unless the actor has particularly well-developed muscles that will be used extensively during the production. **Forearm (19)** Just below the elbow at largest part. **Wrist (20)** Below the wrist bones.

Armseye (21) Circumference of the join between the arm and torso.

Underarm to waist (22) Start directly in the armpit.

Waist to thigh (23) Above the hipbone to the bottom of the buttocks on the side. **To knee (24)** To midknee. **To floor (25)** To the floor if the actor is shoeless, otherwise to the bottom of the body heel.

Inseam to floor (26) High in the crotch to the floor or the bottom of the body heel if shoes are worn. To avoid embarrassment it may be easier to hand the actor one end of the tape and ask him to place it as high as possible at the inside top of his leg with the measurer taking care of the end of the tape at the floor.

Crotch (27) Center front of the waist through the legs to the center back of the waist.

Girth (28) Shoulder through the legs and back to the shoulder.

Thigh through ankle (29–33) Largest circumference at all these points.

Neck—Base (34) Where neck joins body at the point where planes change and a collar would be attached. **Mid (35)** Slightly below the jawline, at about the top of a standing collar.

Head (36) Circumference around the forehead, just above eyebrows.

Hat (37) The actor or actress may know his or her hat size. Hat size is approximately the head circumference divided by pi, which equals the diameter. For example, a 23-inch head is $23 \div 3.14 = 7.3248 = 7\text{-}3/8$. Hat sizes come in eighths. Conversion charts are available from hat companies.

Dress or suit (38) An actor may know his suit size. It is based on the chest measurement, but the size of the shoulders can make a difference. Having a few jackets of known sizes handy for the actor to slip on is useful. Women's dress sizes can vary considerably. More expensive clothes often carry smaller sizes than cheaper ones. A regular size 10 could be a size 6 in a designer garment.

Shirt or blouse (39) May be the same as dress sizes or convert to bust size. A size 10 is a 32, a 12 is a 34, a 14 is a 36, and so on. Men's shirt sizes come in neck and sleeve length; the average is about 15–33, or a 15-inch neck and a 33-inch sleeve. The sleeve length is taken from the center back below the neck base over the extended bent elbow and back to the wrist.

Trousers (40) Inseam and waist—the size the actor buys and feels most comfortable in may not exactly coincide with the measurements taken. Men seldom wear their trousers at their actual waistline.

Glove (41) Around the knuckles, excluding the thumb.

Stocking/Tights (42) For dancers, even the brand might be useful.

Shoe (43) Be sure to include width.

Ballet slipper (44) Almost always smaller than shoe size.

Bra (45) Cup size is particularly important. A woman with a 36-inch circumference around her chest could wear a 36A or a 32D. The former will seem somewhat flat chested; the latter will not.

Other. Check the sketch for any additional information that will be needed. It is sometimes useful to know if the actress has pierced ears. Any fabric allergies should be noted. If a wig is to be made, the measurement around the hairline and from the forehead to the nape of neck will be needed, as well as the measurement across the top of the head from earlobe to earlobe.

Not all these measurements will be needed for every show, of course, but it's a good idea to take all measurements that might be even vaguely useful, for the measurement not taken is the one needed first. If the actor is to be with the company for a while, his or her complete measurements should be on file. Be sure to fill in the date and change it if the measurements are updated. It often is useful to know when a set of measurements was taken.

◆ The Three-Piece Bodice

The basic three-piece bodice may not be used often in intricate period construction, particularly for women, but it is extremely valuable as a handy visual reference for a specific body. A basic bodice fitted carefully and snugly to the body can be pulled out and used as the starting point for any number of shapes, even if the contour of the body is to be changed. This pattern is usually done in muslin or a fairly thin cotton. When heavier fabric is used for the actual costume the pattern should be expanded slightly, for the thicker the fabric the more distance needed to encase the body.

The patterns in this chapter are drawn to scale and done for a woman wearing a size 10 and a man wearing a size 38. The relationship of the basic bodice size to the measurement chart is provided.

The male and female bodice can open either center front or center back. The opening should be a straight line if at all possible. The straight of the fabric, which follows the line of the weave, is indicated on each pattern piece. Any change in the straight can alter the way the garment will fit.

Figure 9.6 shows the pattern for the male bodice. If the waist is quite a bit smaller than the chest, a back dart will ensure a good line without diagonal pulls toward the side seam. A back dart should not go higher than the bottom of the shoulder blade. If the shoulders are rounded, a shoulder dart will help the fit. The darts and extensions that will be needed at the shoulder are indicated with a dotted line. If possible, front darts should not

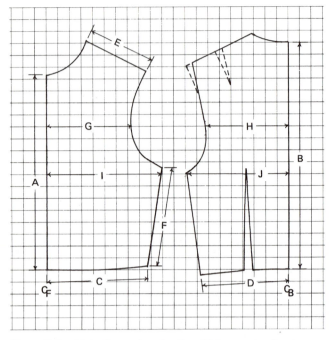

Figure 9.6 Male three-piece bodice. Either center front or center back should be cut on the fold. Scale 1 square = 1″.
A   Neck to waist front
B   Neck to waist back
C and D   1/2 Waist plus dart
E   Slightly less than one shoulder
F   Underarm to waist minus 1″ to 1-1/2″
G   Width of chest front
H   Width of chest back
J and I   1/2 chest

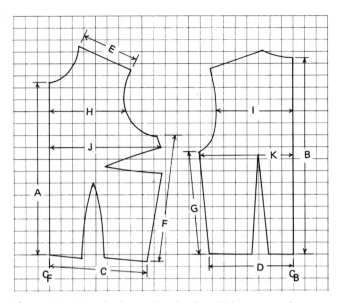

Figure 9.7   Female three-piece bodice. Either center front or center back should be cut on the fold. Scale 1 square = 1″.
A   Neck to waist front
B   Neck to waist back
C and D   1/2 Waist plus darts
E   Slightly less than one shoulder
F   Underarm to waist minus 1″ to 1-1/2″ plus dart
G   Underarm to waist minus 1″ to 1-1/2″
H   Width of chest front
I   Width of chest back
J and K   1/2 bust

be used on the man's bodice. If the front will not fit well in one piece, seams should be added rather than darts.

The basic female bodice (Figure 9.7) is quite similar to the male except, as might be expected, bust darts are added to the front. These are placed by locating the point of the bust and placing the ends of the darts no closer than one inch from the point. The darts for an average size bust are about 1-1/2 to 2 inches, more for a large bust and less for a smaller one.

◆ Creating the Proper Body Shape

The basic bodice provides a record of the body as it is. Often what is needed is the body as it isn't.

Padding

Padding out the figure should be done with careful attention to the way the body naturally grows on its own and how the appearance of extra weight will relate to the body of the actor. If the legs, arms, and neck show, the torso can only be so thick to still seem realistic, or the impression will be that of a small body lost inside a mattress.

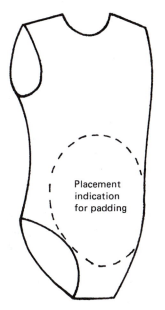

Figure 9.8 Full torso base for padding.

Padding should be constructed to hold its shape through heavy use and frequent cleaning. Made of layers of cotton and dacron, the padding can be quite warm because it is worn right next to the body. While the undergarment can be aired out, it will need frequent washing.

Padding that is to add considerable poundage to the figure should be made on some type of full-torso base of light but sturdy wash-and-wear fabric (Figure 9.8). The crotch strap is quite important to keep the tummy in place, but as a kindness should hook toward the front so the actor can undo it himself. The back of the garment may zip or tie. Areas to be padded should be marked and noted where they need to be the thickest. A smaller padding could be made on a T-shirt or leotard. This does not stand up as well, but it is a fast approach to a washable base.

Dacron or polyester batting is the best material to use for the thickness as it is lightweight and washes and dries easily and quickly. Wadding, or fibers that come in a more pillowlike mass, are more suitable for stuffing rather firm, presewn shapes, such as hip rolls, Elizabethan shoulder rolls, and teddy bears. The batting should be applied in flat, smooth layers, each a bit smaller than the one before, until the desired thickness is reached. Long, fairly loose padding stitches should be used to attach the batting to the base all over the area as well as around the edges. This will hold the fluff in place but not tighten it down to distort the shape.

Figure 9.9 shows the basic potbelly, which is constructed as one area since the genuine article grows as one area. Figure 9.10 is the body of a matronly woman with five separately padded areas: two breasts sagging with age, a protruding tummy, and two buttocks that should extend a bit to the side to suggest heavy thighs. After the batting is securely tacked so it will not shift when washed, the padded areas are covered with a soft stretch fabric such as cotton jersey to smooth the edges and hold everything firmly together (Figure 9.11).

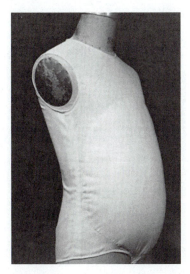

Figure 9.9 Basic belly padding.

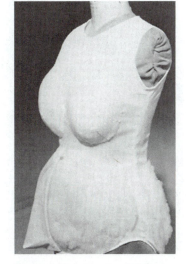

Figure 9.10 Layers of dacron batting are used to create the padded area for a matronly woman's figure.

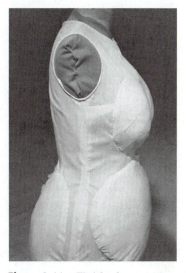

Figure 9.11 Finished areas covered with a soft jersey.

Corseting

For more than four centuries women were tightly confined in some form of boned corset. This had a great influence on the way they moved and the look of their bodices. While the 17-inch waist is usually not possible with today's woman, a controlled figure with the appearance of a small waist can be achieved. The natural waistline is oval (Figure 9.12). Corseting brings the waist to a circular shape so that from the front the waist appears much narrower, accented by the spring of the hips. Because of this, bringing in the waist just an inch or two can produce a rather striking effect (Figures 9.13 and 9.14). The corset should not restrict the diaphragm to a degree that will hinder breathing. As the corset is laced on, an actress should keep her ribcage expanded so the space for a breath will be there. The more she wears the corset the more she will become accustomed to it and learn to deal with it, if not love it.

The best source for corset patterns is Norah Waugh's *Corsets and Crinolines*. The text traces the change in women's shape through the centuries and the illustrations provide clear layouts for a number of corsets based on examples from various periods.

Patterns for the corsets displayed in Figures 9.13 and 9.14 are shown in Figures 9.15 and 9.16. Figure 9.15 is more suitable for the sixteenth, seventeenth, and eighteenth centuries, where the bodice line was quite straight and the bustline was either confined or pushed up. Figure 9.16 shows a corset that might be used in the nineteenth century, in which the curves of the body are more evident. The eighteenth-century corset in particular will need fairly wide shoulder straps to keep the side front line smooth and the bust pushed toward the center to enhance the cleavage. If at any time more

Figure 9.12 The natural waistline is oval.

Figure 9.13 The eighteenth-century corset pulls in the waist and pushes up the bust.

Figure 9.14 The nineteenth-century corset molds more of the torso than the one in Figure 9.13.

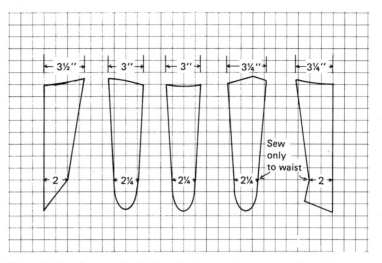

Figure 9.15   Corset suitable for the sixteenth, seventeenth, and eighteenth centuries. Bones on each seam and between each seam. Scale 1 square = 1″.

emphasis is needed at the bust than the actress is able to provide, bust pads should be added inside the corset but to the outside and slightly under the bust to push what is natural in where it will have the most effect.

Corsets should be made of tightly woven strong fabric that washes easily and does not have much thickness, which would add bulk. An extra layer should interface the area under the grommets. The corset should be fully lined, the lining and outside sewed together along the front, top, and back, then turned. Bone channels are sewed through both layers, the bones slipped in, and the bottom bound off. Both front and back may be grommeted, but the corset will be easier to wear if a corset fastener or heavy-duty

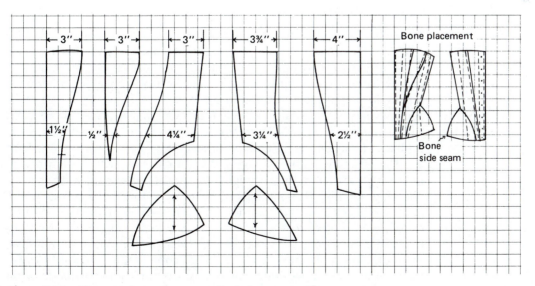

Figure 9.16   Nineteenth-century corset. Scale 1 square = 1″.

zipper is used in front, for it can then be taken off without completely un-lacing the back. Grommets with a fairly wide lip, not eyelets, should be used so they will not pull out easily under the strain. A narrow bone between the grommets and the edge of the fabric will strengthen the area under the most stress when the corset is tightly laced. Metal boning in various lengths and widths can be acquired from companies that supply them for thera-peutic corsets and trusses.

Though it might seem redundant, there are occasions when it is nec-essary to both pad and corset the same figure. The well-endowed, well-established matron could need an ample body that is obviously controlled by serious engineering.

Petticoats

The most commonly used underpinnings are petticoats. While identical petticoats may be used for a number of different periods, a petticoat should be chosen because it reinforces the line of the costume. An empire gown needs petticoats that fall from under the bust; a princess-line underskirt must fit smoothly to the hipline. Full skirts will commonly need more than one petticoat, and if the overskirt has a bit more flair at the bottom or heavy trim on the lower portion, the top petticoat could have a deep flounce to add support. While particularly decorative petticoats may be needed for specific costumes, the standard stock of these underskirts should be out of sturdy but easily laundered fabric with a good amount of body. Some skirt shapes require padding or boning as well as petticoats to create the proper shape. Waugh's *Corsets and Crinolines* is again an excellent reference for these undergarments.

The proper petticoats, corsets, and padding must be available when working up patterns because the outer garment is very much dependent on the underpinnings to give it the right line.

Period Bodices

The cut of a period bodice should reinforce the design line, not fight with it. Except for the neckline, the lines of the bodice usually follow the verti-cality of the figure, so most seams and darts are vertical. A horizontal seam may add a design line, such as a yoke, but horizontal darts are seldom at-tractive in period garments, and in most cases can be avoided. Vertical or diagonal darts may be quite useful in fitting, but in many cases where a dart is all right a seam might be better, for it extends the line and eliminates the problem of making the dart disappear smoothly.

The seven-piece bodice (Figure 9.17) is quite effective for any period where the body line is fairly straight, the bust is pushed up, and the neck-line is not too high. It is particularly common to those periods that would use the earlier corset, such as the sixteenth, seventeenth, and eighteenth centuries. The piece that may need special attention is the side front, for the bustier the woman the more the top of that piece must curve away from the neck. This problem shows up as extra fabric around the armhole. Re-lease the shoulder, smooth the side front up, repin it, and redraw the neck-line. Also be sure that the last inch of the center front curves in slightly to

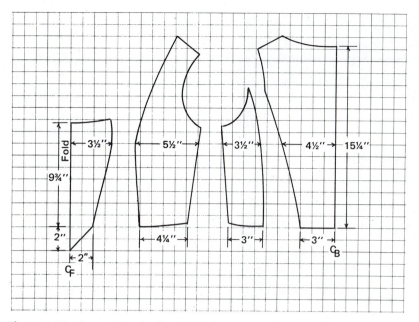

Figure 9.17   Seven-piece bodice. Scale 1 square = 1″.

tighten across the bust and keep everything in place. Figure 9.18 shows the completed bodice pattern.

The nine-piece bodice can be the basis for a costume that has a higher neck and more curves to the bustline, such as those common in the nine-teenth century (Figure 9.19). The extra piece in the front allows for more contouring. Again, the side front piece may need to curve more for the

Figure 9.18   Seven-piece bodice in muslin.

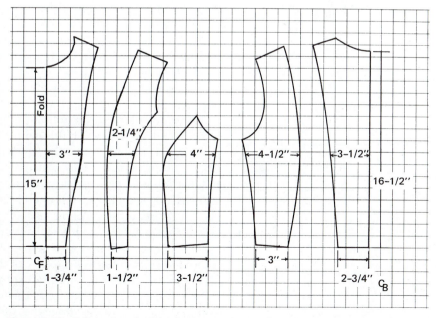

Figure 9.19   Nine-piece bodice. Scale 1 square = 1″.

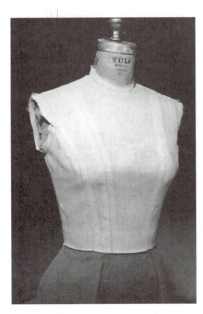

Figure 9.20 Nine-piece bodice in muslin.

fuller figure. If the side front/side seam puckers, it may well smooth out by taking in the upper part of the side front/front seam. To do this, loosen half the shoulder and take out the side front/front seam down to about the bust point, smooth the side front piece up to get rid of the puckers, and repin it. The seam line on the center front will probably remain almost the same; the adjustment is in the side front piece. Figure 9.20 illustrates the assembled nine-piece bodice pattern. The back of the bodice could be as shown or could be constructed like the back of the seven-piece bodice, with the shoulder and center back extended to the neck.

When patterning it is often wise to cut inch-wide seam allowances on all pieces, with two inches at the opening and waist. This usually provides enough fabric for adjustments when necessary. Very wide seam allowances can hinder the fit, particularly on curves. The pattern should be initially drafted showing only the seam lines so the eye can see the shapes to be used. Seam allowance should be considered when the pattern is ready to cut. Much time can be saved if the eye is trained to gauge the one and two inches automatically.

The seams on these bodices are easily adjusted to accommodate variations in the lines of the design, if the shape still allows for the fullness of the body where it is needed. The difference between the bust and waist needs to come in under the bust area. It cannot be taken in at the side without causing the fabric to pull strangely.

Period Skirts

A skirt can be a straight piece of fabric bunched in at the waist, but it is more often made up of gores that are narrower at the waist and wider toward the hem. The way these gores are shaped determines the fall of the skirt. As fabric is suspended along the straight of the weave it falls close to the body in a very organized fashion. A gore that widens toward the hem cuts across the weave of the fabric diagonally or on the bias (Figure 9.21). True bias is on a 45-degree angle from the straight. The bias will fall into folds and flow more away from the body. Because fabric cut more to the bias will fall more away from the body, gores can be made to give a skirt a very particular drape and flow. Pleats and darts can also be used to control the shape.

Most skirts have more fullness to the sides and back than in the center front. The degree to which this happens varies considerably from the basic period skirt, which is full all around with just a bit more in back than in front, to some bustle gowns, which are almost straight in front with all the fullness behind. Period skirts usually close center back with no center front seam except when the skirt is open in front to show the underskirt.

The skirts in this section are patterned for someone 44 inches from waist to floor and do not have a hem included.

Gores in a basic skirt with general fullness (Figure 9.22) could be symmetrical. A nice fullness for a skirt of this type would allow for three times as much fabric as needed in the waist and about five yards in the hem. If the waist is 27 inches, the total size of the waistline would be 81 inches and the hem 180 inches. In a skirt done in six gores, each gore has 13-1/2 inches at the top and 30 inches at the bottom (Figure 9.23). This could be pleated so

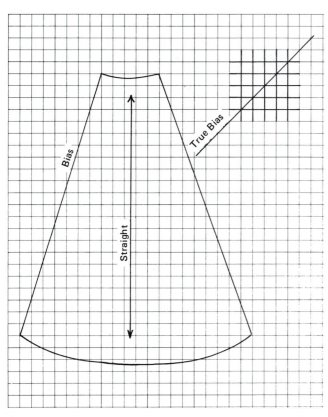

Figure 9.21   The gore.

Figure 9.22   Basic full period skirt in muslin.

the fullness is the same all around (9.24a), or so more of the skirt is to the side and back (9.24b). Pleats that fall into general fullness as these do should not be too deep at the waistline. The center back gore of this skirt would be cut with a center seam to accommodate the opening.

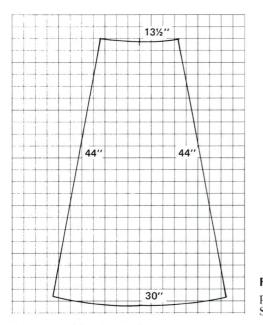

Figure 9.23   Gore pattern for basic skirt. Scale 1 square = 1″.

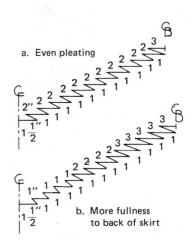

Figure 9.24   Possible pleating diagrams for the basic skirt. Each has 13-1/2″ on the outside of the skirt, with 27″ used in the pleating.

Figure 9.25   Muslin period skirt done in seven gores with eight deep pleats.

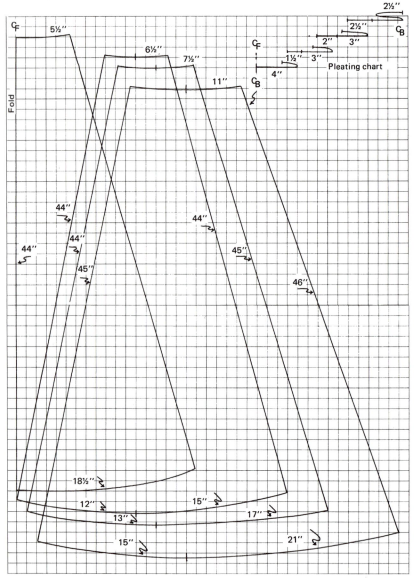

Figure 9.26   Pattern for the pleated skirt shown in Figure 9.25. Scale 1 square = 1″.

Figure 9.27   Muslin of full, high-waisted skirt with back pleats.

A full skirt that will have pleats that hold their fold from waist to hem without being pressed will need gores more specifically shaped for this purpose. The skirt illustrated in Figure 9.25 has a six-yard hem with eight pleats achieved in seven gores. The gores get fuller as they move to the back and are shaped so the front of the gore will fall straighter and the back of the gore will flow out (Figure 9.26). This causes the skirt to flow naturally toward the back of the figure. The offset of the fullness of each gore is indicated by a line dropped from the center of the waistline. The skirt lengthens slightly as the pieces approach the center back because it will be falling out more from the body. Petticoats are, of course, under the skirt.

Figure 9.27 shows a skirt that falls from under the bust, has some fullness in front, and a great deal more in the back controlled by six pleats. Because each pleat is a gore the fall is easily controlled. The skirt has a 6-1/2-yard hem and 6-inch train, and is made for a 30-inch underbust (Figure 9.28).

Deep pleats such as those used in these two skirts need to maintain the fold of the fabric from waist to hem. This means they must be carefully laid in on the form with the petticoats in place or they will not fall properly. Often the outside fold of the pleat must be raised so it will fall smoothly from the

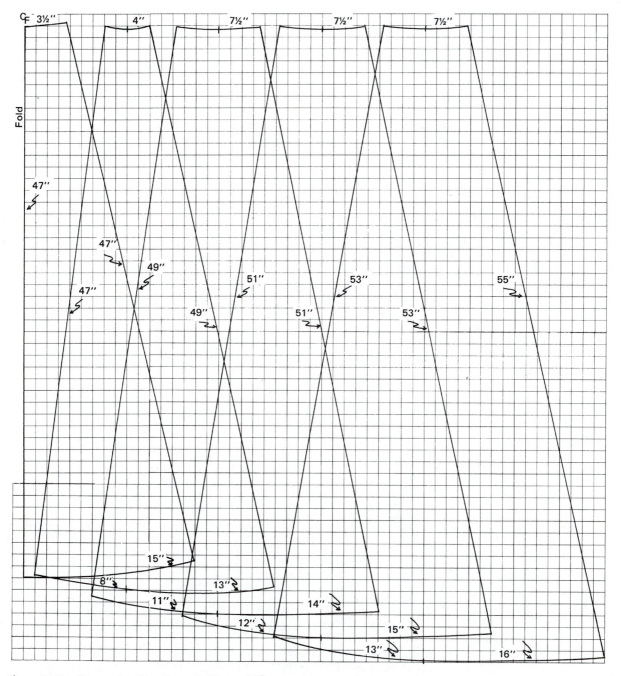

Figure 9.28   Pattern for skirt shown in Figure 9.27.

waist and not pooch out awkwardly. Once the pleat has been arranged the waistline must be remarked and if taken apart would no longer be the smooth curve indicated on the pattern. This cannot be accurately plotted ahead of time and is an adjustment that can be easily made on the form.

A skirt that fits the waist and hipline smoothly is shown in Figure 9.29. In this skirt the front fullness is controlled to the knee, then flares; the back falls out from just below the hipline and is much fuller. The hem is six yards. The tops of these pieces must contour the body more than those skirts that have fullness beginning at the waistline (Figure 9.30a). The waist is 27 inches and the hipline 39 inches, a measurement now necessary to

Figure 9.29   Muslin of period skirt that fits the hip smoothly.

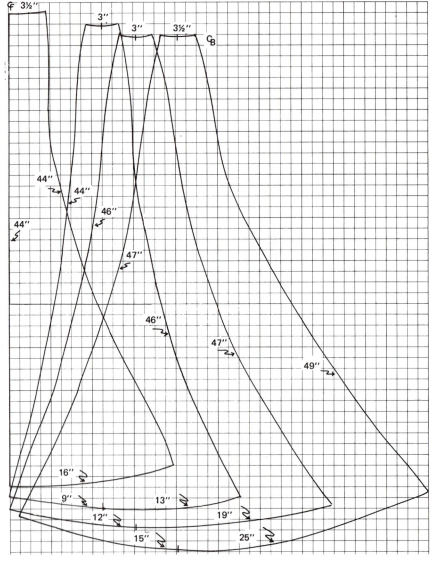

Figure 9.30   Pattern for skirt shown in Figure 9.29. Side back and back pieces that can be used with center front and side front pieces of the same skirt. Scale 1 square = 1″.

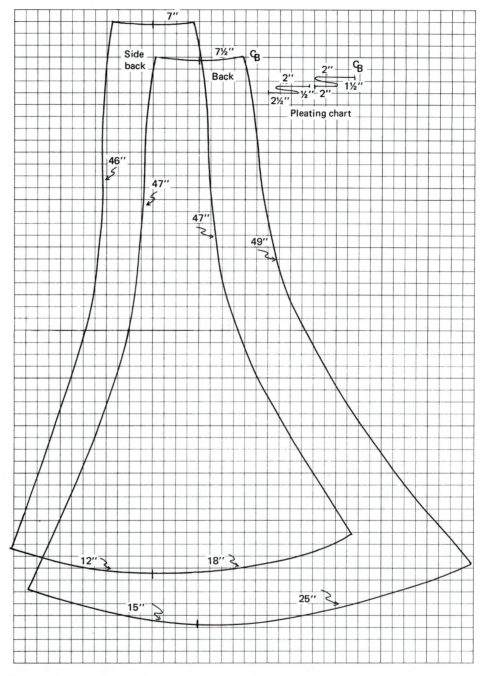

Figure 9.30 Continued

consider because of the smooth fit to this point. A skirt with a similar line but easier to fit is created by substituting the two back pieces shown in Figure 9.30b. In this skirt, a pleat two inches deep that uses four inches of fabric is added to each of the back pieces. These can be pleated in on the figure and sewn down to the hipline to maintain the smooth top to the skirt.

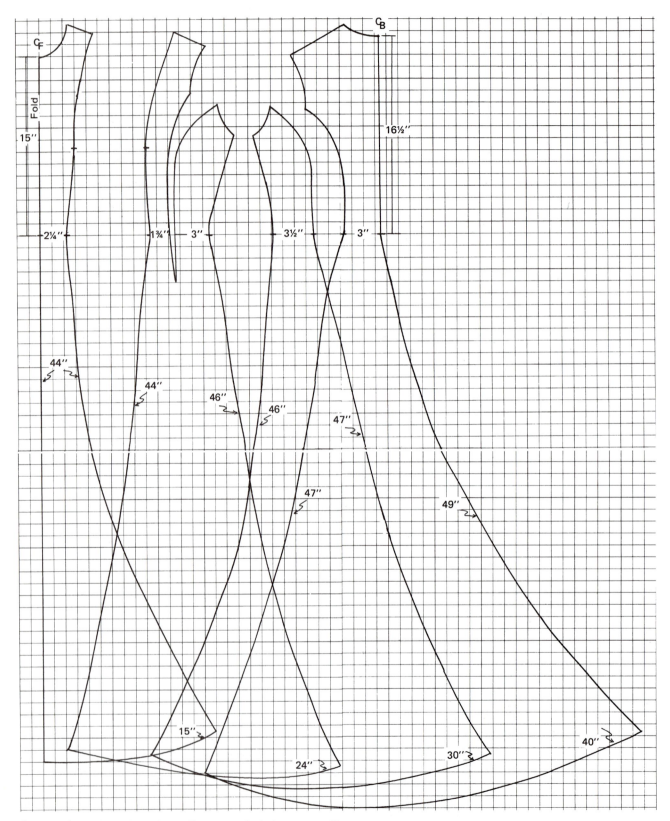

Figure 9.31 Pattern for princess-line gown. Scale 1 square = 1″.

Figure 9.32   Muslin of princess-line gown.

The Princess-Line Gown

A combination of the skirt and bodice that is often used and can be a bit of a challenge to fit is the princess-line gown. A very attractive gown can be done in seven pieces; it uses a skirt similar to the one illustrated in Figure 9.30 and a nine-piece bodice rearranged to become seven (Figure 9.31). The side front and the side pieces are joined with a long dart extending into the skirt. This skirt fits smoothly to the flare of the hip, then goes into fullness. The hem is 5-1/2 yards (Figure 9.32).

Trousers

Figure 9.33 shows a basic trouser pattern. Many commercial patterns for trousers are available that explain various pockets and the way the belt and fly front are done. These can be easily adjusted to construct most styles of trousers with a fly front or back zipper if the primary way they fit is understood.

The crotch seam is longer in the back than the front because on most people there is more back than front. Tight trousers fit and move better if the crotch seam is toward the front for this causes the upper part of the

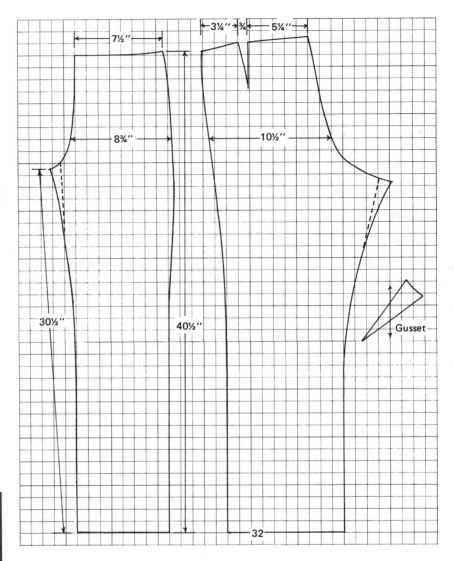

Figure 9.33   Basic trouser pattern. Scale 1 square = 1″.

Figure 9.34   Muslin of full fall breeches.

back inside leg seam to be cut more toward the bias, which will give and mold with movement. The front curve may be about four inches shorter than the back. A dart is needed to fit the back of the trousers in to the waist. The side seam may curve in slightly, but not too much because the side of the body does not curve in a great deal. The fullness is more in the center of the buttock; the dart must be placed there. A yoke in back can eliminate the need for a dart, for it is cut on a curve to shape the top into the body. Women sometimes need a front dart as well because they have a greater difference between hip and waist. Very tight trousers may need gussets, or triangular bias insets, at the top of the inside leg seams. These will allow for more stretch as the leg moves and extends. They are usually about two inches wide and six inches long, and are set in to the body of the garment,

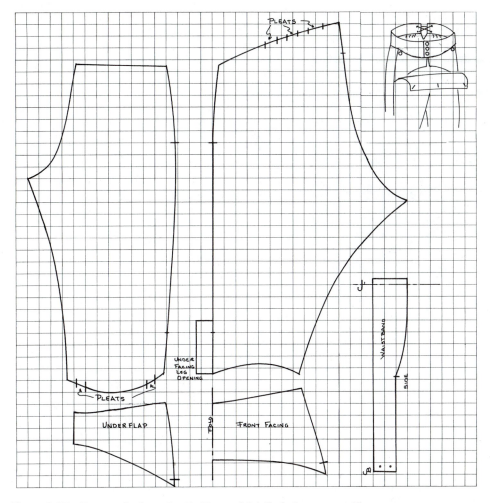

Figure 9.35 Pattern for breeches in Figure 9.34. Scale 1 square = 1″.

not added on as extensions (see the dotted line in Figure 9.33). The need for the gusset is not as common now as it used to be, for if the crotch and inside leg seams are sewn with a stretch stitch the trousers may give enough so they will not rip out with every jump. Don't do this, however, until the fit is set. This type of stitch is not easy to remove.

Fitted knee breeches that fasten below the knee must have a bit more length at the knee in front and at the waist in back to allow for movement. As the leg bends, the distances over the knee and around the backside from the waist get longer.

In the eighteenth century and early nineteenth century knee breeches were fastened in front with fall closings. Figure 9.34 shows full fall breeches in which the whole front unbuttons and drops down. The waistband, done in two pieces and left open in the back to lace together, slopes down in front so the third button on the waistband also buttons up the front flap.

Figure 9.36   Muslin of small fall breeches.

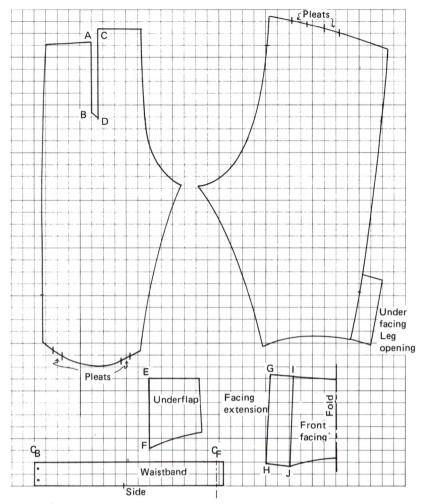

Figure 9.37   Pattern for breeches in Figure 9.36. Scale 1 square = 1″. Fall facing is formed by sewing crotch seam, then stitching CD to GH on both sides. With right sides together the facing extension is folded so GH is over IJ and the top of the fall is stitched, as well as the 1″ seam at the bottom of the extension on each side, from JH to fold. The fall is turned right side out and the bottom of the extension topstitched to the main body to reinforce the end of the opening.

Underflaps extend from the side to the center front, attached to the waistband (Figure 9.35). There are three pleats on each side of the back of the breeches and one pleat on each side of the knee with a narrow band finishing the bottom. The breeches are for a figure with a 32-inch waist, 39-inch hips, and 25 inches from waist to knee.

A later version is the small fall breeches (Figure 9.36), in which only part of the front drops down. A half-inch opening on each side provides the seam allowance for the underflap and the fall facing, which is two inches longer on each side to form an inch-long extension to cover the slit. The waistband is straight and the fall one inch higher so it can overlap and button up to the waistband (Figure 9.37). The back could be the same as in Figure 9.35. This type of closing can also be used for the full-length trousers of the early nineteenth century.

Sleeves

Sleeves bring more variations to costumes than any other single element, and the proper way to construct them is often misunderstood. The top of the sleeve has two parts, the cap and the underarm. BCD is the cap in Figure 9.38 and DEA is the underarm. CD is slightly smaller than CB because more space is needed at the back of the arm to allow for forward movement. ACE is a bit larger than the corresponding area in the body of the garment, about one and a half to two inches, so the sleeve can ease in slightly over the deltoid muscle at the shoulder. The rise in the cap is usually five to six inches, and the width, just above points B and D, usually needs to be eight inches or more so the cap over the upper arm muscle does not tie the arm into the body. Fullness can be added to the sleeve by slitting it up the middle and spreading the two pieces the desired amount. The top curve should be adjusted slightly so it remains a curve and does not flatten out.

These patterns are sized for an arm 22 inches long and of medium build.

A tighter one-piece sleeve must be changed to accommodate the bending arm, so small darts are put in at the elbow area. This makes a little pocket for the bent elbow, which takes up more space than the straight one (Figure 9.39). Elbow darts are functional, but not too attractive. A tight sleeve with a better line and a period look is done in two pieces with the bend of the arm built in (Figure 9.40). The cap of the sleeve is on the upper arm, the underarm curve on the underarm piece, and the seams follow the natural bend of the arm, ending on each side of the wrist (Figure 9.41). This type of seaming is much more useful when developing period sleeve patterns because the seams relate more to where fullness and control are needed. Few exciting things relate to the underarm seam. Any tight sleeve attached to a tight bodice might need a gusset. The gusset is cut on the bias and sewn as indicated in Figure 9.39. It is not sewn directly to the seam lines, but about an inch inside them. The gusset for the two-piece sleeve has a rounded top since there is no underarm seam on the sleeve. Another solution to the movement problem is to cut a gusset right into the sleeve. To do this, added fabric is cut into the underarm piece (Figure 9.41). This is not quite as effective as the separate, sewn in gusset for there is no bias to give, but it is simpler to do.

Fullness and length are added to a sleeve at the back of the arm, not the underarm. Two styles of puffed sleeves attached to the straight two-piece sleeve are shown in Figures 9.42–9.45. In Figures 9.42 and 9.43 fullness is added by extending the upper part of the sleeve and adding more fullness plus length to the back seam. The shortest part of the puff is the underarm, where extra fabric is awkward and gets in the way. This sleeve is gathered over the cap with more fullness slightly to the back. The sleeve in Figures 9.44 and 9.45 is similar but does not have the extra width in the cap. To make the top smaller but with the same dimension at the bottom the puff is made in two pieces like the undersleeve. Both puffs are attached ten and a half inches up from the wrist (Figure 9.41). Panes could be added

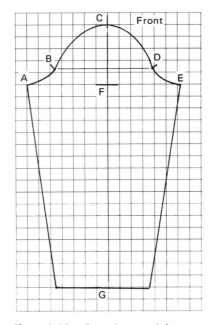

Figure 9.38 One-piece straight
sleeve pattern. Scale 1 square = 1″.
ACE   Armseye plus 1-1/2″ to 2″
AB and DE   3″ to 3-1/2″ each
CG   Length of arm
CF   5″ to 6″

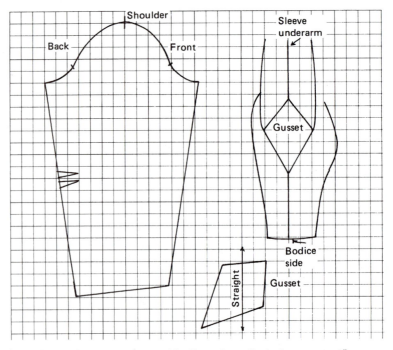

Figure 9.39 One-piece sleeve with elbow darts. Scale 1 square = 1″.

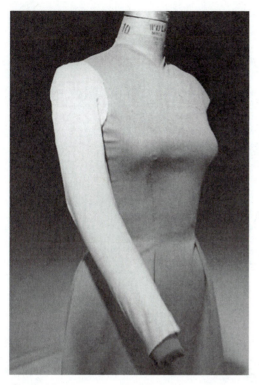

Figure 9.40 Muslin of two-piece tight sleeve.

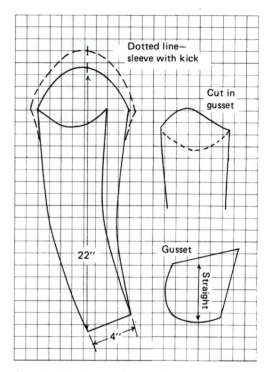

Figure 9.41 Two-piece tight sleeve pattern. Scale 1 square = 1″.

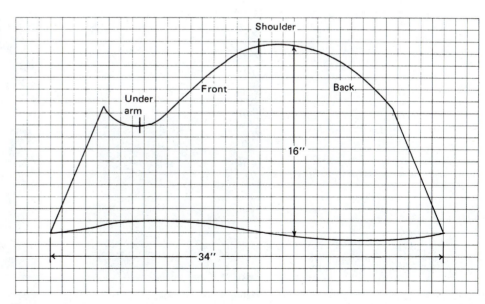

Figure 9.42 Pattern for one-piece upper arm puff. Scale 1 square = 1″.

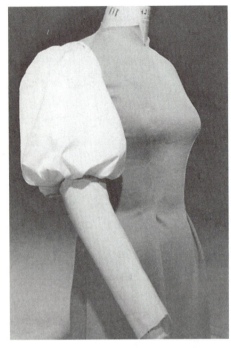

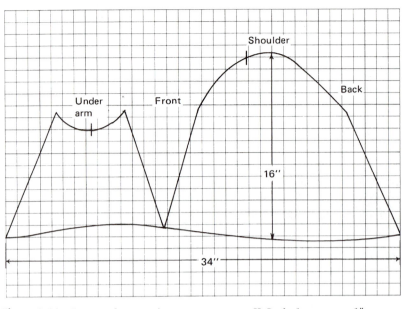

Figure 9.44 Pattern for two-piece upper arm puff. Scale 1 square = 1″.

Figure 9.43 Muslin of pattern in Figure 9.42 added to two-piece tight sleeve.

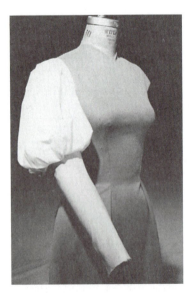

Figure 9.45 Muslin of pattern in Figure 9.44 added to two-piece tight sleeve.

Figure 9.46 Muslin of tight sleeve with kick.

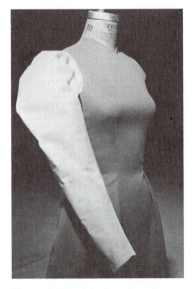

Figure 9.47 Muslin of moderate leg-of-mutton.

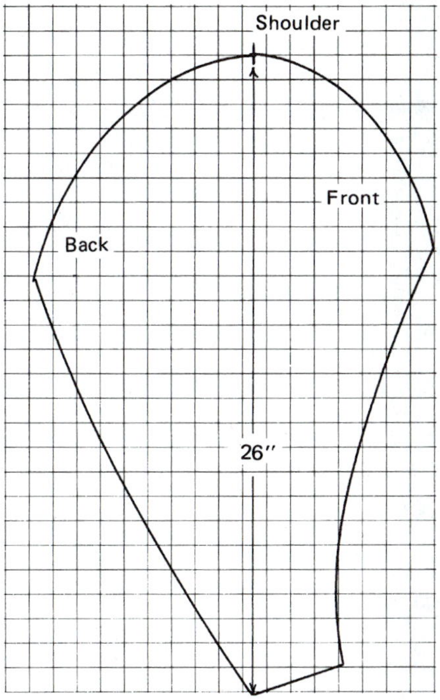

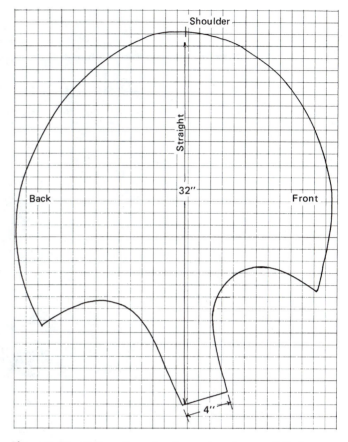

Figure 9.48 Pattern for outer sleeve piece used for Figure 9.47. Scale 1 square = 1″.

Figure 9.49 Pattern for outer sleeve piece for very full gigot sleeve. Scale 1 square = 1″.

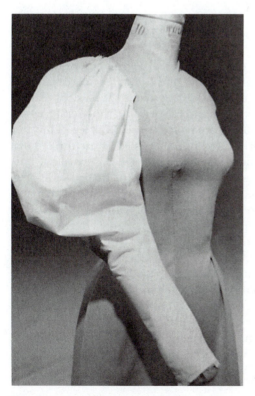

Figure 9.50 Muslin of gigot sleeve.

Figure 9.51   Muslin of funnel sleeve.

over the puff, each pane varying in length the way the puff does with the longest in back and the shortest under the arm. These must be carefully angled into the armhole to fall properly.

The two-piece straight sleeve can expand into the leg-of-mutton style. If the cap of the sleeve is made slightly higher and the outer sleeve widens a bit (dotted lines in Figure 9.41), the head of the sleeve will have a kick to it (Figure 9.46). If the outer sleeve widens and raises more, a moderate leg-of-mutton will result (Figure 9.47). The pattern for the very full leg-of-mutton or gigot sleeve is shown in Figure 9.49. Both outer sleeves use the regular undersleeve piece shown in Figure 9.41. The gigot sleeve is extremely full at the top but fits the forearm and wrist (Figure 9.50). If the sleeve is to have a certain amount of fullness all the way down it may be possible to cut it in one piece, with the wrist and forearm sections of Figure 9.49 widening. These sleeves will need crisp interfacing to hold them out. Patterns for simpler, full sleeves are available with modern patterns.

The funnel sleeve, illustrated in Figure 9.51, is very long on the back seam, only arm length in front, and quite wide at the opening. The bottom curve reverses itself so there will not be extreme points at either the wrist or the bottom of the back seam (Figure 9.52). The back seam joins the body rather high, more toward the shoulder seam, to position the long point gracefully at the back of the arm. If the sleeve has a front slit it should be cut with a seam on the center line, which indicates the front of the arm, slightly ahead of the top of the shoulder.

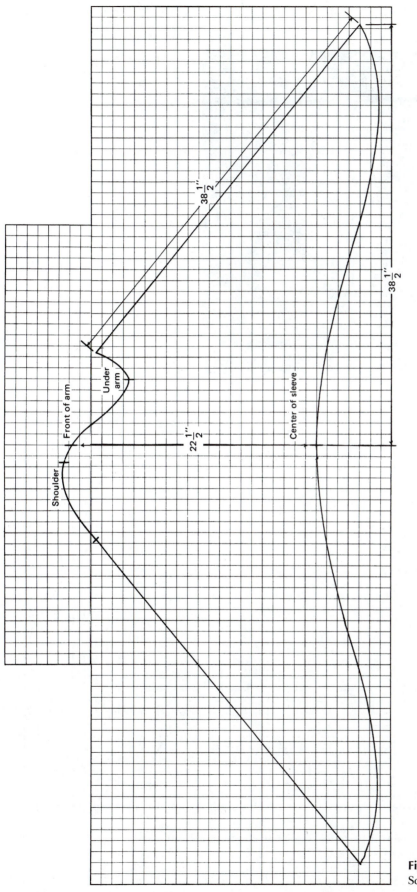

Figure 9.52 Pattern for funnel sleeve. Scale 1 square = 1″.

Figure 9.53 Muslin of bagpipe sleeve.

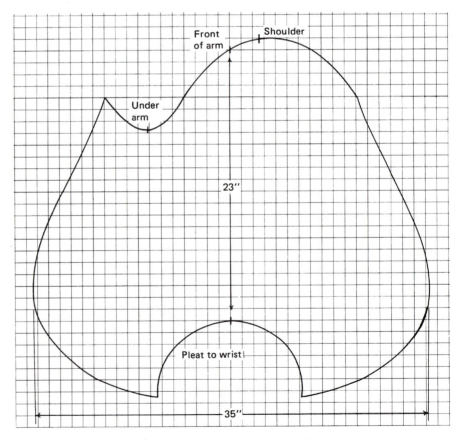

Figure 9.54 Pattern for bagpipe sleeve. Scale 1 square = 1″.

The bagpipe sleeve (Figure 9.53) has a top curve like that of the funnel, but the cap is extended and pleats more into the armseye. The back seam curves out, then in toward the wrist, and is pleated into the wristband. The center of the sleeve is slightly longer than the arm to allow a bit of fullness (Figure 9.54).

The long slit sleeve (Figure 9.55), could be cut straight with the only seam on the front of the arm if a great deal of fullness is not needed at the bottom. If more fullness is needed, a back seam that flares out could be added. This sleeve is quite full at the cap and pleats into the armseye (Figure 9.56). The pleats in any full sleeve should be carefully angled into the body of the garment or they may poke out quite unattractively.

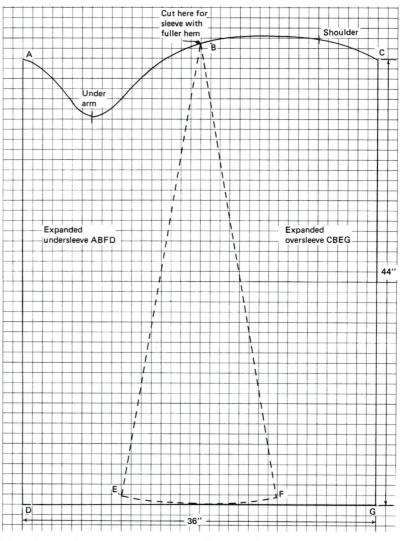

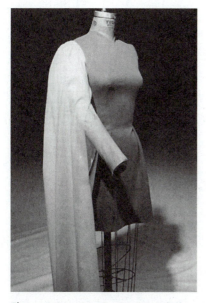

Figure 9.55 Muslin for long slit sleeve.

Figure 9.56 Pattern for long slit sleeve. Scale 1 square = 1″.

◆ Men's Coats and Tailoring

Men's garments up to the cavalier styles of the seventeenth century are often simpler to construct than women's. Costumes from more recent periods that require tailoring can be much more difficult. The cotehardie, doublet, and jerkin are easily developed from the basic bodice. The cotehardie is extended to the hipline and will need both a center front and center back seam, particularly if the chest has a bit of padding (Figure 9.57). The pleated jerkin uses the flat basic as the body for the costume; the good fabric is pleated over it, attached in place, and the excess fabric trimmed away. The skirt is pleated to match the top from a slightly curved gore to allow it to flair properly over the hip (Figure 9.58).

Men's tailored coats began to appear in the seventeenth century and brought with them more complex sewing techniques. Special interfacing and tacking are necessary to create and hold the proper shape. A thorough explanation of tailoring would require a book unto itself, or at least a very long chapter. Figures 9.59 through 9.66 show the basic shapes on a few

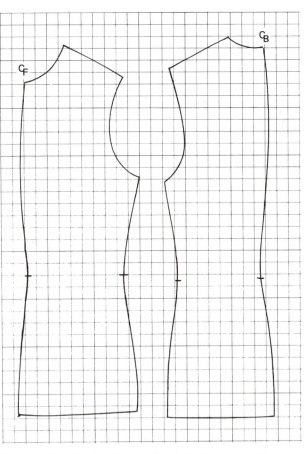

Figure 9.57 Cotehardie pattern. Scale 1 square = 1″.

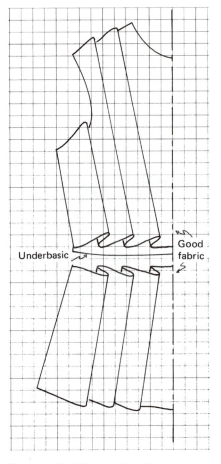

Figure 9.58 Diagram for pleated bodice and skirt assembly.

Figure 9.59   Restoration coat.

men's coats from different periods. These shapes can be useful but the costume will not be effective if it is not tailored properly. An idea of what is included in tailoring follows, but for in-depth knowledge of the field, refer to sources such as *Basic Tailoring* from the Time-Life series *The Art of Sewing*. A good designer pattern for a man's jacket available from one of the better commercial companies can also be very helpful in explaining the step-by-step approach to such construction. An excellent exercise for understanding how a coat really goes together is to find a well-tailored jacket at a used-clothing store and take it apart, carefully noting down each tailoring step that has been done as it is discovered. Two good references for patterns for men's garments are *The Cut of Men's Clothes* and *The Blue Book of Men's Tailoring,* the latter of which has some construction techniques included.

The Restoration coat of the late-seventeenth-century shapes to the body to a degree and has moderate pleats at the side (Figure 9.59). This is one of the earliest styles of tailored coat (Figure 9.60). It should be interfaced throughout to hold the flair and pleats in place. Coat fronts, which are premade interfacings for the chests of suit coats, can be purchased from a tailoring supply shop and give a good shape to the front of the coat. These are made for the modern suit coat, but can be added to or trimmed away as necessary. Shoulder pads, which help a good shoulder line, are centered over the top of the shoulder and extend 5/8-inch past the seam line, with a long, narrow pad called a sleeve head also attached to the seam line

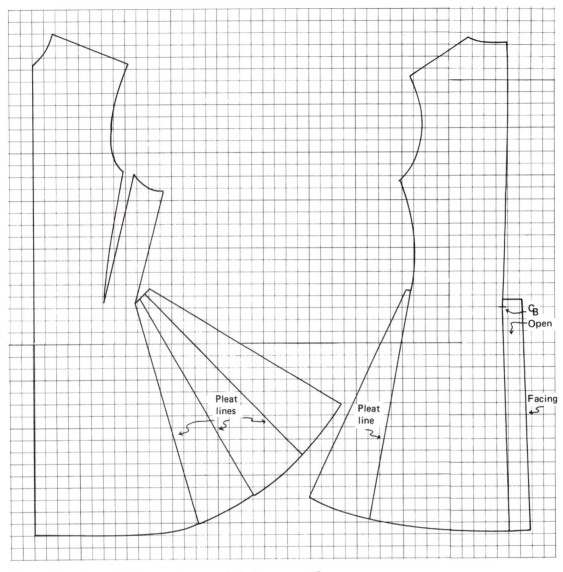

Figure 9.60 Pattern for Restoration coat. Scale 1 square = 1″.

to help shape the top of the sleeve. A narrow twill tape should be sewn around the neckline, which is collarless, before the facing is attached. The twill holds the neck curve so it will not stretch out. This coat did not meet center front. If it is to button the front should be extended 2″ plus a front overlap added, that would go 3/4-inch past the center front line. The vest for this period is cut like the body of the coat, with the front overlap, but usually with only one pleat at the side. The back could be shorter and does not have to be interfaced.

The coat in Figure 9.61, which could come from the second quarter of the eighteenth century, fits more closely to the chest and has a side seam and pleats that are nearer to the side back. The shaped dart from the arm-hole to the pocket flap will give a better fit to the front, though this was not

Figure 9.61 Muslin of early-eighteenth-century coat.

done during the period. The coat has three pleats on each side and one on each side of the center back slit (Figure 9.62). Basic construction notes are similar to those for Figure 9.60. The vest has a straight center front that can button closed, is a few inches shorter than the coat, has two side pleats, and is often shorter in the back. The vest front is heavily interfaced to help hold out the coat front.

The coat body in Figure 9.63 is somewhat similar but has been adapted for later in the century by cutting back the front even more, narrowing the pleats, and eliminating one of them altogether. The side back seam has been moved even more toward the center back and the pleat on each side of the back slit has been eliminated (Figure 9.64). This coat is not as stiff as the earlier ones and, while it should be fully lined, it only needs interfacing in the front over the chest and down the opening. A modern coat front can be adapted to this by adding horsehair interfacing four to five inches wide extending down the front edge. Since the entire armhole is no longer interfaced a twill tape stay should be sewn in to keep it from stretching. This coat could have a standing collar that steps back about an inch from the center front.

Tailoring men's coats was honed to a fine art in the nineteenth century as the aristocrat turned from the gaudy peacock to the impeccably structured, much more conservative gentleman. Figure 9.65 is an early-nineteenth-century style that shows some of the trends that were beginning

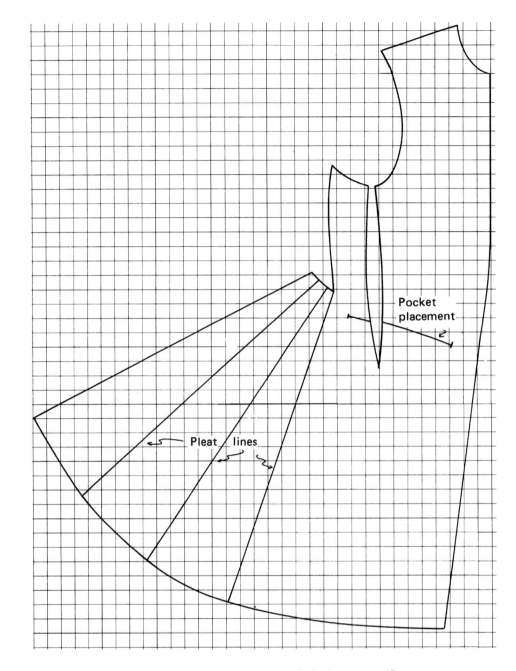

Figure 9.62   Pattern for early-eighteenth-century coat. Scale 1 square = 1″.

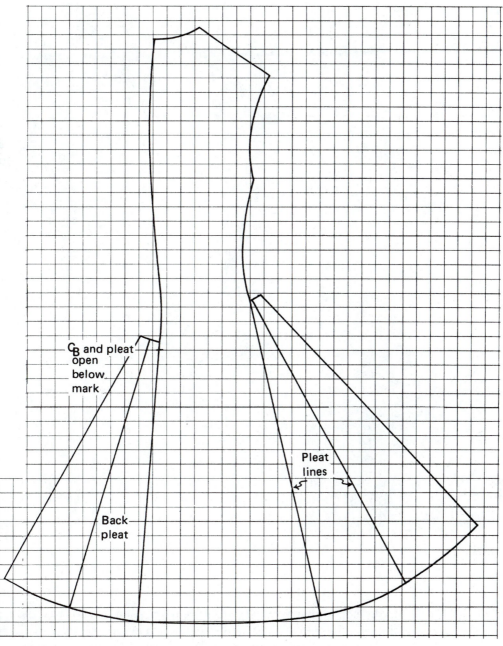

Figure 9.62 Continued.

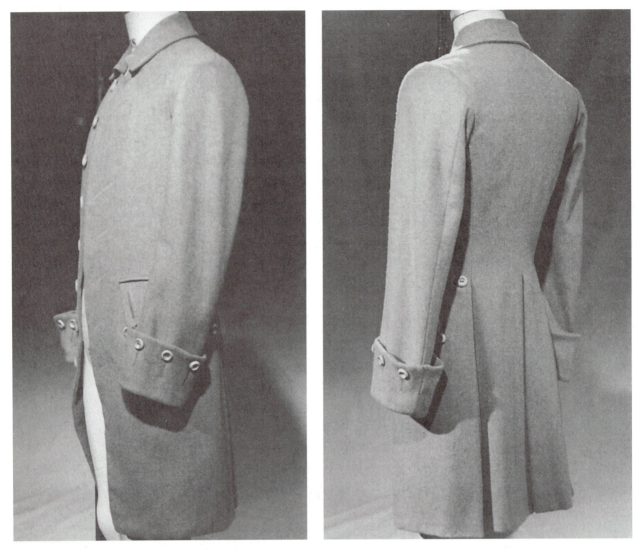

Figure 9.63 Later-eighteenth-century coat.

to develop at that time. The front shoulder seam extends past the top of the shoulder into the back of the coat, which lowers accordingly. The body of the coat molds the chest and waist closely. The side back seam curves into the center back even more and the pleat becomes much smaller (Figure 9.66). The lapel develops on the front of the coat and the standing-falling collar is added. The collar and lapel must be handled very carefully to fall correctly on the body. Both have the fabric and interfacing attached together with padding stitches, which are stitches applied while the two parts are curved in the way they will fall. These stitches go over the interfacing, through to barely catch the good fabric and out over the interfacing again in a regular fashion all over the area. A narrow twill tape is also sewed on to define the actual fold line. To thoroughly understand this and

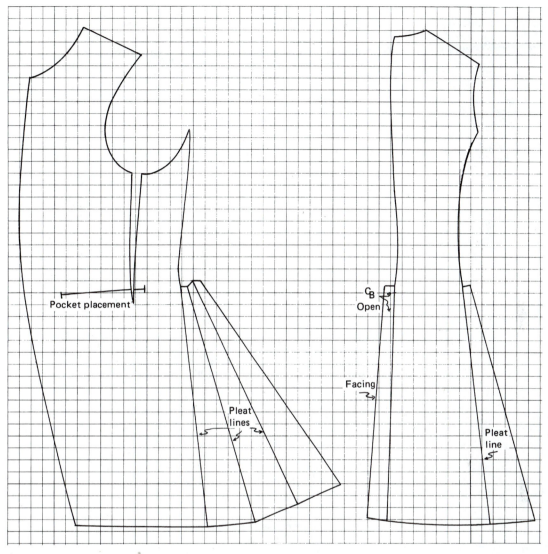

Figure 9.64 Pattern for later-eighteenth-century coat. Scale 1 square = 1″.

the other tricks of the tailoring trade, refer to the tailoring reference books mentioned earlier.

Men's tailcoats, frock coats, and suit jackets were cut in many interesting ways in the nineteenth century and can often be developed from a good modern commercial coat pattern. Coats can be mocked up in muslin, but it is quite difficult to get some of the steps to work and to refine the shape unless a fairly decent-quality wool is used. Good pressing is often as important as good sewing when tailoring, so never skimp in this area. Pressing may even involve a board or tailor's clapper used to beat the seams or edges. While some shortcuts can be developed for costume purposes, tailoring is a time-consuming process and cannot be rushed if a professional-looking garment is to be created.

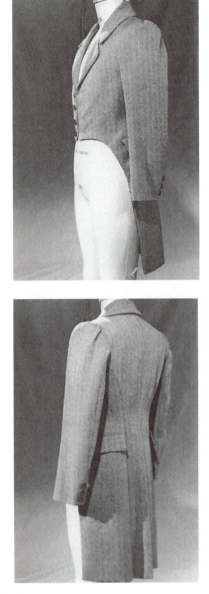

Figure 9.65 Early-nineteenth-century coat.

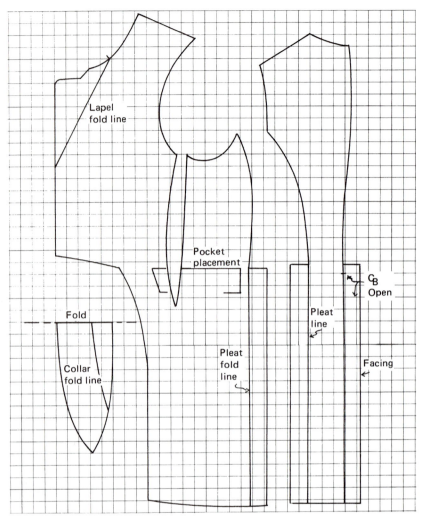

Figure 9.66 Pattern for early-nineteenth-century coat. Scale 1 square = 1″.

◆ Mocking Up the Patterns

Enlarging small-scale patterns is a fairly mechanical process and usually done on brown paper because the line can be drawn or erased easily. Brown paper is also relatively inexpensive. Patterning paper with a grid can speed up the process but is more costly. Skirt patterns are drawn as easily on the plain paper.

When drawing a pattern, whether enlarging or creating from scratch, never stop thinking about what the lines mean and how they will go together. Some patterning books—*The Blue Book of Men's Tailoring,* for example—have very carefully listed step-by-step formulas. The following is an excerpt from the "Systematical Outline for Sack Coat" to establish various points on the center back line:

Square out and down from A

A to V is 1/3 the breast measure.

V to B is 3 in.

A to C is 1/4 of total height plus 1/2 in.

A to D is 1/3 of height plus 1 in.

A to E is 1/2 height minus 5 in.

It continues for 80 steps. Following these steps can create a coat pattern, but rote copying does not develop patterning skills that can then be applied to the next problem. The designer's eye must gauge distances and understand outlines and how they will react when draped on the body. If a pattern is tried and altered, the designer must endeavor to understand what changes the alterations make in the original shapes. Careful attention to detail is a great boon to the well-developed patterning imagination. Soon a pattern drawing that once took two agonizing hours to create can be accomplished with ease in 15 minutes.

◆ Fitting the Actor

Costume fittings should be well organized and efficiently handled if everyone involved is to remain as happy as possible. The actors should not be called more often than necessary and their time well used while they are there. If actors realize the shop is functioning smoothly and will not waste their time, they are much more likely to be prompt and cooperative and to make a special trip should an emergency arise. In a professional company an actor is only required to come in for a very short time, usually two hours a week, outside the regular rehearsal-call time. In this case efficiency is absolutely necessary, for it becomes a question of economics.

Before an actor is called, all the components of his or her costume should be checked so that as many different elements as possible can be fitted at the same time.

The patterns and garments that are to be fitted should be assembled— together with all the shoes and underpinnings that might be needed. Ideally the fitting should take place in a separate area large enough for the actor, those who will need to work with him or her, a mirror, table for equipment, a chair, and a hanging area. Unfortunately this lovely little room is often not available and the fitting takes place in the middle of the shop, which always eats into the time needed to get the costumes built. Those people in charge of the costume must stop what they are doing to work with the actor, and others who are working around the area often find the fitting much more interesting than the seam or button they should be sewing.

For the actual fitting, as much of the pattern as seems logical should be machine-basted together. For example, the body parts should probably be together, and, the sleeve, but not attached to each other. After the fit of the chest and shoulder has been set, the sleeve can be pinned on. In most cases it is useful to baste the pieces together slightly past the end of the seam, but do not backstitch unless the stitching will be under a great deal of tension. The seam thus can be easily ripped open if necessary without endangering the fabric.

◆ Creating a Good Atmosphere

It is almost as important to be able to handle a fitting well from a psychological point of view as it is to be skillful with pins and fabric. The costume is a work in progress. The actor must realize that changes may be necessary and that the alterations being done will present him or her in the best possible way. The crew member in charge of the costume must also realize that some areas may need to be reworked. This is not necessarily because he or she has not done a good job but perhaps because something else might be more effective. During a fitting is not the time to assign blame or make accusations. Should there be a problem, solve it in a pleasant way and find out why it happened later. If the craftsmanship is shoddy, speak to the crew member privately. Don't create a fuss in front of the actor. It will embarrass the crew member and make the actor feel insecure about the final outcome of the costume. If a pattern works well, say so. An encouraging word can work wonders.

Fittings are excellent times for meaningful communication between the designer and the actor. Though the sketch was discussed as work began on the production, both now have a more realistic point of reference, for actual costume shapes have been developed and rehearsal is in progress. Concerns can be explored, questions answered, ideas explained. Should a problem arise that cannot be completely resolved for both parties, at least a thorough airing of the issues can happen and aid those involved to understand the best solution.

Extraneous comments during the fitting can sometimes create difficult situations. Someone casually looking up from his work and remarking "Gee, Phil, that really makes you look fat" or "What's that funny pucker in the back?" can start the actor worrying about something that might never have occurred to him. It's not considered too democratic to put a muzzle on the crew and if someone thinks something really looks good it's nice for him or her to say so. It is not out of place, however, to remind the crew that the costumes are still being developed during the fittings and actors are sometimes a bit insecure about their appearance. If anyone spots a problem, he or she should quietly mention it to someone in charge and not announce it to the world. This approach will probably work very well with the crew. The remaining fly in the ointment is the friend of the actor who walks into the room and feels obliged to make some sort of crack.

Fitting problems also can happen simply because there are too many bodies in the shop at the same time. Know how many people the crew can take at once and schedule no more than that. If three people can be handled efficiently, don't let the stage manager send up eight at once just because there is a rehearsal break. The other five will waste their time and could slow the process by being in the way.

◆ Adjusting the Pattern to the Body

The costume sketch should be available during the fitting so the pattern can be compared to the drawing for both fit and placement of specific costume elements. Memory can be erratic; the designer should check the sketch to verify exactly what he or she had in mind for this costume.

Set the pattern on the actor as squarely as possible and pin up the closing so the work can be done on a well-situated piece that will not shift. Check the armholes and neck hole to make sure the curved-seam allowance does not catch against the body in a way that keeps the fabric from lying properly. This almost always happens at the front of the base of the neck and where the arm joins the chest and back. The seam allowance must be clipped at these points before any other adjustment can be accurately made; it must be clipped in far enough to release the tension but must not go into the body of the garment. Do not clip more than necessary, but if a clip is needed, make it deep enough to count.

Try to pin fairly symmetrically and for alterations locate the area that most logically needs the adjustment. If a bodice is too big it could be tightened by taking in the center back seam, but this might bring the side seams toward the back, create diagonal pulls, and do nothing for the bust area. Another solution could be to take in both side seams or the side front and side back seams. If a seam is replaced or a dart taken, make sure the pin line continues until the line tapers off or goes into the seam allowance.

When a satisfactory fit has been achieved, mark the seam line at the neck, the waist, and both armseyes. One side might do if the pattern has been taken in quite evenly, but if the usual variations occur two will be better. These marks should move continuously around the body, so be particularly attentive where the line crosses a seam. Watch out for ticklish actors. Check the costume design for any particular markings that should be indicated. If lines are drawn for more than one costume, which is entirely possible, do them in different colors and write on the muslin which line corresponds to which drawing.

Sleeves should be pinned in place carefully and checked for movement and length. The cap of the tight sleeve must be wide enough across the upper arm muscle to allow forward and upward movement. The length of the full sleeve should be carefully set. If it is too short the effect of the fullness is lost and it may hinder movement; if it is too long the fabric will droop on itself and look awkward. The fabric should be just long enough to hold out the fullness and slightly longer to the outside and back than under the arm. Soft, heavier fabrics will droop more than crisp ones. If a sleeve is too long in the fitting, pin a tuck in the middle of it until the right length is achieved.

The general length of a skirt can be estimated, but the actual hem usually cannot be taken until the skirt is constructed in the real fabric because the weight of the fabric can cause a variation. The movement capability in tight trousers should be checked as well as the way the seams fall down the leg. Should the seams twist, open them on both sides, allow the fabric to fall straight, and repin. The front length of knee breeches should be marked with the actor seated to allow enough fabric to go over the bent knee and the back length marked when he is standing.

This checklist will be useful when organizing the fittings for a show:

1. Patterns should have as many pieces basted or pinned together as possible, with body pieces and sleeves separate. Seams should be basted past the end, but not backstitched.
2. Everyone who might need to see the actor should be notified that the actor has been called.
3. All the elements that might be needed for the fitting should be gathered into one space, including the costume sketch.
4. Someone should be available to take notes as the fitting progresses.
5. The pattern should be set squarely on the body and pinned in place.
6. Any area with a curved seam allowance that may keep the fabric from lying properly on the body, such as arm and neck holes, should be checked and clipped.
7. The garment should be pinned as evenly as possible from side to side and in logical places to solve the fitting problems.
8. Neck, waist, armholes, lengths, and any design lines should be marked as soon as a good fit has been achieved.
9. The pattern should be checked immediately after the fitting to make sure all areas are clearly marked. It should be organized as soon as possible.

◆ Finishing the Pattern

As soon as possible after the fitting the pattern should be finalized. What seems obvious and easy to remember at the time can become quite fuzzy and vague a few more fittings and hundreds of questions later. Each alteration should be carefully marked and each piece labeled with its position, the name of the actor or costume, and the top, bottom, front, or back if there is any chance confusion could arise. The pattern should then be taken apart, pressed if necessary, and organized so cutting can be done easily and accurately.

The best way to organize a pattern in most cases is to "even it up." Though the human body is never actually symmetrical, it is usually wise to make a costume that is. Once a garment starts to go askew all kinds of problems can arise: trim lines off center, pleats at different intervals, the true center front obscured—one variance seems to beget three more.

No matter how carefully a fitting is done there are usually differences from side to side. These can easily be evened up by using the following method. Matching pieces should be laid on top of each other, seam lines coinciding and on the outsides. If the pieces were cut and marked together, matching the cut edges will also match the seam lines. Any new lines drawn on one piece should be traced to the other so the changes on both sides are now visible on one piece. The final seam line can be marked halfway between what was done on side A and what was done on side B. An example may help clarify this process.

A system for the colors of pattern lines should be established for the shop. A useful code is to mark all the preliminary patterns in red, the intermediate evening-up lines in yellow, and the final seam lines in blue. If a line has not been changed the red will stand; if it has been changed the blue line will supersede it.

Figure 9.67a shows the two side front pieces of a seven-piece bodice with the original pattern lines and the pencil lines drawn in the fitting. In Figure 9.67b the two pieces have been pinned together and the lines from the left side transferred to the right with yellow tracing paper. In Figure 9.67c the blue line is located halfway between each correction. Note the underarm seam. Since this was not changed on the left side, the final blue line is located halfway between the pencil correction on the right and the red line, which was the good line on the left. Most of the front seam was not changed so the red line remains. The mark on the front seam indicates where the center front piece joins on. This too is evened up. Darts are done in the same way. Perhaps it should be noted that the blue line is actually created by placing the blue tracing paper under the pieces as they are seen in Figure 9.67b and the tracing wheel is used to draw in the line, which will appear on the left side. The piece can then be flipped and the blue copied to the right so the final lines will appear on all the pattern pieces.

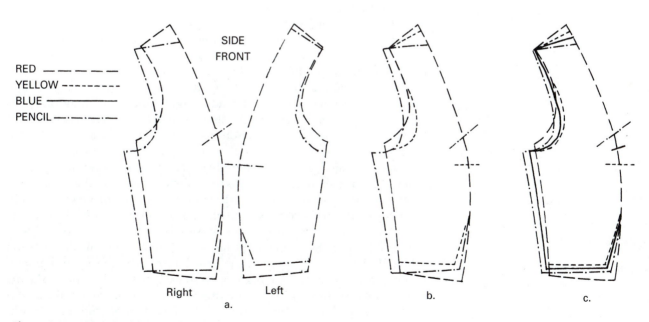

Figure 9.67 A method for evening pattern pieces after the fitting.

Occasionally an actor is shaped quite differently from side to side, so much so that the pattern should not be evened but fitted very carefully on the body and marked so the pieces fitted on the left will always be on the left, and so forth.

◆ Constructing the Costume

Basic sewing methods will not be discussed in this book since this type of information can be found in many other sources. Costume construction begins with the same type of sewing skills used in making regular garments, but they often need to be sturdier because they get quite a workout during the production and may be used over and over again as part of the stock of a continuing company.

Bodices and sleeves should be flat lined, often with broadcloth, unless this will interfere with the drape of the primary fabric. Seams should be sewn with a moderate-length stitch. A long stitch will be loose and may not hold; if alterations are necessary removing short, tight stitches is time-consuming and may cause the fabric to be ripped in the attempt. Ample but not bulky seam allowances should be left wherever possible for future use, and the allowance should be finished in some way to keep it from raveling. Closings must be quite sturdy. All grommeted edges should be interlined, and if they are under pressure, the edges must be boned. Any stress points should be reinforced or they will need frequent mending.

Garments with complex pleating, tucking, or draping on the outside need a flat lining next to the body to hold the shape firmly in place. Large draped pieces should be carefully tacked to retain their shape. Complex sleeves should be built on a fairly tight undersleeve so they will not shift out of place and will be easy to put on.

Any trim applied to the costume must be attached firmly. Collars and cuffs that might get heavily soiled can be made as finished pieces that can be removed for laundering. The inner layer of all costumes that can't be washed regularly should be supplied with dress shields.

The key thought behind building any costume is quite simple. Construction should be careful and solid. The method of working may vary from that found in a dressmaker's shop—a machine stitch may be substituted for handwork or on occasion even glue may be used—but careful craftsmanship must be employed if the result is to be successful.

One extremely important ingredient for a well-built costume is a crew that really cares about the work. It's up to the designer and the head of the shop to integrate all those who work with them into the production and to let them know how vital their contribution is to the success of the show. The designer should present the designs to the entire shop, explain his or her ideas, display the fabrics and trims, establish the schedule that must be followed, describe any special problems that must be solved, and in general let everyone know what is going on so each can see how he or she fits into the picture. Designers can't be cheerful every moment, but those who try most of the time will be forgiven a few cranky periods and the crew will be more inclined to put extra effort into building the show. If the designer is not prepared and has careless work habits, this attitude may soon pervade the entire crew and the results can be devastatingly lackluster.

◇ The Costume Shop

The costume shop can almost become home during a busy show. If it is a well-equipped, well-organized, pleasant place, the push to get things done will not seem too much like drudgery.

The size and location of shops vary considerably. The area is seldom too large, and often is smaller than ideal, so careful thought needs to go into the layout for the most efficient use of the available space.

Basic Sewing Equipment

The basic sewing supplies needed in a costume shop are similar to those found in most professional sewing situations. The following is a list of items most commonly used, with indications where costume use may be different from other situations.

Thread.　Regular weight, heavy-duty, and button thread are needed. Silamide is very useful for hand sewing.

Machine Needles.　A medium size is satisfactory for most sewing, but lightweight and heavy needles should be available for special problems. Leather needles should be available for leatherwork.

Hand Needles.　A variety of sizes of needles with long eyes are the most useful. Heavy-duty upholstery needles and curved needles are occasionally necessary.

Straight Pins.　Medium-size rustproof pins are most commonly used, but longer, heavier pins are desirable for heavy fabrics.

Safety pins.　All sizes are needed in quantity.

Tracing Paper.　At least four colors should be stocked, including white and probably blue, red, and yellow because they are easily distinguished from each other.

Tracing Wheels.　Regular tracing wheels are the most useful, but smooth and pointed ones are sometimes called for. The very pointed tracing wheels can mark most easily through heavy fabrics, but they can also rip up the surface of the tabletop.

Seam Rippers.　Small ones are the easiest to use. Some people prefer razor blades. These are fine in skilled hands but can be very dangerous to the fabric if the wielder is not careful.

Shears and Scissors.　Bent-handled shears with 8- to 10-inch or even 12-inch blades are used for most cutting chores. Good shears are expensive and generally worth it, for they keep a better edge. Fabric shears should be used only on fabric; other materials will dull the blades. A supply of inexpensive shears and smaller scissors should be available for nonfabric use. Leather shears will be a welcome tool for heavy-duty cutting.

Tape Measures, Yardsticks, Hem Gauges, Plastic Rulers. All measuring devices should be of fairly good quality. Cheap ones, or free ones with a bit of advertising included, are sometimes calibrated inaccurately, and the yardsticks are inevitably warped. The measuring tools should be marked on both sides with the numbers reversing so the handiest end may be used. Large aluminum rules 48 and 72 inches long are convenient for laying out skirt and cape patterns. The tailor's square, tailor's curve, and French curve can be used for drafting patterns.

Tailor's Chalk. Both wax and clay can be stocked, in white and various colors. Clay brushes out of fabric, white wax will melt off with the iron but may stain some synthetic fabrics.

Fasteners. A wide variety of fasteners should be available. Here are some of the most common.

- *Hooks and Eyes.* All sizes may be used. The larger, size 3 or 4, are better for closings. Very large or skirt hooks and eyes are often needed.
- *Snaps.* All sizes should be stocked, from extra-small to the big, heavy "whopper poppers."
- *Velcro.* Available in 12-yard rolls, both white and black Velcro is useful; colors also available. The white can be dyed, though one side takes much better than the other.
- *Zippers.* Specific zippers will probably be bought for the show, but a good store of emergency zippers should be available.

Twill tape and bias tape. Twill tape in 1/4-, 1/2-, and 1-inch widths, both black and white, can be an asset to the well-equipped shop. Bias tape can be stocked in black and white spools.

Elastic. This is needed in widths of 1/4 inch to 1 inch in both black and white. Elastic thread also should be available for special problems.

Thimbles. Often resisted by many, they can speed up sewing with practice and are essential for some heavy materials.

Hangers. Both wire and wooden are needed. Wooden hangers are particularly useful for heavier garments, which tend to lose their shape if supported by only the thin wire.

Most of these materials can be purchased from tailoring suppliers and wholesalers in bulk. This should be done whenever possible since the savings can be quite significant.

Larger Equipment

Sewing Machines. A number of good, sturdy, straight-stitch machines, such as the old black metal Singers, are invaluable. These are almost indestructible, no matter how inexperienced the user. A modern zigzag machine such as the Bernina, Elna, Pfaff, or Viking is necessary for specialty

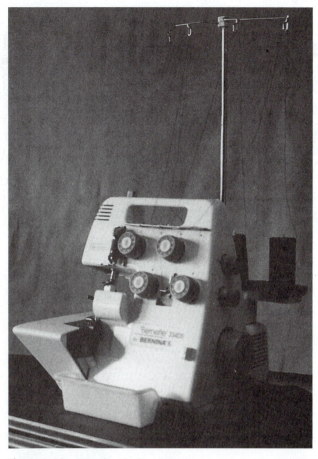

Figure 9.68 The overlock machine or serger is now readily available at reasonable prices and is invaluable for finishing edges. The machines come in three-, four-, and five-thread versions.

stitches. Overlock machines are now reasonably priced and very useful (Figure 9.68). Embroidery machines capable of intricate, multicolored patterns are becoming more affordable (Figure 9.73). A heavy-duty walking foot machine can make its way through practically anything and might be shared with the scene shop. The blind stitch machine (Figure 9.69) only does hems, but it does them very rapidly and with a stitch that is easily removed.

Irons. Industrial irons (Figure 9.70) are far superior to the domestic ones because they are heavier and deliver much more steam. As might be expected they are also much more expensive. This is somewhat counterbalanced by a longer life span.

Ironing Boards. Large heavy-duty boards will minimize tipping accidents. A vacuum board will pull the steam and heat down through the fabric and away from the ironer (Figure 9.70).

Figure 9.69 The blind stitch machine can hem yards of fabric in a few minutes, and the hem easily can be removed if necessary.

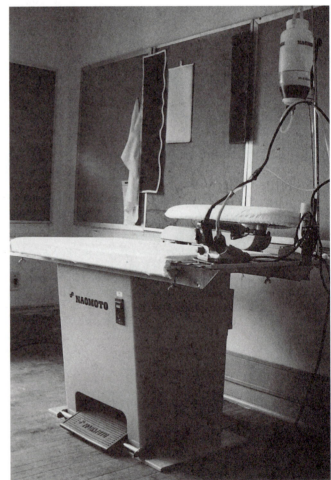

Figure 9.70 Industrial irons are efficient for the costume shop; they provide more steam and are heavier than household irons. The vacuum ironing board pulls the heat through the garment, increasing ironing efficiency and decreasing the heat that comes back at the ironer.

Specialty Ironing Equipment. Sleeve board, needle board for velvets, pressing ham, clapper for pounding seams, distilled water to prolong iron life, and iron cleaner for the sole plate.

Steamer. The table model is useful for work on hats; the floor model is good for large costumes and drapes (Figure 9.74).

Washing Machine and Dryer. These are vital for both maintaining the costumes and for dyeing fabrics. If one set is used for both purposes, care must be taken to keep them clean so that the lighter garments don't spot. A good supply of liquid bleach is recommended to clean out both machines. The washer should top load and have a number of water levels and temperature combinations. The dryer could have an automatic sensor but also needs a timed dry cycle, permanent press, and air fluff. Large-capacity heavy-duty models are the best.

Hot Plate or Stove. Used for heating water to dye, the hot plate should be large and heavy- duty. A 30-inch stove is even better because it is sturdy with a large flat surface and has an oven available if it is needed.

Dye Vat. Wonderful for dyeing large quantities, these can be quite expensive. A soup kettle available from restaurant suppliers is still costly but much less than a dye vat and can be used for the same purpose (see Figure 9.71).

Laundry Sink. This must have two deep tubs and a mixer faucet.

Figure 9.71 The dye vat below was actually a soup kettle and holds 40 gallons of water, which it can heat to boiling in less than 20 minutes.

Cutting Tables. These should be 6 to 8 feet long, at least 42 inches wide, and 36 inches high. The top should be smooth enough to lay fabric out easily but not so slick that the fabric slides to the floor the minute the cutter's back is turned. The surface should have a bit of give for easy marking. Upson board covered with vinyl can be quite practical. Cork coated with polyurethane makes an excellent though more expensive surface.

Dressmaker's Dummies. Good dummies are expensive but can sometimes be found used or collected one or two a year when the money is available. A variety of sizes for both men and women can be used. New dummies, including the hanging dummy with legs, can be purchased with detachable arms and collapsible shoulders (Figure 9.73). Inexpensive home sewing dummies are useful only if nothing better is available.

Computer. A good computer with programs for organizational and bookkeeping tasks and drawing, modeling, and rendering. Necessary peripherals include a printer, scanner, fax, and network hookup.

General Equipment

Racks. Rolling racks with large casters are the most practical way to hang the costumes. One style, called the Z-Truck, is sturdy and good where space is a problem, for the racks nest together well for storage.

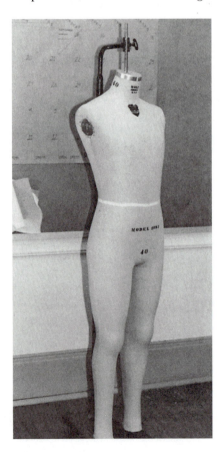

Figure 9.72 A hanging dummy is very useful for many construction problems.

Mirrors.   A three-fold mirror is best for fittings, but a full-size wall mirror can be used.

Hemming stand.   Not essential, but certainly a boon to the person marking the hem, for it raises the actor about 12 inches off the floor.

Bulletin boards.   These are necessary to hang up sketches, patterns, notes, trinkets, etc.

Brown paper and squared patterning paper

Muslin and other stock patterning fabric

Interfacing and lining fabrics

Buckram.   This can be used in both regular and heavy weight for hats and other items that need a stiff base.

Polyester or dacron batting and wadding

Boning—both metal and plastic or feather boning

Wire.   Milliner's wire in both medium and heavier weights is useful, as well as lightweight spool wire for jewelry and accessory work.

Basic tools.   Hammers, screwdrivers, wrenches, awl, wire cutters, rasps, and files for distressing costumes. Also nails, screws, and anything else the scene shop might not want to lend.

Hot glue gun and pellets

Flexible white glue, such as Sobo

Dress shields, bust pads, shoulder pads, and sleeve heads

Buttons.   Always handy to have around, common types should be purchased in bulk whenever a sale is encountered.

Laundry soap, starch, antistatic spray, bleach, clothes brushes, and lint removers

Cleaning fluid

Dye and dye remover.   These are much less expensive when purchased in bulk from a wholesaler.

Grommets and setters

Leather tools and dyes

Rhinestone setter

Paints, brushes, and sprays

Shoe polishes, brushes, and sprays

Plasticene or clay for molding shapes

Celastic and acetone.   Acetone may be available in bulk from a chemical supply company or the chemistry department of a university.

Scrap boxes.   Medium to large boxes are needed, one for muslin pieces too large to throw away, and at least one for the scraps from the current show. These should be saved until the show closes in case a repair is needed.

Combs, brushes, hair and bobby pins, dryers, curlers, and other wig and hair-setting materials.

Wig blocks and hat stands

Notebooks for measurement sheets and show organization
Filing system for catalogs, patterns, and reference materials

The size of the shop, the money available, and the type of production work usually done should be considered when deciding which items need to be acquired first and what will be the most useful. Careful planning has two definite advantages: work can be done more efficiently in a well-equipped space and items purchased in bulk are almost always less expensive.

If at all possible, the shop floor should be wood or cushioned tile, not cement which can be hard on feet and legs. The lighting should be incandescent, or at least a combination of incandescent and fluorescent. Exclusively fluorescent light distorts the colors of the fabrics and trims. The dye area in particular must have some incandescent illumination.

A few more items are really essential, though they don't tie in directly to constructing costumes. There are often times when a number of people are spending a great deal of time in this area. A coffeepot makes life a lot easier, as does a small refrigerator and a microwave. With these supplies, the crew can camp out in the shop for days.

◆ Laying Out the Costume Shop

Each space will have its own problems and its own potential and will need to be considered with a good logical eye to discern the best ways to place the equipment for the most efficient use.

Cutting tables should be placed away from the walls so they can be approached from all sides. Shelves for fabric storage or scrap boxes can be kept underneath the tables. Sewing machines should relate to both the cutting tables and the irons and, if possible, should have sewing tables large enough for big costumes and lots of yardage. Tables and chairs should be available for those doing handwork.

A shelf unit can hold clearly labeled containers for all the small sewing equipment. Shelves near the ironing boards will organize all the ironing accessories. Deeper shelves can be used for fabrics and storage boxes of the trims and accessories most commonly used. Floor space should be allotted for racks and dummies. The bulletin boards need to be on walls that can be reached easily. The mirror should be located in an area that allows maneuverability in front of it.

The dye area should be separated from the shop if at all possible because the moisture it produces can be hard on the machines and dyeing itself can be quite messy. A worktable and storage shelves are needed, as well as a space to hang fabrics that cannot go into the dryer. A floor drain is always best in this area. If the space is also used to spray costumes or if work with any toxic materials is done, it should have excellent ventilation. Many new materials can be quite hazardous to the health and should be used with extreme caution. Either the dye area or another separate space is needed for the costume craft work such as the making of armor, shoes, jewelry, headdresses, and the like. This, too, can be very messy work involving different types of materials, tools, paints, and glues and is better done away from the regular costume construction (See Figure 9.74.) Filing cabinets

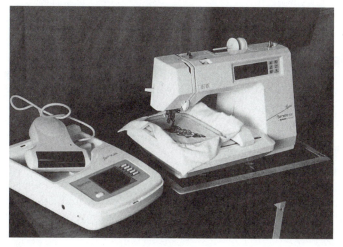

Figure 9.73 Embroidery machines are now available that can produce complex, multicolored patterns. The one shown has a scanner that can be used to created original designs. Other patterns can be purchased on premade computer disks.

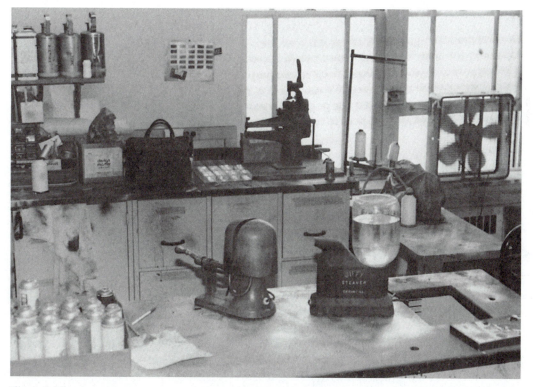

Figure 9.74 A separate area is necessary for the craft work since it is often messy and uses different types of tools and materials. Pictured are a tabletop steamer and hat block.

are very convenient for pattern storage and catalogs. Large wastebaskets located at regular intervals are a must.

If no office is available in conjunction with the shop, a desk will have to provide a headquarters area for the designer and costume shop foreman.

The arrangement of all the costume shop's equipment is seldom easy because such a variety of activities take place when the crew is constructing costumes. A logical arrangement should be made and tried with an eye always open for an even better way of doing things. Sometimes it can be quite refreshing to rearrange the shop and try something different.

A clear system of methods and procedures is not a physical item used in the shop, but it must be established and understood by all who work in the space. Such a system can make life easier because those working together know what to expect of each other. Remember, though, that because a method has been devised and written down does not mean that it may never be improved. Just as the physical space may sometimes need to be reorganized, new systems can be tried. If they improve the work or the result, so much the better; if not, little has been lost.

Flexibility can often be the key to both happiness and success in all phases of the costume field. Anyone who wants a completely orderly world and is inflexible when it comes to change should not be in the costume profession. Every show is a new challenge. New methods and techniques can continually be tried. It's an area where one can always learn and grow, from the first approach to the production to the last stitch on the costume.

A Guide to the History of Clothing

A knowledge of the history of clothing is an essential tool for the costume designer who must be aware of the basic shapes as they develop and change through the centuries. This guide will help the designer understand the development of the garments of the Western world. He or she will then be able to go to more detailed sources to do extensive research for a particular project and understand the information that is presented. The guide is not a research source in itself. No section of a book, or any single book, can provide enough information to familiarize a designer with a complete era. The principal forms are presented here to give a starting point. Other sources are suggested that can be used as the designer moves on to an in-depth investigation. This section can only be a brief overview, for no period in the history of clothing should be thought of as an island but must be considered in terms of its development from what came before and its affect on what follows.

The designer who begins a serious investigation of a period may discover that the terminology varies from source to source. There are few fixed definitions, and many different languages have contributed to the nomenclature of costumes. Various costume-history books use different terms for the same garment. This is not really a problem. What is important is an ability to comprehend the source material and to interpret it in a sketch that will communicate ideas successfully.

◆ The Four Basic Types of Costumes

In terms of construction, all clothes fall into four basic types. These categories delineate the costume by the way it is worn on the body, or the way it is cut to fit the body contours.

The Draped Costume

In this style the fabric remains in the rectangular shape in which it was woven. The draped costume can provide the wearer with great freedom of movement if the fabric is suspended from the shoulders or waist, or greatly

FOUR BASIC TYPES OF COSTUMES

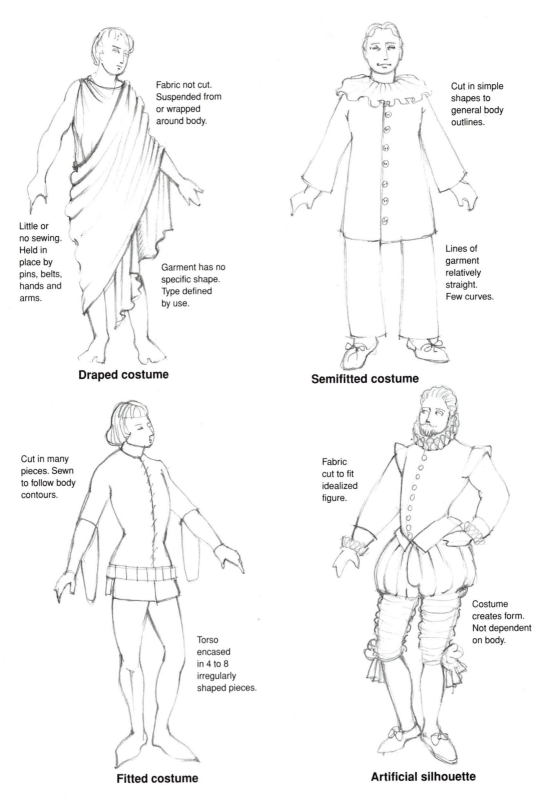

Fabric not cut. Suspended from or wrapped around body.

Little or no sewing. Held in place by pins, belts, hands and arms.

Garment has no specific shape. Type defined by use.

Draped costume

Cut in simple shapes to general body outlines.

Lines of garment relatively straight. Few curves.

Semifitted costume

Cut in many pieces. Sewn to follow body contours.

Torso encased in 4 to 8 irregularly shaped pieces.

Fitted costume

Fabric cut to fit idealized figure.

Costume creates form. Not dependent on body.

Artificial silhouette

constrain the wearer if the garment is wrapped around the body in such a way that the arms must hold it in position.

The Semifitted Costume

Semifitted costumes are generally cut simply—trousers are loose and shirts, tunics, and dresses are constructed in a T-shape.

The Fitted Costume

The fitted costume, which is more complex to construct than the draped or semifitted, does not appear often in history. This is not because of construction difficulty but because it reveals so much of the actual body shape. The youthful figure is much more suited to this type of treatment than one beginning to show the usual effects of age.

The Artificial Silhouette

A costume can create an artificial silhouette in which the body may be corseted or padded, and the fabric interlined, wired, or stiffened to create the shape of a particular historical fashion. Most costumes for the stage fall into this category because certain construction techniques can better realize the line of the design and create the best shape for the actor.

◆ Greek Costumes

The Greek costume required almost no cutting. Rectangular pieces of fabric were draped to become particular garments, distinguished by the way they were worn. They wrapped around or were suspended from the body, held in place by pins, belts, hands, or arms. A well-formed body was the ideal, with drapery used to enhance its contours.

The Greek "business suit" was the *himation,* an important garment that could be worn alone. Its method of draping could restrict movement, so it was impractical and not used by the lower classes. The *himation* had no fastenings and was held in place by the way the body was carried. For men it could be the only garment worn. For women, the *himation* was an outer drape. A simple tunic form could be used to cover the torso and legs of both men and women. For men, the most common was the *Doric chiton,* a garment usually thigh- or knee-length with the waist most often belted in, but the girdle was neither ornamental nor conspicuous. The women's most common tunic form was the *Doric peplos* which was similar to the *chiton* but much longer. The garment was floor-length and often had an overfold at the top. It was belted at the waist, sometimes both under and over the overfold, and often had a blousing over the belt called the *kolpos.* The *Ionic chiton* was a tunic-type garment worn by both sexes, though principally by women and older men. It was usually made of linen or a crepelike material that was crinkled or finely pleated. The garment was girdled in around the slightly raised waist and over the shoulders in such a manner that it gave the appearance of sleeves, but no sleeves were cut in.

GREEK

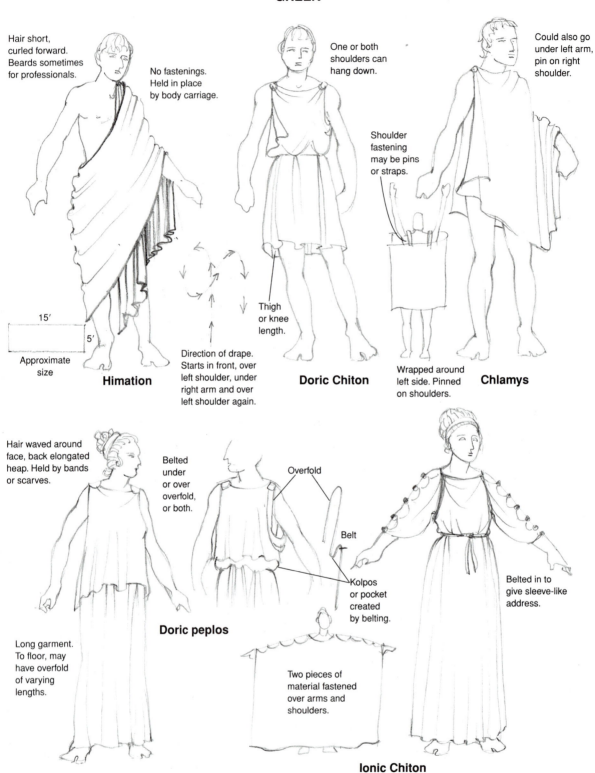

Hair short, curled forward. Beards sometimes for professionals.

No fastenings. Held in place by body carriage.

15′

5′

Approximate size

Himation

Direction of drape. Starts in front, over left shoulder, under right arm and over left shoulder again.

One or both shoulders can hang down.

Thigh or knee length.

Doric Chiton

Could also go under left arm, pin on right shoulder.

Shoulder fastening may be pins or straps.

Wrapped around left side. Pinned on shoulders.

Chlamys

Hair waved around face, back elongated heap. Held by bands or scarves.

Belted under or over overfold, or both.

Long garment. To floor, may have overfold of varying lengths.

Doric peplos

Overfold

Belt

Kolpos or pocket created by belting.

Two pieces of material fastened over arms and shoulders.

Belted in to give sleeve-like address.

Ionic Chiton

Wools, cottons, and linens in a variety of thicknesses were used in many colors, although only women wore yellow. Dyed and bleached fabrics were worn by the upper classes; the lower classes wore garments in natural tones. The fabrics were decorated with embroidered borders and sometimes all-over spotting. Headbands, necklaces, bracelets, earrings, pins, and narrow functional belts were common. Worked metals, such as bronze, comprised Greek jewelry; few precious stones were used. Sandals were worn outdoors, and boots were worn for hunting. No footwear was worn indoors. Hats were worn only for travel and work, though women often donned veils.

◆ Roman Costumes

The founding date of Rome is believed to be 753 B.C. For the first six or seven centuries, Roman garments were similar to those of the Greeks, although without the same reverence for the well-developed body. The more truly Roman style existed from the first century B.C. to A.D. 200. More garments were used to complete the costume, more cutting was needed, and there were more costume differences between men and women.

The most important male garment was the *toga,* a costume of distinction required in formal situations and worn by all Roman aristocrats and free men. It was denied to peasants and foreigners, though possibly bestowed as an honor on visiting dignitaries. The toga had a curved edge and was cut according to the size of the wearer with the width at the deepest part of the curve equal to the height of the man and the length three times as long. Draped around the body in a fashion similar to the *himation,* the folds were very specifically set in place by a slave to give dignity to the wearer, who was controlled by this garment that required he stand erect and move with a slow stately walk. Disarraying the folds of a gentleman's toga could be a deliberate insult, the equivalent of a slap in the face. The several types of togas varied in color and material, but not in shape, and were worn over a *tunic.* The tunic was usually belted in an inconspicuous manner and might be decorated by a deep wine-colored stripe down the center front or over each shoulder. Women, too, wore one or more tunics, with the top one referred to as the *stola* and the undertunic called the *tunica interiore.* Over these the *palla* might be draped, but not the *toga,* which was exclusively a male garment.

The *lacerna* and *abolla* were short cloaks similar to the short Greek cloak or *chlamys;* the *paludamentum* was a large purple cape of consequence, and the *paenula* was a protective overgarment similar to a modern hooded poncho. Fine wools, cottons, silks, and linens were used, sometimes woven with gold threads. Many real and false jewels were worn. Stones were round, not faceted, so produced a luster, not a sparkle. Sandals were the ordinary footwear both indoors and out and men sometimes wore boots.

Men's hair was worn short and brushed forward over the forehead with no part. Women's hairdressing could be quite elaborate, pulled to the back to elongate the head with the front raised in a diadem of artificial hair or metal ornaments.

ROMAN

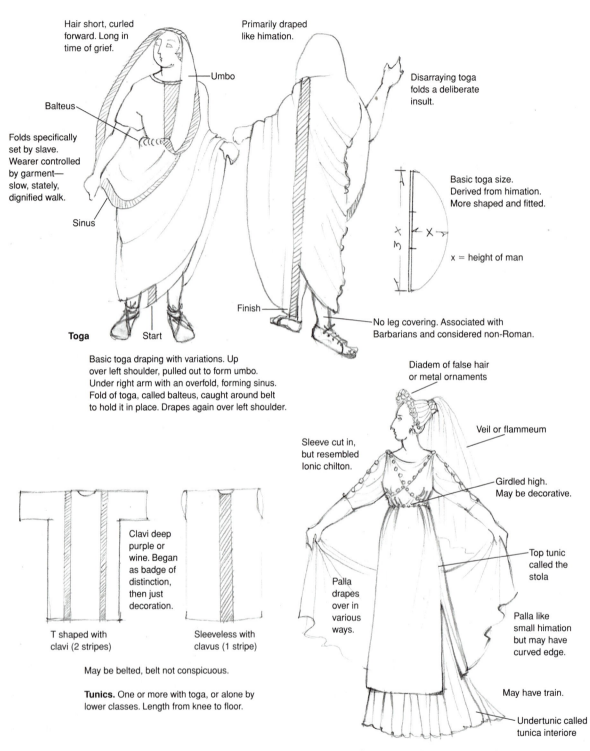

Hair short, curled forward. Long in time of grief.

Primarily draped like himation.

Umbo

Balteus

Disarraying toga folds a deliberate insult.

Folds specifically set by slave. Wearer controlled by garment— slow, stately, dignified walk.

Basic toga size. Derived from himation. More shaped and fitted.

Sinus

x = height of man

Toga   Start

Finish

No leg covering. Associated with Barbarians and considered non-Roman.

Basic toga draping with variations. Up over left shoulder, pulled out to form umbo. Under right arm with an overfold, forming sinus. Fold of toga, called balteus, caught around belt to hold it in place. Drapes again over left shoulder.

Diadem of false hair or metal ornaments

Veil or flammeum

Sleeve cut in, but resembled Ionic chilton.

Girdled high. May be decorative.

Clavi deep purple or wine. Began as badge of distinction, then just decoration.

Top tunic called the stola

Palla drapes over in various ways.

Palla like small himation but may have curved edge.

T shaped with clavi (2 stripes)

Sleeveless with clavus (1 stripe)

May be belted, belt not conspicuous.

May have train.

Tunics. One or more with toga, or alone by lower classes. Length from knee to floor.

Undertunic called tunica interiore

Roman matron in one or more tunics which may or may not have sleeves.

◈ Early Christian, Byzantine, and Romanesque Costumes

Simple tunic, shirt, and mantle shapes predominated in Europe from the second to the twelfth centuries. The Roman Empire declined and power moved east to Constantinople and the Byzantine Empire. Western Europe was ruled by various barbarian nations who wore simple garments influenced first by Rome, then Byzantium. In the Early Christian era, the second to fifth centuries, the *toga* declined in popularity for regular dress and was worn only as a symbol of office. The *pallium* took its place as an overdrape and was considered something of a badge of learning, for it was associated with the Greek philosophers. The principal tunic styles were the *talaris*, with long tight sleeves; the *dalmatica*, based on the loose, flowing Asiatic tunic; and the loose and sleeveless *colobium*. Overgarments included the *paenula*, the larger *amphibalus* and the *cuculla*, a rectangular poncho-like garment with a hole in the middle for the head. Women's tunics were not particularly graceful as the three basic forms of the *dalmatica* were all rather large and ill-fitting. Jewelry, worn by both sexes, included pearls, polished stones, and goldsmith's work. Cosmetics were in general use.

The center of fashion and civilization moved to Byzantium from the sixth to twelfth centuries. The basic forms developed in the fifth and sixth centuries and stayed much the same throughout the entire period. The new state garment was the *paludamentum,* worn only by men and the empress. It was seen in practically all colors on high officials, with imperial purple reserved for the emperor. Leg coverings were previously worn only by Asians and northern savages, but *hosa* now became part of regular clothing. They were cut and seamed from silk, wool, or linen, not knitted. Because of this, hose that fit the body tightly and smoothly could restrict movement. Women wore garments that were simple in form and rich in fabric. Jewelry had an Oriental influence, employing intricate gold work with pearls, polished gems, and mosaic stonework. Pearls were sometimes sewn to the garments with gold threads.

Romanesque costumes were seen in Western Europe from the eighth to the twelfth centuries, developing from the simple wraps and animal skins of the barbarians. They were decorated with embroidered bands and medallionlike trims, often in a mosaic style, reflecting the Byzantine influence. Both sexes wore layers of tunics and mantles; the quantity and quality of fabric varied with the occasion.

EARLY CHRISTIAN

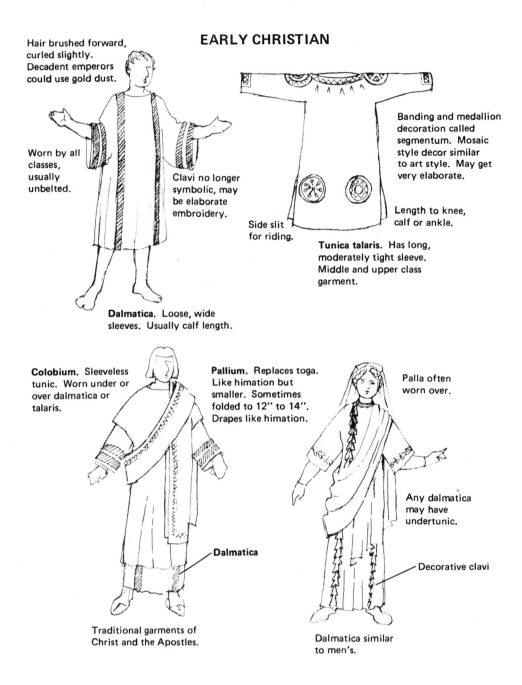

Hair brushed forward, curled slightly. Decadent emperors could use gold dust.

Worn by all classes, usually unbelted.

Clavi no longer symbolic, may be elaborate embroidery.

Banding and medallion decoration called segmentum. Mosaic style decor similar to art style. May get very elaborate.

Side slit for riding.

Length to knee, calf or ankle.

Tunica talaris. Has long, moderately tight sleeve. Middle and upper class garment.

Dalmatica. Loose, wide sleeves. Usually calf length.

Colobium. Sleeveless tunic. Worn under or over dalmatica or talaris.

Pallium. Replaces toga. Like himation but smaller. Sometimes folded to 12" to 14". Drapes like himation.

Palla often worn over.

Any dalmatica may have undertunic.

Dalmatica

Decorative clavi

Traditional garments of Christ and the Apostles.

Dalmatica similar to men's.

EARLY CHRISTIAN

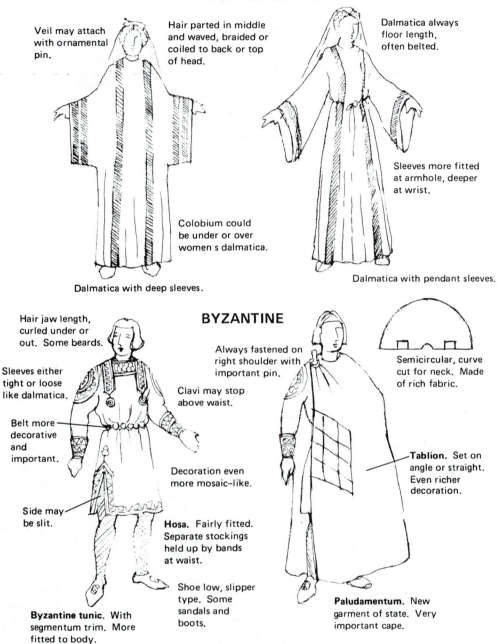

Veil may attach with ornamental pin.

Hair parted in middle and waved, braided or coiled to back or top of head.

Dalmatica always floor length, often belted.

Colobium could be under or over women's dalmatica.

Sleeves more fitted at armhole, deeper at wrist.

Dalmatica with deep sleeves.

Dalmatica with pendant sleeves.

BYZANTINE

Hair jaw length, curled under or out. Some beards.

Sleeves either tight or loose like dalmatica.

Belt more decorative and important.

Side may be slit.

Always fastened on right shoulder with important pin.

Clavi may stop above waist.

Decoration even more mosaic-like.

Hosa. Fairly fitted. Separate stockings held up by bands at waist.

Shoe low, slipper type. Some sandals and boots.

Semicircular, curve cut for neck. Made of rich fabric.

Tablion. Set on angle or straight. Even richer decoration.

Byzantine tunic. With segmentum trim. More fitted to body.

Paludamentum. New garment of state. Very important cape.

BYZANTINE

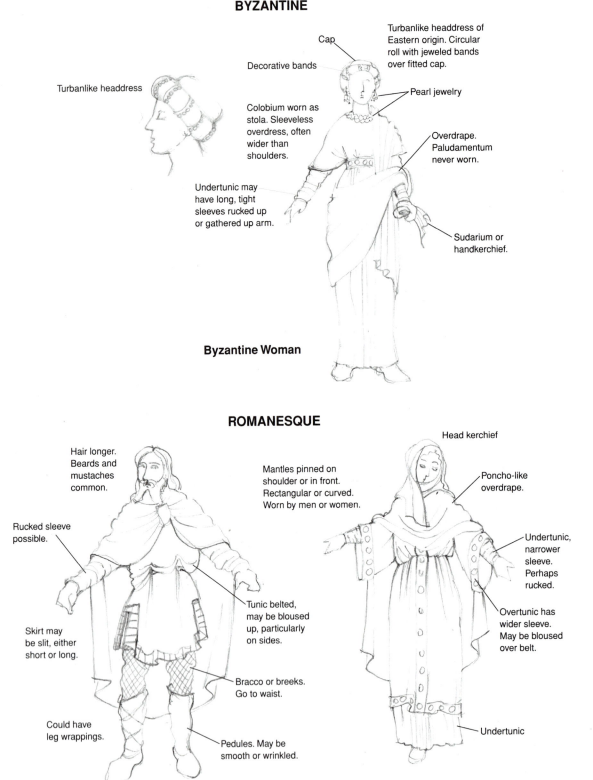

Turbanlike headdress

Cap

Decorative bands

Turbanlike headdress of Eastern origin. Circular roll with jeweled bands over fitted cap.

Pearl jewelry

Colobium worn as stola. Sleeveless overdress, often wider than shoulders.

Overdrape. Paludamentum never worn.

Undertunic may have long, tight sleeves rucked up or gathered up arm.

Sudarium or handkerchief.

Byzantine Woman

ROMANESQUE

Head kerchief

Hair longer. Beards and mustaches common.

Mantles pinned on shoulder or in front. Rectangular or curved. Worn by men or women.

Poncho-like overdrape.

Rucked sleeve possible.

Undertunic, narrower sleeve. Perhaps rucked.

Tunic belted, may be bloused up, particularly on sides.

Overtunic has wider sleeve. May be bloused over belt.

Skirt may be slit, either short or long.

Bracco or breeks. Go to waist.

Could have leg wrappings.

Pedules. May be smooth or wrinkled.

Undertunic

◇ Thirteenth-Century Costumes

The costumes of both sexes in thirteenth-century France and England used an excess of material to reveal a sober grandeur with long, flowing lines. Elaborate bands were gone and class distinction was revealed in the quantity and quality of fabric. Men's costumes consisted of layers of tunics with new variations developing in the overtunic or supertunic. Mantles went from small to very long and ample. Both sexes were quite adept at handling the large draperies. The most common men's headgear were the coif and hood. Hose were still separate pieces tied to the waist, and a purse was often attached to the belt. Women also wore tunics in a new form called the *kirtle,* shaped more to the body. Stockings were gartered above the knee and close-fitting slipper-style shoes were worn. The hair was parted in the middle and braided around the head or curled in ram's-horn fashion on each side. The headdresses often employed veiling, which tended to formally encase the woman.

THIRTEENTH CENTURY

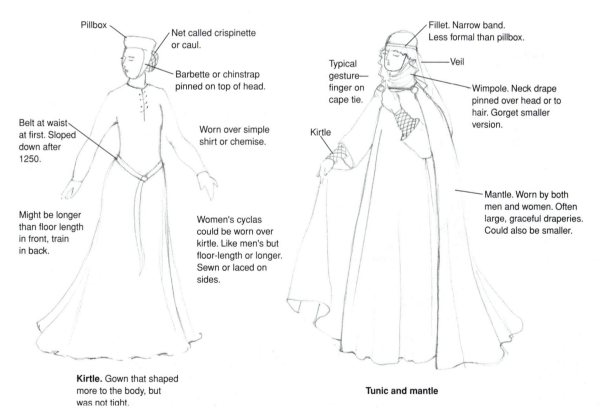

Pillbox

Net called crispinette or caul.

Barbette or chinstrap pinned on top of head.

Belt at waist at first. Sloped down after 1250.

Worn over simple shirt or chemise.

Might be longer than floor length in front, train in back.

Women's cyclas could be worn over kirtle. Like men's but floor-length or longer. Sewn or laced on sides.

Kirtle. Gown that shaped more to the body, but was not tight.

Fillet. Narrow band. Less formal than pillbox.

Typical gesture— finger on cape tie.

Veil

Wimpole. Neck drape pinned over head or to hair. Gorget smaller version.

Kirtle

Mantle. Worn by both men and women. Often large, graceful draperies. Could also be smaller.

Tunic and mantle

THIRTEENTH CENTURY

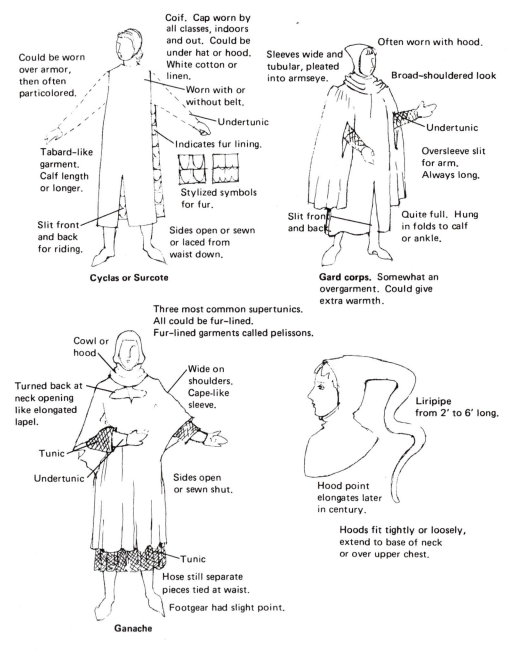

Coif. Cap worn by all classes, indoors and out. Could be under hat or hood. White cotton or linen.

Could be worn over armor, then often particolored.

Worn with or without belt.

Undertunic

Indicates fur lining.

Tabard-like garment. Calf length or longer.

Stylized symbols for fur.

Slit front and back for riding.

Sides open or sewn or laced from waist down.

Cyclas or Surcote

Often worn with hood.

Sleeves wide and tubular, pleated into armseye.

Broad-shouldered look

Undertunic

Oversleeve slit for arm. Always long.

Slit front and back

Quite full. Hung in folds to calf or ankle.

Gard corps. Somewhat an overgarment. Could give extra warmth.

Three most common supertunics. All could be fur-lined. Fur-lined garments called pelissons.

Cowl or hood

Wide on shoulders. Cape-like sleeve.

Turned back at neck opening like elongated lapel.

Tunic

Undertunic

Sides open or sewn shut.

Tunic

Hose still separate pieces tied at waist.

Footgear had slight point.

Ganache

Liripipe from 2' to 6' long.

Hood point elongates later in century.

Hoods fit tightly or loosely, extend to base of neck or over upper chest.

◈ Fourteenth-Century Costumes

The height of the fourteenth century in England and France, from 1325 to 1375, was a time of extravagant and eccentric styles. Garments were cut and shaped closer to the body as the fitted style gained popularity. Flowing robes were still worn for ceremony and by the elderly, but aristocratic attire accentuated the physique and emphasized youth. The man's *doublet* was now an undergarment padded to give a deep-chested look. The *hosen,* still separate pieces, tied to the waist of the doublet with strings called *estaches* that ended with decorative tips, or *poynts.* The process of pulling the hose up tightly to give a smooth, fitted leg was called *trussing the poynts* and produced a tension from shoulder to foot. The *cotehardie* replaced the supertunic for the gentry and was worn over the doublet. This was a tight-fitting garment that conformed quite snugly to the padded chest, waist, and hips, often so tight that a man required assistance getting it on. The cotehardie was belted at the hipline, often with the *knightly girdle,* which consisted of a series of ornamental plaques made of worked metal and jewels. Women also wore a version of the cotehardie that fit the upper body smoothly and fell into fullness. The neckline was moderately low and wide, stressing the horizontal, and the garment could button or lace up the front or back. The new headdress style also emphasized the horizontal, with the hair parted in the middle and brought to the sides of the head where it was drawn through jeweled metal ornaments that created a square shape. The positioning of the headdress, the bodice neckline, and the weight of the garments encouraged the development of the "Gothic slouch": chin tucked in, shoulders back, and pelvis thrust forward.

Colors were bright, fabrics rich with embroideries, damasks, and silks. Heraldic motifs were common in particolored garments that followed the colors of a noble house. Many decorative elements adorned these costumes. Any edge might be cut in a tonguelike shape called *dagging,* rows of small buttons were common, as were ornamental garters, sometimes supporting a row of small *folly bells*—which could also be worn on a band over the shoulder.

FOURTEENTH CENTURY

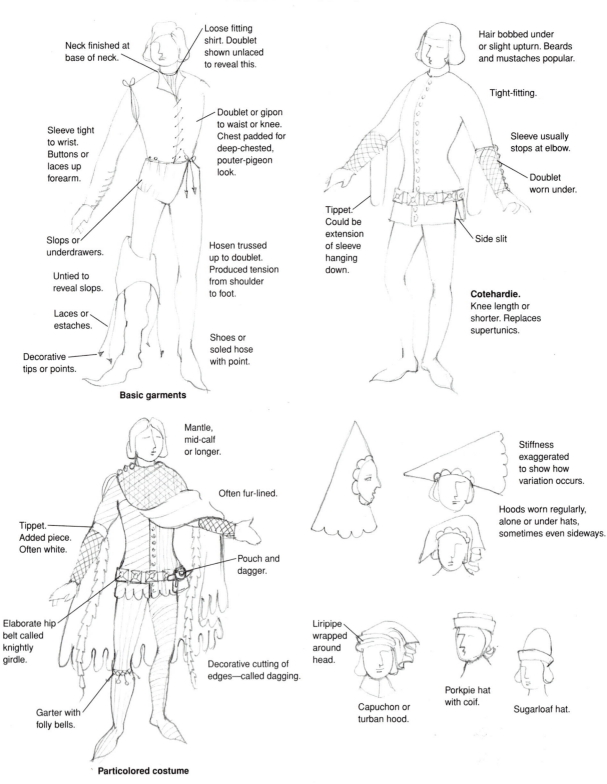

Neck finished at base of neck.

Loose fitting shirt. Doublet shown unlaced to reveal this.

Sleeve tight to wrist. Buttons or laces up forearm.

Doublet or gipon to waist or knee. Chest padded for deep-chested, pouter-pigeon look.

Slops or underdrawers.

Untied to reveal slops.

Hosen trussed up to doublet. Produced tension from shoulder to foot.

Laces or estaches.

Decorative tips or points.

Shoes or soled hose with point.

Basic garments

Hair bobbed under or slight upturn. Beards and mustaches popular.

Tight-fitting.

Sleeve usually stops at elbow.

Doublet worn under.

Tippet. Could be extension of sleeve hanging down.

Side slit

Cotehardie. Knee length or shorter. Replaces supertunics.

Mantle, mid-calf or longer.

Often fur-lined.

Tippet. Added piece. Often white.

Pouch and dagger.

Elaborate hip belt called knightly girdle.

Decorative cutting of edges—called dagging.

Garter with folly bells.

Particolored costume

Stiffness exaggerated to show how variation occurs.

Hoods worn regularly, alone or under hats, sometimes even sideways.

Liripipe wrapped around head.

Capuchon or turban hood.

Porkpie hat with coif.

Sugarloaf hat.

FOURTEENTH CENTURY

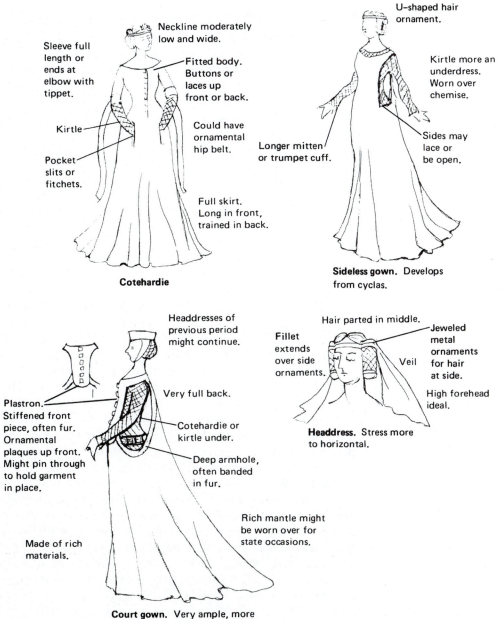

Coteharadie

Neckline moderately low and wide.

Sleeve full length or ends at elbow with tippet.

Fitted body. Buttons or laces up front or back.

Kirtle

Could have ornamental hip belt.

Pocket slits or fitchets.

Full skirt. Long in front, trained in back.

U–shaped hair ornament.

Kirtle more an underdress. Worn over chemise.

Longer mitten or trumpet cuff.

Sides may lace or be open.

Sideless gown. Develops from cyclas.

Headdresses of previous period might continue.

Very full back.

Plastron. Stiffened front piece, often fur. Ornamental plaques up front. Might pin through to hold garment in place.

Cotehardie or kirtle under.

Deep armhole, often banded in fur.

Made of rich materials.

Rich mantle might be worn over for state occasions.

Court gown. Very ample, more elaborate version of sideless gown.

Hair parted in middle.

Fillet extends over side ornaments.

Jeweled metal ornaments for hair at side.

Veil

High forehead ideal.

Headdress. Stress more to horizontal.

◆ Fourteenth- and Early-Fifteenth-Century Costumes

The years between 1375 and 1425 saw a transition from the styles of the fourteenth century to those of the fifteenth century. The young continued to reveal the figure with tight-fitting garments while a stately robe more suitable to the older figure became popular. The man's doublet was now definitely an underdress, stopping at the waist. The body might be cheaper fabric than the sleeves, which showed through the overgarment. Hose took on a new shape to accommodate the rising hemline of the overgarments and were joined together in back and laced up the front with a baglike piece called the *codpiece* tied over the lacing.

The new garment that developed was the *houppeland,* a gown for men and women that was worn at both state and ordinary occasions. This was a very ample gown that fit the shoulders and top of the chest, then fell away in a funnel shape, becoming fuller as it approached the hem. It was caught at the waistline in formal or casual pleats by a belt no longer as ornamental as the knightly girdle. Made of wool, velvet, satin, or damask, the houppeland was usually lined and frequently had dagged edges or fur borders. Hoods were still occasionally worn, as were many styles of caps and hats, including the fez, porkpie, and sugarloaf. The distinctive headgear of the period was the *chaperon.* Shoes that fit close to the ankle, soled hose, or long laced boots were worn, all having a point that could extend out in front of the foot. Occasionally this point became so long that it needed to be attached by a gold chain to the garter. This period was known more for rich fabrics than for jewelry, but jeweled collars were worn at the base of the neck, or long chains were worn over the shoulders. The pouch and dagger were usual accessories, with folly bells still fairly common.

Women continued to wear the gowns stylish in the fourteenth century as well as the *houppeland.* The neck opening might reveal the *kirtle* or a more decorative insert piece called the *stomacher.* The silhouette continued to display the "Gothic slouch." Head covering became even more elaborate, as this time began a period of extraordinary fantasy in headdresses. The accent remained on the horizontal; the hair was generally concealed and sometimes shaved off the forehead, with eyebrows plucked to a thin line or shaved off. Many headdresses were based on the *templers* made of metal and jeweled latticework that began at the temples and covered the ears. The more intricate head coverings were common in England and France, while in Italy braided and twisted hairstyles interwoven with jewels were more often seen.

FOURTEENTH TO FIFTEENTH CENTURY

Rounded, padded chest.

Stops at waist.

Could be mitten cuff.

Hose sewn up back, front laced with codpiece added.

Shoes or soled hose quite pointed.

Doublet. Worn under other garments.

Belted in at waist. Formal or casual pleating.

Funnel sleeve.

Edges frequently dagged or with fur borders.

Ample gown fits shoulders. Widens to hem. Body always has fullness.

Gown length varies. To floor plus train, to calf, to knee, or to thigh.

Houppeland. Formal gown of the period worn for regular or state occasions.

Bottleneck collar.

Body always tight-fitting.

Cotehardie shorter, belted at natural waist.

Doublet

Funnel sleeve

Doublet

Bagpipe sleeve

Any sleeve can be worn with either cotehardie or houppeland. Both sleeves would match.

Long, straight sleeve with slit.

Gathered sleeve with cuff.

Wooden undershoe or pattern

Long point fastened up to garter— called crackow

Cotehardie

FOURTEENTH TO FIFTEENTH CENTURY

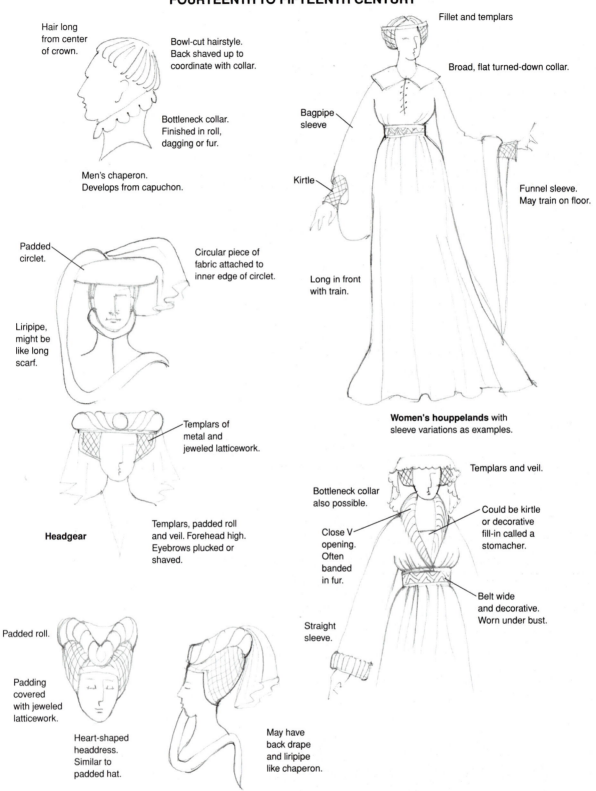

Hair long from center of crown.

Bowl-cut hairstyle. Back shaved up to coordinate with collar.

Bottleneck collar. Finished in roll, dagging or fur.

Men's chaperon. Develops from capuchon.

Padded circlet.

Circular piece of fabric attached to inner edge of circlet.

Liripipe, might be like long scarf.

Templars of metal and jeweled latticework.

Headgear

Templars, padded roll and veil. Forehead high. Eyebrows plucked or shaved.

Padded roll.

Padding covered with jeweled latticework.

Heart-shaped headdress. Similar to padded hat.

May have back drape and liripipe like chaperon.

Fillet and templars

Broad, flat turned-down collar.

Bagpipe sleeve

Kirtle

Funnel sleeve. May train on floor.

Long in front with train.

Women's houppelands with sleeve variations as examples.

Templars and veil.

Bottleneck collar also possible.

Could be kirtle or decorative fill-in called a stomacher.

Close V opening. Often banded in fur.

Belt wide and decorative. Worn under bust.

Straight sleeve.

◆ Mid- to Late-Fifteenth-Century Costumes

The height of this period in France and England was from 1450 to 1485. The elite costume was rich, dignified, elegant, mannered, brilliantly colored, and elaborately patterned. The masculine stress was basically vertical with broad shoulders, deep chest, narrow waist, and fine legs. The feminine stress emphasized the vertical curve with a high waist. Fantastic headdresses were worn. This style began the artificial silhouette that continues more or less to this day. The new man's garment was the *jerkin* which featured full sleeves to give a broad shoulder. The long gown was similar to the jerkin and remained an upper-class garment until the late sixteenth century. It then added a hood and became an official costume of dignitaries. It is the model for the legal and academic gowns. Hose and shoes were as before; the toe point was quite long in the 1560s and 1570s. *Pattens* were worn

FIFTEENTH CENTURY

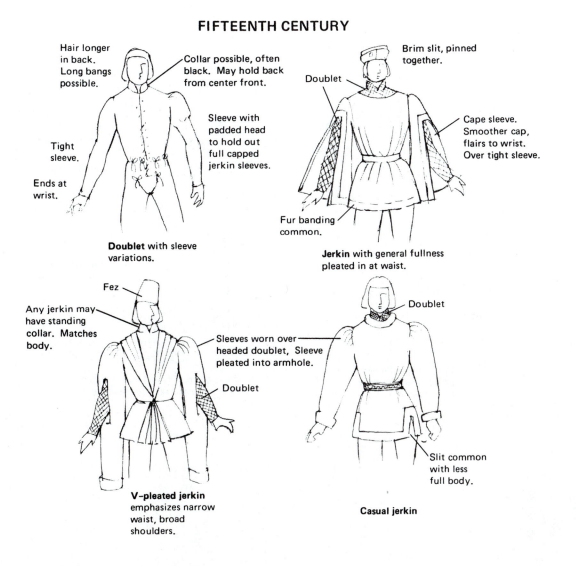

Hair longer in back. Long bangs possible.

Collar possible, often black. May hold back from center front.

Sleeve with padded head to hold out full capped jerkin sleeves.

Tight sleeve.

Ends at wrist.

Doublet with sleeve variations.

Brim slit, pinned together.

Doublet

Cape sleeve. Smoother cap, flairs to wrist. Over tight sleeve.

Fur banding common.

Jerkin with general fullness pleated in at waist.

Fez

Any jerkin may have standing collar. Matches body.

Sleeves worn over headed doublet. Sleeve pleated into armhole.

Doublet

V-pleated jerkin emphasizes narrow waist, broad shoulders.

Doublet

Slit common with less full body.

Casual jerkin

FIFTEENTH CENTURY

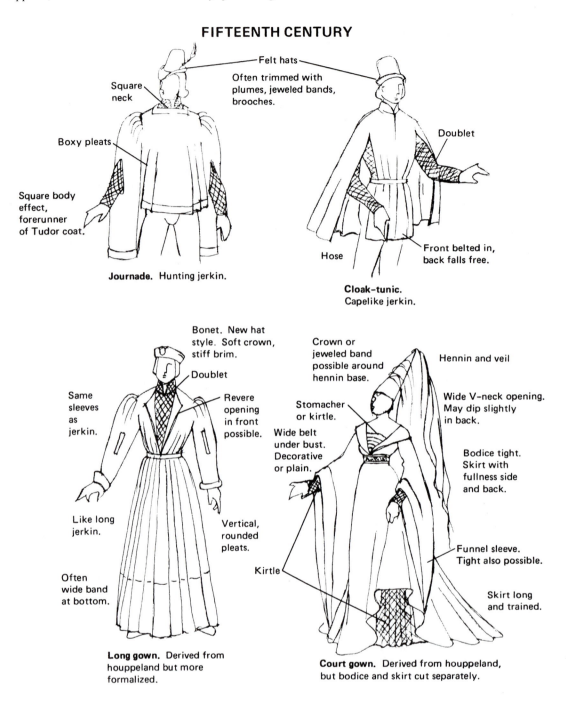

Felt hats
Often trimmed with plumes, jeweled bands, brooches.

Square neck

Boxy pleats

Square body effect, forerunner of Tudor coat.

Journade. Hunting jerkin.

Doublet

Hose

Front belted in, back falls free.

Cloak–tunic. Capelike jerkin.

Bonet. New hat style. Soft crown, stiff brim.

Doublet

Same sleeves as jerkin.

Revere opening in front possible.

Like long jerkin.

Vertical, rounded pleats.

Often wide band at bottom.

Long gown. Derived from houppeland but more formalized.

Crown or jeweled band possible around hennin base.

Hennin and veil

Stomacher or kirtle.

Wide belt under bust. Decorative or plain.

Wide V–neck opening. May dip slightly in back.

Bodice tight. Skirt with fullness side and back.

Kirtle

Funnel sleeve. Tight also possible.

Skirt long and trained.

Court gown. Derived from houppeland, but bodice and skirt cut separately.

under the shoe for protection from mud, and delicate walking sticks and gloves were important accessories. The extraordinary part of the woman's style was the *hennin* (also called steeple headdress), which varied from truncated to long and pointed. It was made of stiff, buckramlike material covered with decorative fabric. It had no visible fastening, though the black U-shaped wire on the forehead may have provided support.

FIFTEENTH CENTURY

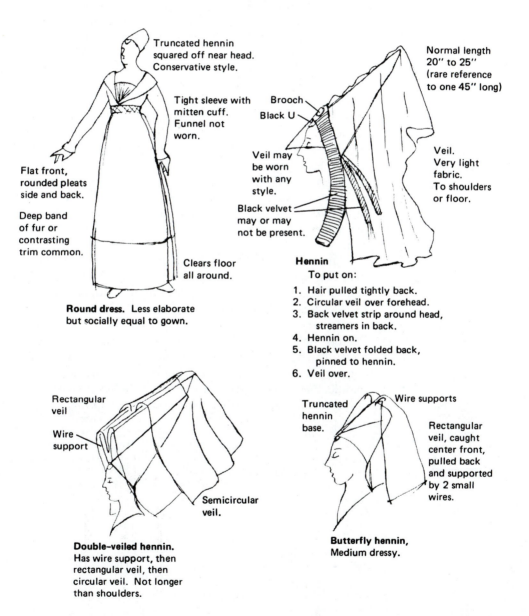

Truncated hennin squared off near head. Conservative style.

Tight sleeve with mitten cuff. Funnel not worn.

Flat front, rounded pleats side and back.

Deep band of fur or contrasting trim common.

Clears floor all around.

Round dress. Less elaborate but socially equal to gown.

Normal length 20″ to 25″ (rare reference to one 45″ long)

Brooch
Black U

Veil may be worn with any style.

Black velvet may or may not be present.

Veil. Very light fabric. To shoulders or floor.

Hennin
To put on:
1. Hair pulled tightly back.
2. Circular veil over forehead.
3. Back velvet strip around head, streamers in back.
4. Hennin on.
5. Black velvet folded back, pinned to hennin.
6. Veil over.

Rectangular veil

Wire support

Semicircular veil.

Double-veiled hennin. Has wire support, then rectangular veil, then circular veil. Not longer than shoulders.

Truncated hennin base.

Wire supports

Rectangular veil, caught center front, pulled back and supported by 2 small wires.

Butterfly hennin, Medium dressy.

◇ Fifteenth- to Sixteenth-Century Costumes

At this time, from about 1485 to 1515, men's costume had a more casual air with less emphasis on the vertical line. The silhouette displayed an irregular, shorter line; the costume looked a bit as if it were falling apart and the stress began heading toward the horizontal. Women however, became even more encased and nunlike. The men's costumes in England and France were very much influenced by the Italian fashions, while women's costumes reflected the feeling of the northern countries.

Men's garments had a generally casual air, with shirts important, low necks, open sleeves, loose casual coats. They wore their hair long and flowing. The doublet now became street dress, often worn merely with hose and perhaps a short cape. For the most part, padding was gone from the chest. The shirt became more important, for much more of it was seen. Made of fine cottons or silks, it was cut full and gathered into the neck opening, which was often square, and into bands at the wrists. Hose became more decorative, with particoloring, and the upper part, around the hips, was often trimmed in contrasting braid. This was the first sign of what was to become a separation of the upper leg covering and lower leg covering. The hose were trussed up to the doublet with very decorative lacings and the shirt was sometimes allowed to puff out between the two garments. An important decorative element was called *cuttes,* the slashing of the outer garment to allow the shirt or other material (such as lining fabric at the hips) to show through. The ornamental costume feeling was enhanced by heavy metal and jeweled shoulder collars, massive chains, brooches, pendants, and rings.

The basic silhouette of the women's garments changed from a mannered elegance and a striking effect to one that was restrained, reserved, and subdued. Before there had been an upward, outward movement; now the look was tightly encased, closing in. Under the gown, the woman wore a stiffened corset, a lightweight shift, and petticoats or underdresses with the top one made of rich fabric since it would show as the skirt was lifted to move. The boned hoop, which was in common use by the Spanish nobility, began to be worn in France and England. Hair was generally parted in the middle, then pulled back, perhaps with a slight wave over the temples, to be covered by a headdress that could be quite enclosing.

FIFTEENTH TO SIXTEENTH CENTURY

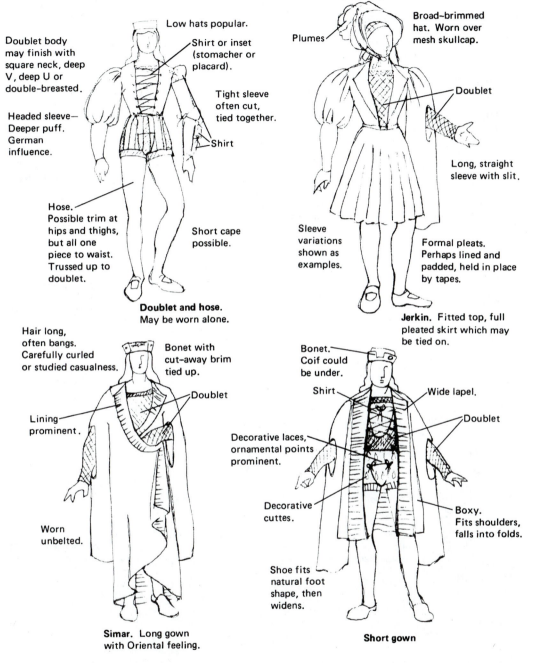

Low hats popular.

Doublet body may finish with square neck, deep V, deep U or double-breasted.

Shirt or inset (stomacher or placard).

Headed sleeve— Deeper puff. German influence.

Tight sleeve often cut, tied together.

Shirt

Hose. Possible trim at hips and thighs, but all one piece to waist. Trussed up to doublet.

Short cape possible.

Doublet and hose. May be worn alone.

Broad-brimmed hat. Worn over mesh skullcap.

Plumes

Doublet

Long, straight sleeve with slit.

Sleeve variations shown as examples.

Formal pleats. Perhaps lined and padded, held in place by tapes.

Jerkin. Fitted top, full pleated skirt which may be tied on.

Hair long, often bangs. Carefully curled or studied casualness.

Bonet with cut-away brim tied up.

Doublet

Lining prominent.

Worn unbelted.

Simar. Long gown with Oriental feeling.

Bonet. Coif could be under.

Shirt

Wide lapel.

Doublet

Decorative laces, ornamental points prominent.

Decorative cuttes.

Boxy. Fits shoulders, falls into folds.

Shoe fits natural foot shape, then widens.

Short gown

FIFTEENTH TO SIXTEENTH CENTURY

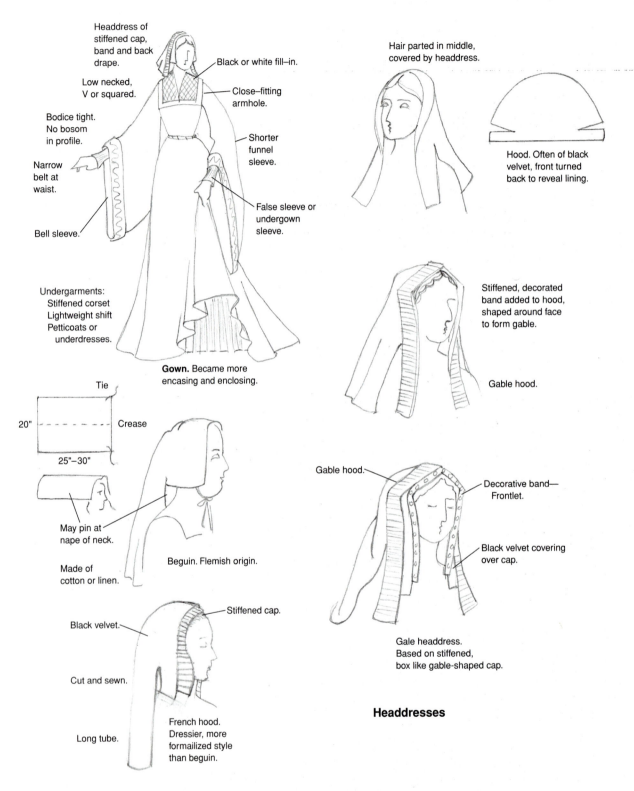

Headdress of stiffened cap, band and back drape.

Black or white fill–in.

Low necked, V or squared.

Close–fitting armhole.

Bodice tight. No bosom in profile.

Shorter funnel sleeve.

Narrow belt at waist.

False sleeve or undergown sleeve.

Bell sleeve.

Undergarments:
Stiffened corset
Lightweight shift
Petticoats or underdresses.

Gown. Became more encasing and enclosing.

Tie

20"

Crease

25"–30"

May pin at nape of neck.

Made of cotton or linen.

Beguin. Flemish origin.

Black velvet.

Cut and sewn.

Stiffened cap.

Long tube.

French hood. Dressier, more formailized style than beguin.

Hair parted in middle, covered by headdress.

Hood. Often of black velvet, front turned back to reveal lining.

Stiffened, decorated band added to hood, shaped around face to form gable.

Gable hood.

Gable hood.

Decorative band— Frontlet.

Black velvet covering over cap.

Gale headdress. Based on stiffened, box like gable-shaped cap.

Headdresses

◈ Early Sixteenth Century—Tudor Costumes

The period from 1515 to 1545 in France and England was one of German influence. Fairly clear outlines gave a feeling of solidity and bulkiness. There was a squareness and breadth for men and a cone shape for women. The gentlemen were massive, strong, broad-shouldered, and arrogantly masculine. Women became enclosed, inactive, and protected.

The men's costume tended to extend away from the body on the horizontal plane. The doublet again became an undergarment and was not worn alone. It might have been padded, though men seemed to follow the trend set by Henry VIII and were heavier. Trunk hose developed from the prominent decoration around the hips of the hose. The embroidered bands became separate pieces called *panes* that opened to reveal the contrasting material beneath. The codpiece was still present, but no longer functional. It was now padded and trimmed, and considered almost obscene in its own time. Panes, lining, and codpiece were permanently attached to the full-length hose underneath, and all tied to the doublet as one unit. More and more embroidered banding was used as a decorative element on the costume, and *cuttes,* commonly seen, were more formally set, with the backing material carefully puffed out, surrounded by embroidery and jewels. Hair was bobbed and moderately long until the 1530s, then cut short till past the end of the century. Beards were squared off and mustaches followed natural growth. Hats were characteristically flat, with feathers following the horizontal line. Heavy, wide, jeweled collars were very common, worn out on the shoulders further to stress the horizontal. Jewels were cut and faceted to add sparkle to the costume.

The women's costume continued many of the shapes used in the previous period, but they seem frozen into a rigid form. Much stiffening and unyielding underpinnings produced a figure that moved as if on wheels, with little flow to either fabric or body. The rigid effect of the female costume owed a great deal to the conical hoop or Spanish *farthingale,* and the *corset,* which was stiffened with bone or even constructed of thin iron bands made in two parts and hinged on the side. Hair was still encased by the headdress.

EARLY SIXTEENTH CENTURY—TUDOR

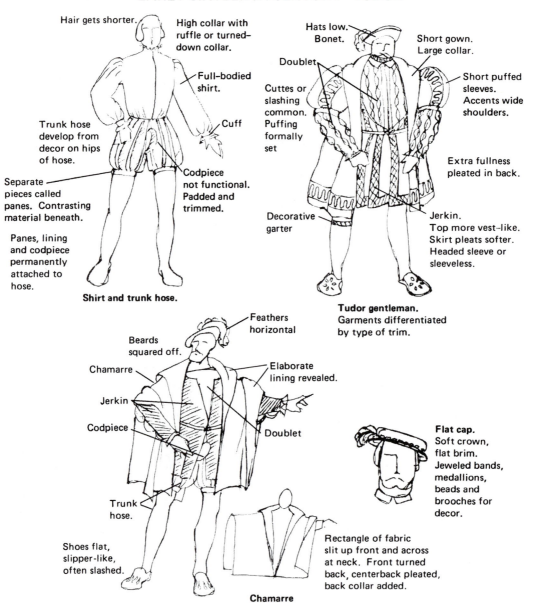

Hair gets shorter.

High collar with ruffle or turned–down collar.

Full-bodied shirt.

Cuff

Trunk hose develop from decor on hips of hose.

Separate pieces called panes. Contrasting material beneath.

Panes, lining and codpiece permanently attached to hose.

Codpiece not functional. Padded and trimmed.

Shirt and trunk hose.

Hats low. Bonet.

Short gown. Large collar.

Doublet

Short puffed sleeves. Accents wide shoulders.

Cuttes or slashing common. Puffing formally set

Extra fullness pleated in back.

Decorative garter

Jerkin. Top more vest–like. Skirt pleats softer. Headed sleeve or sleeveless.

Tudor gentleman. Garments differentiated by type of trim.

Feathers horizontal

Beards squared off.

Chamarre

Jerkin

Codpiece

Elaborate lining revealed.

Doublet

Trunk hose.

Shoes flat, slipper-like, often slashed.

Chamarre

Flat cap. Soft crown, flat brim. Jeweled bands, medallions, beads and brooches for decor.

Rectangle of fabric slit up front and across at neck. Front turned back, centerback pleated, back collar added.

EARLY SIXTEENTH CENTURY—TUDOR

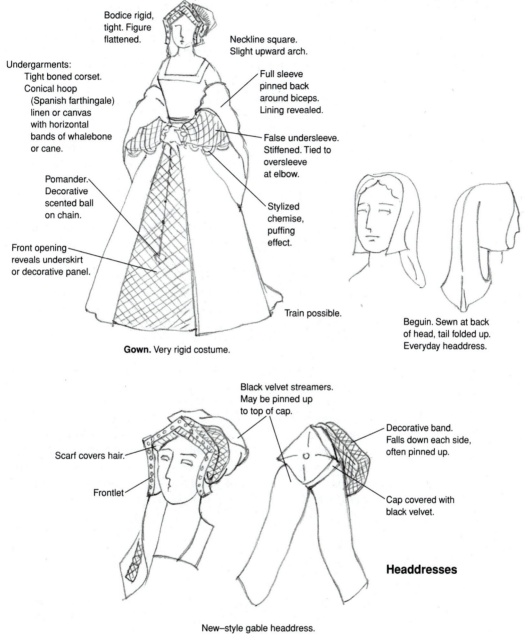

Bodice rigid, tight. Figure flattened.

Neckline square. Slight upward arch.

Undergarments:
Tight boned corset.
Conical hoop
(Spanish farthingale)
linen or canvas
with horizontal
bands of whalebone
or cane.

Full sleeve pinned back around biceps. Lining revealed.

False undersleeve. Stiffened. Tied to oversleeve at elbow.

Pomander. Decorative scented ball on chain.

Stylized chemise, puffing effect.

Front opening reveals underskirt or decorative panel.

Train possible.

Gown. Very rigid costume.

Beguin. Sewn at back of head, tail folded up. Everyday headdress.

Black velvet streamers. May be pinned up to top of cap.

Scarf covers hair.

Frontlet

Decorative band. Falls down each side, often pinned up.

Cap covered with black velvet.

Headdresses

New–style gable headdress. Based on stiffened cap.

◈ Mid-Sixteenth to Early Seventeenth Century— Elizabethan Costumes

Western European costume now followed the lead of Spain, thus the Elizabethan style was one of Spanish influence. As Spain declined as a world power so did its influence wane in clothing styles. The Elizabethan costume developed from 1545 to 1570, was in full flower from 1570 to 1595, and declined from 1595 to 1620. The chief characteristic was extreme rigidity achieved by *bombast,* the padding used to fill out garments. Bombast also included all the stiffening, starching, and wiring used to achieve the epitome of the artificial silhouette. The costume created a shape of its own. As the period declined, the bombast declined and the silhouette wilted.

The ideal gentleman once again had a vertical emphasis, accenting a narrow waist, broad shoulders, and long legs. The shapely leg was now more readily enhanced by the knitted stocking, available because of the invention of the stocking frame. These fit the leg well and still allowed flexibility. The focal point of the costume was the ruff worn at the neck. Overgowns similar to academic gowns were sometimes donned for ceremonial or professional reasons. Gauntlets and regular gloves were commonly worn, ornamental handkerchiefs and delicate walking sticks carried, and masks used by both sexes for incognito situations. The military steel collar, or *gorget,* was sometimes seen with civilian dress. Elaborate jewelry was popular and gems, both false and real, covered garments and hats. Long boots were used for riding.

The rigid woman's costume emphasized a frontal perspective. Bombast created the ideal stiffness and a gliding walk was used, so the fabric had very little flow or movement. The corset was extremely confining and gave the foundation for the long-waisted bodice to extend to a deep point in the center front. The three principal skirt shapes were supported by the funnel farthingale, the cartwheel farthingale, or the bolster and petticoats. Pendant sleeves could be attached behind the regular sleeve for ceremonial occasions. An asymmetrical jewel-and-sash arrangement might be draped over the bodice. Quite a bit of makeup was used.

MID–SIXTEENTH TO EARLY SEVENTEENTH CENTURY—ELIZABETHAN

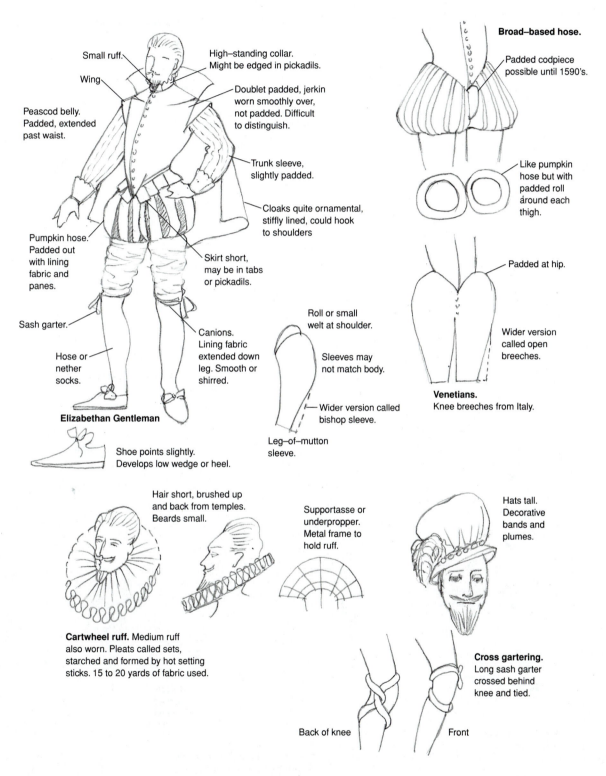

Small ruff.

Wing

High–standing collar. Might be edged in pickadils.

Doublet padded, jerkin worn smoothly over, not padded. Difficult to distinguish.

Peascod belly. Padded, extended past waist.

Trunk sleeve, slightly padded.

Cloaks quite ornamental, stiffly lined, could hook to shoulders

Pumpkin hose. Padded out with lining fabric and panes.

Skirt short, may be in tabs or pickadils.

Sash garter.

Canions. Lining fabric extended down leg. Smooth or shirred.

Hose or nether socks.

Elizabethan Gentleman

Shoe points slightly. Develops low wedge or heel.

Roll or small welt at shoulder.

Sleeves may not match body.

Wider version called bishop sleeve.

Leg–of–mutton sleeve.

Broad–based hose.

Padded codpiece possible until 1590's.

Like pumpkin hose but with padded roll around each thigh.

Padded at hip.

Wider version called open breeches.

Venetians. Knee breeches from Italy.

Hair short, brushed up and back from temples. Beards small.

Cartwheel ruff. Medium ruff also worn. Pleats called sets, starched and formed by hot setting sticks. 15 to 20 yards of fabric used.

Supportasse or underpropper. Metal frame to hold ruff.

Hats tall. Decorative bands and plumes.

Cross gartering. Long sash garter crossed behind knee and tied.

Back of knee

Front

MID–SIXTEENTH TO EARLY SEVENTEENTH CENTURY—ELIZABETHAN

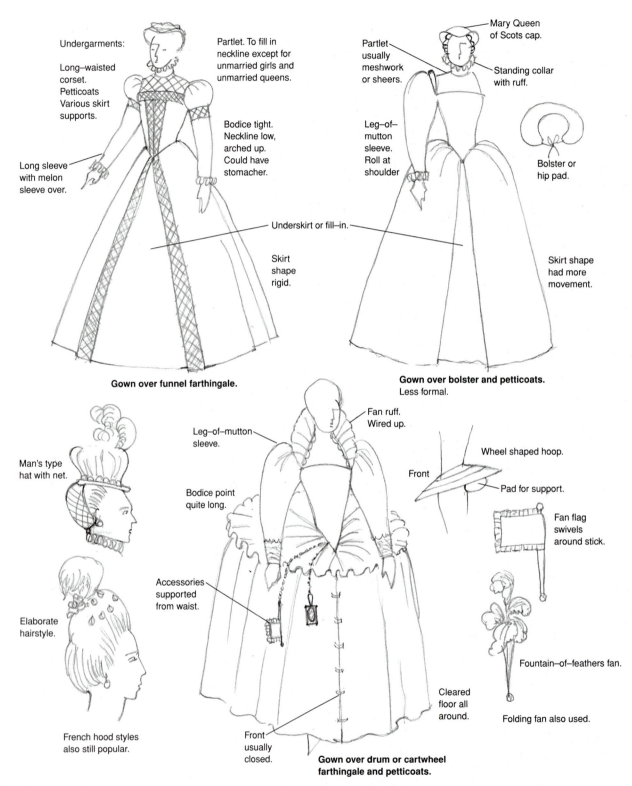

Undergarments:

Long–waisted corset. Petticoats Various skirt supports.

Partlet. To fill in neckline except for unmarried girls and unmarried queens.

Long sleeve with melon sleeve over.

Bodice tight. Neckline low, arched up. Could have stomacher.

Underskirt or fill–in.

Skirt shape rigid.

Gown over funnel farthingale.

Partlet usually meshwork or sheers.

Mary Queen of Scots cap.

Standing collar with ruff.

Leg–of–mutton sleeve. Roll at shoulder

Bolster or hip pad.

Underskirt or fill–in.

Skirt shape had more movement.

Gown over bolster and petticoats.
Less formal.

Man's type hat with net.

Elaborate hairstyle.

French hood styles also still popular.

Leg–of–mutton sleeve.

Bodice point quite long.

Accessories supported from waist.

Front usually closed.

Fan ruff. Wired up.

Gown over drum or cartwheel farthingale and petticoats.

Front

Wheel shaped hoop.

Pad for support.

Fan flag swivels around stick.

Fountain–of–feathers fan.

Folding fan also used.

Cleared floor all around.

◆ Early Seventeenth Century—Cavalier Costumes

The rigid Elizabethan outline became more broken and casual in the Cavalier period, especially for men. The feeling was domestic rather than formal. Spain's domination of the fashion world diminished with its loss of power and France began to regain prestige. Fashion centered in Paris and stayed there to a degree to the present day, though England led in men's clothes after the eighteenth century. The Cavalier period, from 1620 to 1655, showed the influence of the Thirty Years' War fought in Europe during much of this time. Civilian dress reflected the constant presence of soldiers. During the first 20 years of the century, as the Elizabethan costume declined, the shapes stayed much the same but the feeling of bombast was less evident. The Cavalier period seemed to have the starch taken out of it; the costume had a flow, a movement not allowed to happen previously, a feeling for the "swashbuckle" associated with the gentleman soldier.

The doublet became easy-fitting and slightly high-waisted, with little or no padding except over the stomach where belly pieces were the interlinings used to help the garment retain its shape. The jerkin was no longer fashionable and was discarded by 1630. The only remnant was the leather jerkin, or *buff coat* which was of military origin and popular until about 1665. Many types of breeches were worn during this time, though the style that might be thought most typical was long-legged breeches or *Spanish hose.* Two forms not illustrated were *trunk slops,* which were short and quite full, and *open breeches,* which were like long-legged breeches but wider at the knee. Collars and cuffs came in various sizes and shapes but were usually fairly large and decorative. One new form was the *whisk* or *golilla,* a standing-band type with embroidery and lace that lay flat on the tilted wire frame, or underpropper. The image of the dashing gentleman soldier was enhanced by his accessories: sword, baldric, broad military sash, gorget, and gauntlets.

The women of the Cavalier period had a soft, round line and—though the corset continued to be worn—the feeling of extreme rigidity was gone. The waist was raised and the neckline featured a low décolletage with the bosom pushed up by the corset to create a cleavage that was very much a part of the costume. Elaborate lace collars were also quite prominent. Hairstyles began to have a horizontal feeling.

EARLY SEVENTEENTH CENTURY—CAVALIER

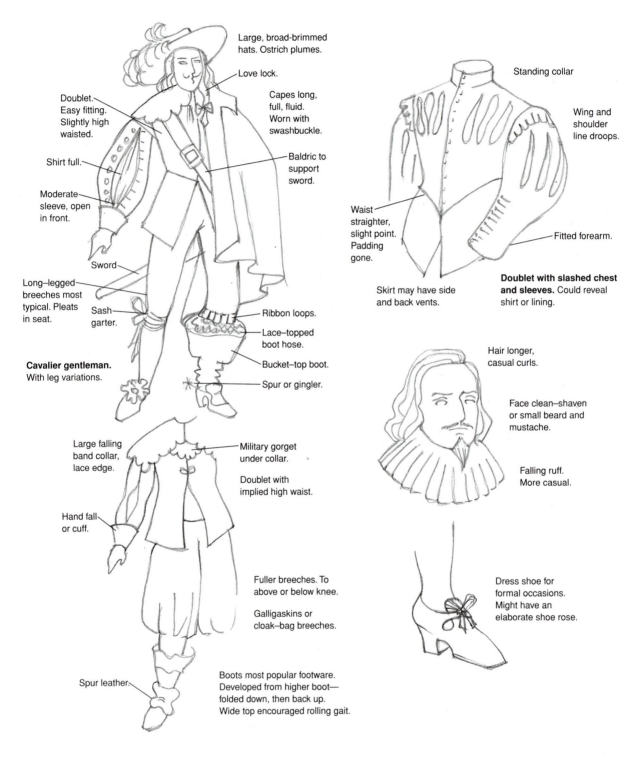

Large, broad-brimmed hats. Ostrich plumes.

Love lock.

Capes long, full, fluid. Worn with swashbuckle.

Doublet. Easy fitting. Slightly high waisted.

Baldric to support sword.

Shirt full.

Moderate sleeve, open in front.

Sword

Long–legged breeches most typical. Pleats in seat.

Sash garter.

Cavalier gentleman. With leg variations.

Ribbon loops.

Lace–topped boot hose.

Bucket–top boot.

Spur or gingler.

Standing collar

Wing and shoulder line droops.

Waist straighter, slight point. Padding gone.

Fitted forearm.

Skirt may have side and back vents.

Doublet with slashed chest and sleeves. Could reveal shirt or lining.

Hair longer, casual curls.

Face clean–shaven or small beard and mustache.

Falling ruff. More casual.

Large falling band collar, lace edge.

Military gorget under collar.

Doublet with implied high waist.

Hand fall or cuff.

Fuller breeches. To above or below knee.

Galligaskins or cloak–bag breeches.

Dress shoe for formal occasions. Might have an elaborate shoe rose.

Spur leather.

Boots most popular footware. Developed from higher boot— folded down, then back up. Wide top encouraged rolling gait.

EARLY SEVENTEENTH CENTURY—CAVALIER

Ballooned underdress sleeve, waisted at elbow. Could be paned.

Undergarments:
Corset
Petticoats
Chemise
Perhaps
    hip roll.

Overgown. Dark, open-up front. Sleeve open and to elbow. (For formal occasions.)

Gowns slightly high–waisted. Rounded point in front.

Fullness to sides and back. Could train.

Underskirt

Cavalier woman. Soft, round line.

Low neck. Cleavage prominent.

Long sleeve. Stops above wrist.

Ribbon sash.

Basques or tabs.

Gown with basqued bodice.

Sleeves set into side back seam for small waist illusion

Hair accents horizontal, curled out at side, up in back.

Standing, spreading collar.

Sheer fill–in, tucker.

Bow or flower highlights décolletage.

Back bun.

Broad Bertha collar (falling band).

Hats worn more by middle class and for travel.

Neck kerchief.

Pearl chokers, bracelets and earrings were popular jewelry.

◆ Mid-Seventeenth Century—Petticoat Breeches

The garments worn by the men of 1655 to 1680 were fairly simple, but a gentleman could become almost useless because of the profusion of detail applied to the shapes, particularly in the French court. The doublet became quite short and skimpy, in some instances almost a bolero. The shorter sleeve could be either plain, open on the front seam, or paned. Much of the shirt could show, so it was very full and made of fine fabric, often with ruffles at the wrist and down the front. Legs might be covered by the Spanish hose, open breeches that were now even looser around the knee, or *petticoat breeches*. Baggy underbreeches that gathered into a band above the knee could be worn with the latter.

The coat and vest, prototypes of those worn today, began to be seen in the mid-1660s. The coat had very little shaping as it fit the shoulders and tapered out somewhat to hang loosely to about the knee. It was worn over first the doublet, then the vest. Cloaks were less commonly seen after 1670 and were often replaced by an overcoat. Boots were less fashionable and worn more for riding. The shoe had a high, square heel, square toe, and squared tongue. Hair was worn long, to the shoulders, till about 1660, when wigs came into fashion and were an essential part of dress. If a gentleman were not rich enough to have a wig, he would dress his hair to look like one. The most popular hair color was blond, appropriate for those living in the court of the Sun King, Louis XIV. In the boudoir, turbans were worn over shaved heads. Hats were fairly large and plumed but not as dashing as before. As the wigs got bigger the hats became less important and were often carried. In addition to all the trim, accessories might include gloves, handkerchiefs, sashes, mirrors, combs, snuff boxes, beauty patches, and paint. There was, however, very little jewelry.

The women of this time period were rather regulated and subdued compared to their male counterparts. The bodice was again long-waisted, close-fitted, and boned, with a medium-low horizontal neckline that had a somewhat off-the-shoulder look. The skirt was closely gathered in small, carefully set pleats that flared out at the hips and provided fullness at the sides and back. The pearl choker necklace and drop earrings continued to be the most popular jewelry, and a few ribbon loops might be used. The fabrics used by women did tend to be more ornamental, since less trim was added.

MID-SEVENTEENTH CENTURY — PETTICOAT BREECHES

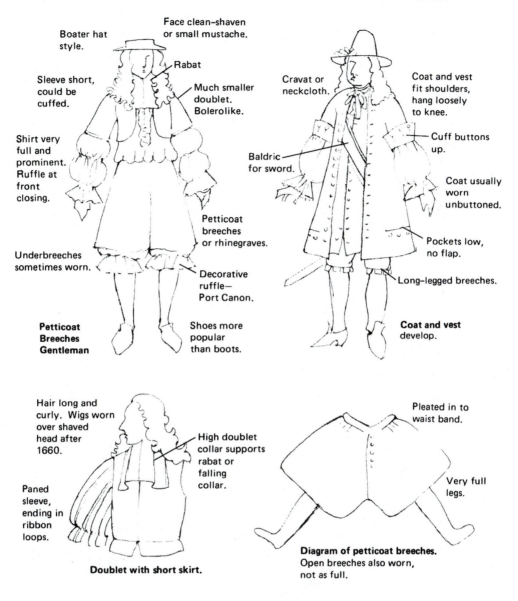

Boater hat style.

Face clean-shaven or small mustache.

Rabat

Sleeve short, could be cuffed.

Much smaller doublet. Bolerolike.

Shirt very full and prominent. Ruffle at front closing.

Underbreeches sometimes worn.

Petticoat breeches or rhinegraves.

Decorative ruffle— Port Canon.

Petticoat Breeches Gentleman

Shoes more popular than boots.

Cravat or neckcloth.

Coat and vest fit shoulders, hang loosely to knee.

Baldric for sword.

Cuff buttons up.

Coat usually worn unbuttoned.

Pockets low, no flap.

Long-legged breeches.

Coat and vest develop.

Hair long and curly. Wigs worn over shaved head after 1660.

High doublet collar supports rabat or falling collar.

Paned sleeve, ending in ribbon loops.

Doublet with short skirt.

Pleated in to waist band.

Very full legs.

Diagram of petticoat breeches. Open breeches also worn, not as full.

MID-SEVENTEENTH CENTURY—PETTICOAT BREECHES

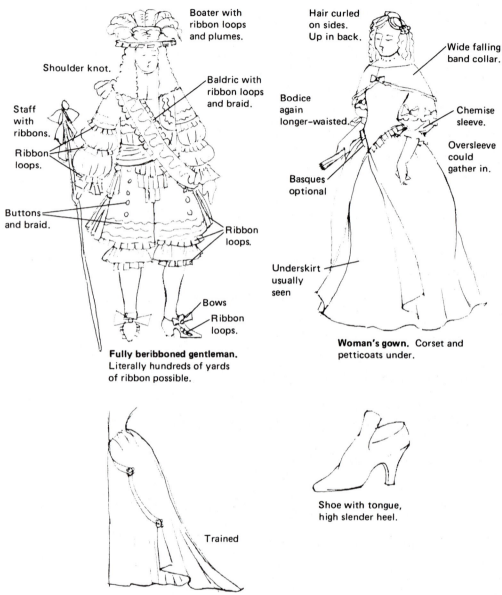

Boater with ribbon loops and plumes.

Shoulder knot.

Baldric with ribbon loops and braid.

Staff with ribbons.

Ribbon loops.

Buttons and braid.

Ribbon loops.

Bows

Ribbon loops.

Fully beribboned gentleman. Literally hundreds of yards of ribbon possible.

Hair curled on sides. Up in back.

Wide falling band collar.

Bodice again longer-waisted.

Chemise sleeve.

Oversleeve could gather in.

Basques optional

Underskirt usually seen

Woman's gown. Corset and petticoats under.

Trained

Skirt can be formally caught back.

Shoe with tongue, high slender heel.

◈ Late Seventeenth to Early Eighteenth Century— Restoration Costumes

The Restoration costume, prominent from about 1680 to 1715, had a heavy opulence and deep, rich colors, similar to the Baroque art of the time. The primary garments for men were the coat, vest, and breeches, which became much more tailored. The art of tailoring developed during this century as clothes were cut and interfaced to maintain a particular shape, no longer relying on the heavy padding and bombast of undergarments to create the form.

The coat was now more fitted and conformed to the chest, defined the waist, then flared out over the hips in pleats that were controlled at the top by stitching hidden by a large button. The vest was cut similarly to the coat though the back panel, usually hidden, could be much shorter than the front and might be made of cheaper material. The shirt was not nearly so prominent in this costume and was often only seen in the heavy lace ruffle that came to the knuckles. Breeches were now closer-fitting, though still with fullness in the seat, and came to below the knee where they buttoned, buckled, or tied. Capes were not as popular as before; when worn they were full, to the knee or calf, and often had rounded collars. Fabrics varied from simple wools to very rich brocades. Rich bands were used to edge the coat front opening, cuffs, and pockets. Baldrics, hip sashes, and muffs were common, and snuff was used extensively, causing spots of discoloration on the jabot.

Women's garments stressed the vertical and took on a feeling of authority and aggressiveness. A bustle was added to the silhouette and a great deal of ornamentation was used. The long-waisted bodice was worn over a very tight corset and the stomacher in the center front extended to a point past the waist. The gathered and trained full overskirt was often turned back and fastened to reveal the rich lining or the inside of fabric that had been woven to be reversible. The primary headdress was the *fontange*. The costume was one of rich embroidery but used very little jewelry, with pear-shaped pearl earrings and a single strand of pearls at the neck the most popular accessories. Very elegant aprons were sometimes worn and the folding fan was a definite part of the ensemble. Parasols and muffs were carried outdoors and the mask was always appropriate for any incognito situation. Elbow-length gloves complemented the shorter sleeve.

LATE SEVENTEENTH TO EARLY EIGHTEENTH CENTURY—RESTORATION

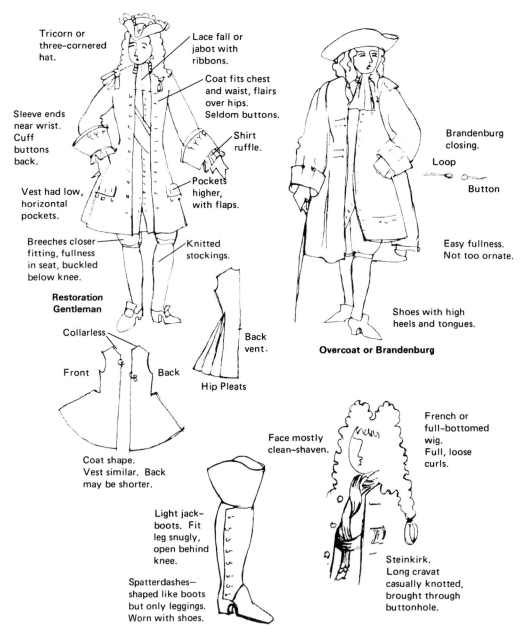

Tricorn or three–cornered hat.

Lace fall or jabot with ribbons.

Coat fits chest and waist, flairs over hips. Seldom buttons.

Sleeve ends near wrist. Cuff buttons back.

Shirt ruffle.

Vest had low, horizontal pockets.

Pockets higher, with flaps.

Breeches closer fitting, fullness in seat, buckled below knee.

Knitted stockings.

Restoration Gentleman

Collarless

Front   Back

Coat shape. Vest similar. Back may be shorter.

Back vent.

Hip Pleats

Brandenburg closing.

Loop

Button

Easy fullness. Not too ornate.

Shoes with high heels and tongues.

Overcoat or Brandenburg

Light jack-boots. Fit leg snugly, open behind knee.

Spatterdashes— shaped like boots but only leggings. Worn with shoes.

Face mostly clean-shaven.

French or full-bottomed wig. Full, loose curls.

Steinkirk. Long cravat casually knotted, brought through buttonhole.

LATE SEVENTEENTH TO EARLY EIGHTEENTH CENTURY—RESTORATION

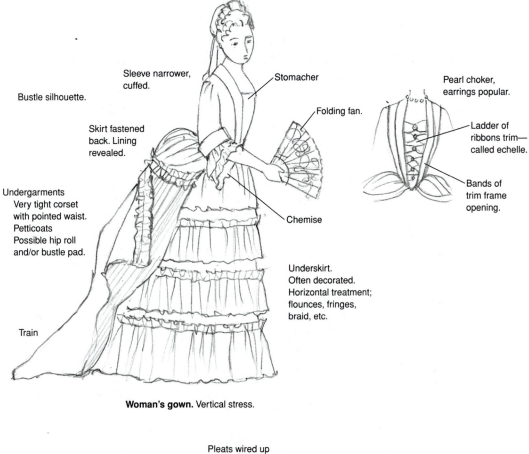

Sleeve narrower, cuffed.

Bustle silhouette.

Skirt fastened back. Lining revealed.

Undergarments
  Very tight corset
  with pointed waist.
  Petticoats
  Possible hip roll
  and/or bustle pad.

Train

Stomacher

Folding fan.

Chemise

Underskirt.
Often decorated.
Horizontal treatment;
flounces, fringes,
braid, etc.

Pearl choker, earrings popular.

Ladder of ribbons trim— called echelle.

Bands of trim frame opening.

Woman's gown. Vertical stress.

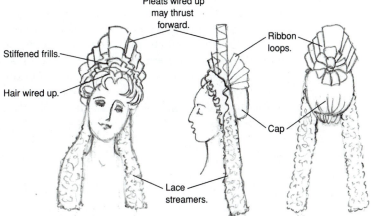

Pleats wired up
may thrust
forward.

Stiffened frills.

Hair wired up.

Ribbon loops.

Cap

Lace streamers.

Fontange. Primary headdress.

◆ The First Half of the Eighteenth Century— Rococo Costumes

The heavy Baroque grandeur gave way to the more informal, intimate atmosphere of the Rococo with its lighter, buoyant silks and cottons in subtle and lighthearted colors. The general mood was soft and reclining as opposed to the heavy, upright opulence of the period before. The basic thrust of this early-eighteenth-century feeling continued to about 1755, though there were no really striking changes until closer to the end of the century. Social pressures at this time had a strong influence on the clothing, for the lower classes became less satisfied with their lot and sought to climb the ladder of society. The dress of the higher ranks was still restrictive, but as the result of social changes there was more mobility of forms between the classes. The dress coat was made of linens, silks, velvets, and brocades, sometimes shot with metallic threads. The frock coat was mostly wool. Cloaks were occasionally worn, often with a collar, buttons down the front, and slits for arms. Queue wigs became popular, so named because the back hair was longer and controlled in a particular way. For example, the back hair of the bag wig was caught in a black fabric bag. The front hair of the wig, called the *foretop* or *toupee*, was brushed back from the forehead and perhaps padded up a bit. The side hair was curled or frizzed in front of the ears. A non-queue style was the bob wig with bushy, curly hair that came to the jawline or shoulder. Wigs were made of human or animal hair and usually powdered white or gray for dress. A gentleman might style his own hair, but this was not considered fashionable. Common accessories included gloves, sashes, handkerchiefs, muffs, swords, canes, watches, and snuff boxes.

Women's garments were also made of more lightweight fabrics and became softer and less formal, with a horizontal feeling. Short capes or large scarves were the most common type of outer garments. Accessories included elegant aprons, ribbon neck bands, ribbon bows, narrow belts, elbow-length gloves, small muffs, handkerchiefs, and folding fans. Necklaces of three or four rows of pearls or gems might be worn at the neck. Makeup and beauty patches were prominent. Outdoors women could wear hoods or hats. Shoes were pointed and had high, slender heels that might be waisted—that is, shaped in from the heel of the shoe, then widened again at the base.

FIRST HALF OF THE EIGHTEENTH CENTURY—ROCOCO

Front straight, usually not buttoned.

Vest buttoned at waist.

All buttonholes may not open.

Skirt interfaced for stiffness.

Stiffened vest under.

Stiffened stock at neck. Steinkirk or cravat possible.

Fit chest and waist closely.

Sleeve tighter.

Closed cuff.

Pockets higher.

Early dress coat. Stress to horizontal. Made of silks, velvets, brocades.

Always had collar called cape.

Cuffless slit sleeve.

Made of plainer wools, tweeds.

Shoe—lower heel.

Frock coat. Adopted from working class. Looser fit, less interfacing. More practical fabric.

Worn in country.

Collarless

Vest shortens. Back much shorter.

1740s dress coat. Coat front and vest begin to cut back.

Coat back. 3 to 6 pleats each side. Perhaps inverted pleat at back slit.

Open cuff. Open on back seam.

Cuff styles possible on any coat style.

Tricorn hat.

Standing collar.

Broad, flat collar.

Deep boot cuff. Popular in 1730s.

Like coat, heavier, looser fit.

Overcoat. Called surtout, great coat, redingote or wrap rascal.

FIRST HALF OF THE EIGHTEENTH CENTURY—ROCOCO

Night cap

Shawl collar

Face usually clean-shaven.

Hair loop.

Campaign or travelling wig.

Pigtail. Hair wrapped in black ribbon.

Wigs with queues

Worn casually at home.

Similar to coat shape but looser.

Waistband laced in back.

Foretop or toupee.

Bow

Solitaire. Black bowtie.

Hair in black bag.

Hair braided.

Dressing gown.

Bag wig

Ramillies

Cut wide in fork. Baggy crotch, pleats in back. Fit thigh and knee.

Variety of wig styles

Full fall breeches.
Full fall closing (like sailor pants).
Small fall possible.

Undergarments:
Tight corset
Petticoats
Various hoop petticoats.

Round-earred cap.

Robings frame opening.

Casaquin jacket.

Stomacher

Bodice back fits to body. English robe style.

Chemise

Open robe gown.
Most common type.

Oblong hoop or panier under. Wide at hips, narrow front to back.

Cupola or bell hoop under. Round shape.

Underskirt

Separate bodice and skirt or petticoat.

FIRST HALF OF THE EIGHTEENTH CENTURY—ROCOCO

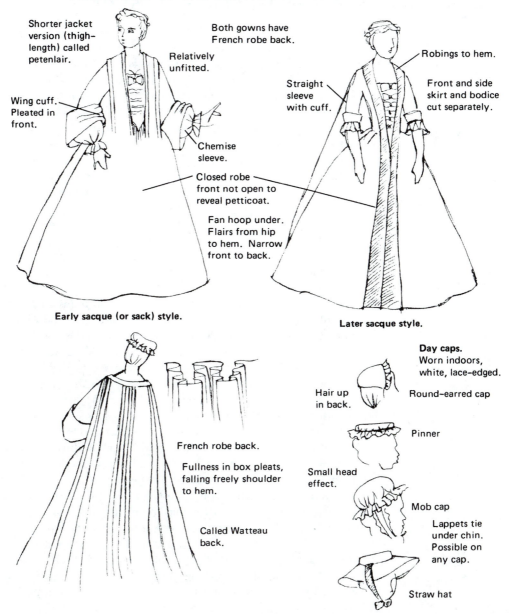

Shorter jacket version (thigh-length) called petenlair.

Both gowns have French robe back.

Relatively unfitted.

Wing cuff. Pleated in front.

Straight sleeve with cuff.

Robings to hem.

Front and side skirt and bodice cut separately.

Chemise sleeve.

Closed robe front not open to reveal petticoat.

Fan hoop under. Flairs from hip to hem. Narrow front to back.

Early sacque (or sack) style.

Later sacque style.

French robe back.

Fullness in box pleats, falling freely shoulder to hem.

Called Watteau back.

Hair up in back.

Small head effect.

Day caps. Worn indoors, white, lace-edged.

Round-earred cap

Pinner

Mob cap

Lappets tie under chin. Possible on any cap.

Straw hat

◆ The Mid-Eighteenth Century—Georgian Costumes

The period from 1755 to 1780 showed a continuation of the trends that began earlier. The men's dress coat fit closer to the body and the frock coat became even more acceptable and was seen everywhere but at court. The skirt of the frock coat was likely to be shorter, especially for sports and riding. The vest was now much shorter than the coat and the breeches, which were more visible, fit the leg quite well while still cut with fullness in the seat. The most popular type of outerwear was the large overcoat called the *surtout, greatcoat,* or *caped coat* that could finish at the neck with one, two, or three broad falling collars or capes. Wigs without queues were not common, though the full-bottomed wig was used by dignitaries. In the 1770s the foretop of the wig was padded up. Jockey boots with a tight turned-down cuff were the most fashionable boot style.

The dandies of the period, called Macaronis, took all fashion elements to extremes. They wore their clothes cut quite tight, their coattails quite short, their shoes very low and slipperlike, and in the 1770s they often had the foretop of the wig padded to excessive heights, topped with a tiny tricorn.

Women's gowns in this period had a great many variations. The sack was still quite popular but now worn as an open robe with robings that framed the bodice opening and continued down the skirt front to the hem. The skirt on any gown might be caught up in some way to reveal more of the underskirt. The new-style gown was the *polonaise,* which had the overskirt permanently sewed up in three puffs and the underskirt shorter—a style that was particularly popular with Marie Antoinette, who found it most suitable for gamboling in her gardens at Versailles. Women's hair also went to extremes in the 1770s and the height of the toupee often exceeded the length of the face and was achieved with such additives as false hair, pads, lard, and pomantum liberally coated with powder and topped with some ingenious decoration. These concoctions might be left in place for a month or two, revealing some unpleasant surprises when dismantled. The *Salisbury Journal* in 1777 advertised "nightcaps made of silver wire so strong that no mouse or even a rat can gnaw through them," being sold because of "the many melancholy accidents that have lately happened in consequence of mice getting into ladies hair in the night time." Shoes continued to have high, slender, waisted heels that might be placed forward under the instep to give the appearance of a tiny foot peeking out from under the ruffled skirt.

MID-EIGHTEENTH CENTURY—GEORGIAN

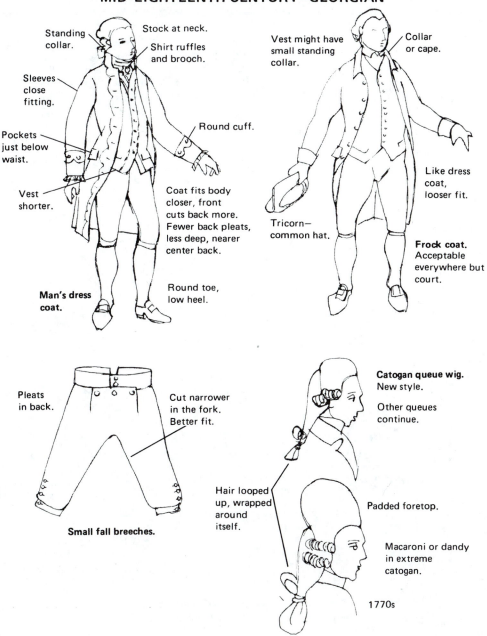

Standing collar.

Stock at neck.

Shirt ruffles and brooch.

Sleeves close fitting.

Round cuff.

Pockets just below waist.

Vest shorter.

Coat fits body closer, front cuts back more. Fewer back pleats, less deep, nearer center back.

Man's dress coat.

Round toe, low heel.

Vest might have small standing collar.

Collar or cape.

Like dress coat, looser fit.

Tricorn— common hat.

Frock coat. Acceptable everywhere but court.

Pleats in back.

Cut narrower in the fork. Better fit.

Small fall breeches.

Hair looped up, wrapped around itself.

Catogan queue wig. New style.

Other queues continue.

Padded foretop.

Macaroni or dandy in extreme catogan.

1770s

MID-EIGHTEENTH CENTURY—GEORGIAN

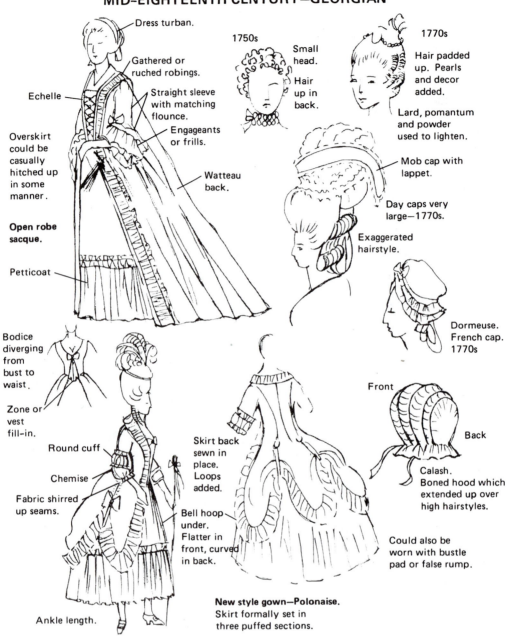

Dress turban.

Gathered or ruched robings.

Echelle

Straight sleeve with matching flounce.

Engageants or frills.

Overskirt could be casually hitched up in some manner.

Open robe sacque.

Watteau back.

Petticoat

1750s
Small head.
Hair up in back.

1770s
Hair padded up. Pearls and decor added.

Lard, pomantum and powder used to lighten.

Mob cap with lappet.

Day caps very large—1770s.

Exaggerated hairstyle.

Dormeuse. French cap. 1770s

Bodice diverging from bust to waist.

Zone or vest fill-in.

Round cuff

Chemise

Fabric shirred up seams.

Skirt back sewn in place. Loops added.

Bell hoop under. Flatter in front, curved in back.

Ankle length.

New style gown—Polonaise. Skirt formally set in three puffed sections.

Front

Back

Calash. Boned hood which extended up over high hairstyles.

Could also be worn with bustle pad or false rump.

◆ Costumes at the End of the Eighteenth Century

The end of the eighteenth century brought a basic change in men's clothing. This change began in the 1780s and was even more evident in the 1790s. Men ceased to be colorful peacocks, and status was shown by clothes that were tailored to perfection out of very good wool cloth, considered the most suitable for the tight styles that became popular. Men's dress became more somber and social superiority was expressed in a much more subtle fashion. The figure accented the chest and shoulders with a small waist and long leg. Underwaistcoats were sometimes worn to give the gentleman three layers to emphasize his chest. Hats included a form of tricorn called *the fantail,* the *bicorn,* and a round hat with a tall, straight crown and small brim.

The styles of the women changed more rapidly than those of the men. The silhouette of the 1780s was quite different from that of the 1770s, and the 1790s had yet another look. In addition to the 1780s styles shown, a chemise gown, which slipped over the head and was casually sashed in at the waist, was worn. The separate jacket and skirt was again quite popular, with the jacket bodice fitting snugly to the waist and flaring to the thigh or knee. False rumps were present under all styles of gowns. Indoor caps and turbans continued. Hats developed into wide, sweepings plumed millinery masterpieces. During the 1790s the high-waisted classical-style gowns became the fashion. White dresses of muslin, cambric, and calico were common. Though the fashion was thought to be very Greek, it was actually quite diluted by many elements retained from the previous period. Shoes were low slippers or sandals and shawls and stoles were the regular outdoor garments.

END OF THE EIGHTEENTH CENTURY

Van Dyck curls.
Longer, casual. 1790s.

Standing collar.

Wide lapel.

Much chest emphasis.
May be padded.

Double–breasted vest.
Shawl collar.

Tight sleeve.

Coat cuts back.
Shallow side-back pleats.

Pantaloon breeches.
Longer, to ankle.
Very tight.

Mid–calf boots popular.

Gentleman in Frock Coat

Standing collar and lapel.

Welt pockets.

Double–breasted vests common, stop at waist.

Fit higher on waist.
Held up by suspenders or braces.

Small fall closure.

Very tight— some too tight to sit.

Knee breeches or smallclothes.

1780s wigs as before but simpler, more casual around face.

High stock.

1780s strained back pigtail wig. Becomes law court style.

Cravat wound around and tied.

1790s Brutus head.
Casual, tousled look.

Large hats.

Soft, full hair.

Buffon and lapels emphasize bust.

Tight sleeves.
Full or 3/4 length.

Sash

Open robe 1780s

Small train.

END OF THE EIGHTEENTH CENTURY

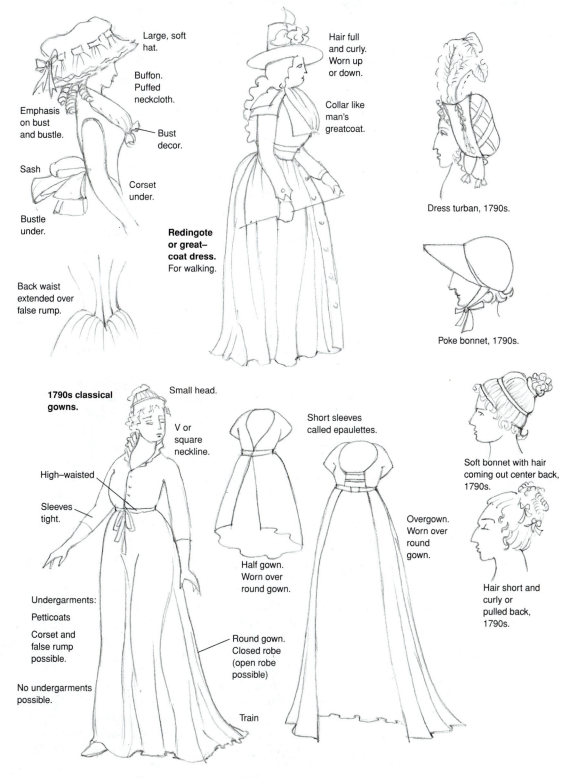

Large, soft hat.

Buffon. Puffed neckcloth.

Emphasis on bust and bustle.

Bust decor.

Sash

Corset under.

Bustle under.

Back waist extended over false rump.

Hair full and curly. Worn up or down.

Collar like man's greatcoat.

Redingote or great–coat dress. For walking.

Dress turban, 1790s.

Poke bonnet, 1790s.

1790s classical gowns.

Small head.

V or square neckline.

High–waisted

Sleeves tight.

Undergarments:

Petticoats

Corset and false rump possible.

No undergarments possible.

Round gown. Closed robe (open robe possible)

Train

Short sleeves called epaulettes.

Half gown. Worn over round gown.

Overgown. Worn over round gown.

Soft bonnet with hair coming out center back, 1790s.

Hair short and curly or pulled back, 1790s.

◆ Nineteenth-Century Costumes

The nineteenth century was a time of rapid changes in both society and clothing styles. A great many books and periodicals were printed and are still available. Detailed sources are not difficult to find and, in most cases, are fairly easy to understand. During this time the Industrial Revolution had its effect on costume as the political, social, and moral power shifted toward the middle class, and the soot and dirt from smokestacks and factories required more practical fabrics. The first 20 years, known as the Regency, were based on classical lines. The rest of the century is thought of as Victorian, and the various styles are considered Gothic.

Men's clothes became less and less distinguished as the century wore on, but in the first two decades the true gentleman was concerned with fine fabric, expert cutting, and skillful tailoring. The emphasis was still on the deep chest, trim waist, and long leg. The neck linen was worn very high, framing the chin and brushing the earlobes. All styles of leg wear were high-waisted. The most popular overcoat was the *Garrick,* with many deep collars or capes and a standing collar. During the decade between 1820 and 1830, the Age of Romanticism began highlighting a pinched waist, rounded hips, and full chest. To aid this look a gentleman might have worn a corset and padding. In the mid-1820s a new style of frock coat became popular, one with a straight front that did not cut back at the waist. It continued to be important throughout the century, with the tailcoat relegated to evening and formal wear by the 1850s. A few gradual changes took place from 1830 to 1840, and during the decade from 1840 to 1850 the last vestiges of the true dandy began to disappear. Rich colors, pleated frills, and smart tailoring faded away and color seemed to be restricted to the vest and tie. In the late 1840s the more conservative suit coat began to appear and for day wear the gentleman was free to choose between it and the frock coat. The smoking jacket was also introduced. Both fitted and loose overcoats were worn. Fitted cloaks were also common; these often included an overcape. Wellington boots were the usual day wear; low shoes were worn for evening dress. The period between 1850 and 1860 was one in which the matched suit of coat, vest, and trousers became widely worn. Called the *ditto* suit, the coat or sack coat was square and boxy. The top hat was still popular and soft felt and straw hats began to appear. The suit from 1860 to 1870 buttoned high up the front to the small collar, eliminating the lapels. *Knickerbockers,* loose breeches gathered into a knee band, began to be worn for sports. Overcoats could be single- or double-breasted. The cloak, called the *Inverness* or *Ulster,* fit fairly closely with a circular overcape and two long openings for the arms. The deerstalker cap in plaid or tweed was used for sports.

The 1870s began an era when more and more factory-produced clothes could be found, with a corresponding decrease in the quality of the garments. Despite the general inelegance that was affecting men's fashions, there was a considerable amount of dandyism in the 1880s. For evening wear the swallowtail coat was worn. The dinner jacket or tuxedo was introduced. A casual jacket worn at sporting occasions was the belted *Norfolk,* usually made of tweed. No striking changes occurred in the last decade of

NINETEENTH-CENTURY MEN

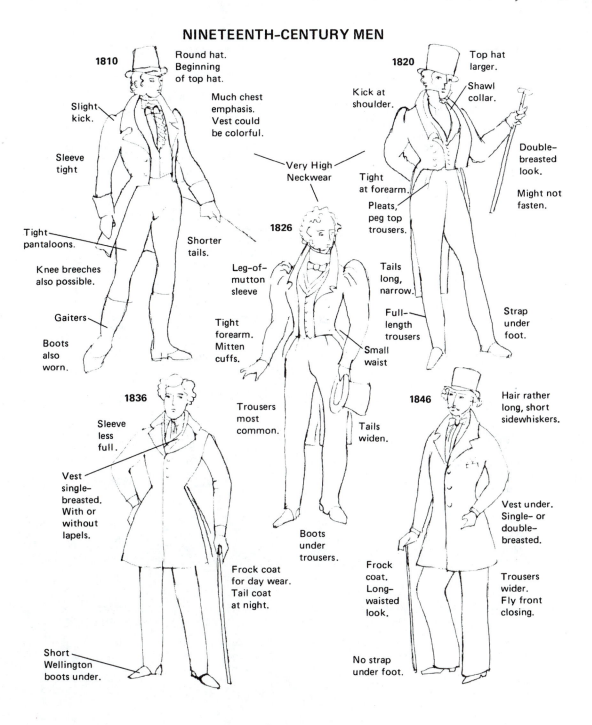

1810

Round hat. Beginning of top hat.

Slight kick.

Much chest emphasis. Vest could be colorful.

Sleeve tight

Very High Neckwear

Tight pantaloons.

Shorter tails.

Knee breeches also possible.

Gaiters

Boots also worn.

1820

Top hat larger.

Kick at shoulder.

Shawl collar.

Double-breasted look.

Tight at forearm.

Might not fasten.

Pleats, peg top trousers.

Tails long, narrow.

Full-length trousers

Strap under foot.

1826

Leg-of-mutton sleeve

Tight forearm. Mitten cuffs.

Small waist

Trousers most common.

Tails widen.

Boots under trousers.

1836

Sleeve less full.

Vest single-breasted. With or without lapels.

Frock coat for day wear. Tail coat at night.

Short Wellington boots under.

1846

Hair rather long, short sidewhiskers.

Vest under. Single- or double-breasted.

Frock coat. Long-waisted look.

Trousers wider. Fly front closing.

No strap under foot.

NINETEENTH–CENTURY MEN

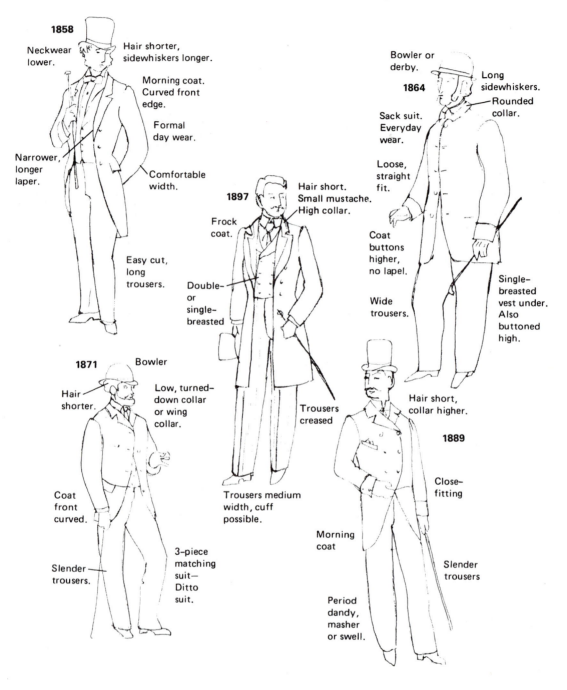

1858

Neckwear lower.

Hair shorter, sidewhiskers longer.

Morning coat. Curved front edge.

Formal day wear.

Narrower, longer laper.

Comfortable width.

Easy cut, long trousers.

1864

Bowler or derby.

Long sidewhiskers.

Rounded collar.

Sack suit. Everyday wear.

Loose, straight fit.

Coat buttons higher, no lapel.

Wide trousers.

Single-breasted vest under. Also buttoned high.

1897

Frock coat.

Hair short. Small mustache. High collar.

Double- or single-breasted

Trousers creased

Trousers medium width, cuff possible.

1871

Bowler

Hair shorter.

Low, turned-down collar or wing collar.

Coat front curved.

Slender trousers.

3-piece matching suit— Ditto suit.

1889

Hair short, collar higher.

Close-fitting

Morning coat

Slender trousers

Period dandy, masher or swell.

the century. Suits had a fairly easy cut and trousers were of comfortable proportions. The clean-shaven look prevailed; more conservative men wore mustaches, while their elders grew beards.

During the first 10 years of the century the chief characteristics of the fashionable woman included a tall, slender, willowy silhouette with a high waistline and light, supple, clinging fabrics; low shoes without heels; scarves; and stoles. Evening gowns were elaborately trimmed. An overcoat, the *pelisse* or *redingote,* could be worn, as well as a short jacket. Gloves, handkerchiefs, and purses were common accessories. The period between 1810 and 1820 was one of transition, with the high waistline continuing but the classical line forgotten in the increasing use of Gothic ornamentation. For walking, a woman could wear a pelisse or woman's Garrick. Gloves were important. In the years between 1820 and 1830 the waistline lowered and the accent moved more to the horizontal as the skirt and sleeves got fuller. Hats, fans, muffs, parasols, and quite a bit of jewelry were usual accessories. The styles of the 1820s continued to expand in the 1830s, reaching their peak around 1836. There was a buoyancy and feeling of outward extension that changed to one of drooping restraint as the years moved toward 1840 and the costume lost its horizontal emphasis, with both sleeves and skirt declining. For outerwear, the pelisse robe or coat dress was often worn as a walking costume. Three-tiered cloaks were also seen, as well as shaped shawls. From 1840 to 1850 the fashionable young woman was quite demure in a fairly controlled costume, though her skirt was still quite full. The evening bodice was worn off the shoulders and usually had some form of deep collar, pleats, or ruffles to accent the horizontal neckline. Shawls and half capes were common overgarments, and some fitted overcoats were worn. Shoes or boots had a low heel. The decade between 1850 and 1860 was prosperous and the silhouette of the day was dominated by the skirt, which was now a large bell shape that increased in size because the hoop petticoat again became popular. Amelia Bloomer introduced her new practical garment for ladies—long, full trousers cuffed at the ankle—but they were not received favorably. Capes were shaped to the waist and flared over the skirt, as were fitted overcoats. Shawls were also popular. The pale complexion was considered proper. The years between 1860 and 1870 continued the extravagant skirt shape, though the excess material gradually moved to the back of the figure. The new bonnet style was the spoon bonnet, which had a peak that raised over the hair with trim inside. Small hats were popular later. The gowns of the 1870s were quite incredible because of the amount of detailing on the skirt. The long molded bodice developed by the middle of the decade and was still present at the end, when the bustle was practically gone and the silhouette was quite slim and tubular. The skirt of the late 1870s, which might be so narrow at the hem that only small steps were possible, was still intricately detailed and swagged toward the back. The slim silhouette that ended the decade did not stay long, for by 1881 the bustle had reappeared. The tailor-made costume appeared during this decade, a business-like ensemble tailored of wool with masculine touches, which was more appropriate for the woman who was now venturing forth into the practical world. Fashions at the end of the century tended to indicate that women were leading a more active life, though many restrictions were still present. In less than 30 years women would

NINETEENTH–CENTURY WOMEN

1810

Classic style walking dress.

Sleeves short or long.

Clinging fabrics.

Small bustle possible.

Parasol

Stoles and shawls worn over.

Neck high day, low evening.

High–waisted. Corset kept bust high.

Not much fullness. Trains early, then disappeared.

Shoes low, slipper-like.

1819 Walking dress.

Classical style diminishes.

Skirt gored, hem wider.

Skirt shorter.

Coal scuttle bonnet.

Hair parted in middle, curls at sides, up in back.

High–waisted.

Wide band of intricate trim at bottom.

Pelisse or coat over gown.

1826 Day dress. Horizontal emphasis.

Neck ruffle or Betsy.

Short sleeves, low neck for evening.

Length almost to floor.

Hats wide-brimmed, many trimmings on top and under brim.

Hair parted in middle, side curls, high back.

Sleeves full. Gigot or leg-of-mutton.

Waist lower, small.

Very corseted. Rounded bust.

Hem wider, skirt trimmed at bottom.

1835 Day dress. Extreme horizontal emphasis.

Small corseted waist.

Hair parted in middle, closer to head. Bonnets popular. Demure look.

Very wide shoulders. Sleeve could be full to wrist.

Neckline low. Filled in for day.

Bouyant, light–weight feeling.

Skirt cleared floor. Many stiff petticoats under.

NINETEENTH-CENTURY WOMEN

1840
Promenade dress.

Controlled, demure hairstyle.

Drooping shoulder.

Ruffle on bonnet.

Bodice tight and simple. V trim to accent small, corseted waist.

Tight sleeve.

Long-waisted look.

Costume less bouyant, more downward feeling.

Skirt to floor. Bell-shaped. 5–6 petticoats under.

Evening bodices very low. Short sleeves.

Hair fuller. Back could be in snood.

1860 Day dress.

Bodice just to waist. May have slight point.

Skirt-and-blouse look possible.

Often highly decorated.

Extravagant skirt over large hoop. Fullness in back.

Could have train.

1850
Day costume.

Bonnet smaller. Set back to reveal hair.

Under-sleeve.

Sleeve widens to wrist.

Not as long-waisted.

Full skirt, often 2 or 3 flounces.

Hooped crinoline and petticoats under.

Long drawers worn under.

Hair piled high. Small hats popular.

1870
Day dress.

Bodice to waist, point in front.

Bustle high.

Many details like 1770s.

Large wired bustle and petticoats under.

Overskirt–underskirt effect common.

Excessive, complicated draping and trims used.

Trained

NINETEENTH-CENTURY WOMEN

1876 Day dress.

Hair up. Hats small.

Corset under, hour-glass figure ideal.

Cuirass bodice molded down over hips.

Smaller bustle.

Jacket bodices popular.

Skirt highly decorated.

High-heeled shoes or boots under.

Trained

1895 Day dress.

Hair piled softly on head. Hats larger.

High boned collar.

Large gigot or leg-of-mutton sleeve.

Very horizontal emphasis at mid-decade.

Some blousing possible.

Fitted over forearm.

Small, corseted waist.

Skirt springs smoothly over hip.

Side and back pleats possible.

Length to floor.

Wide at hem.

Petticoats under.

1886 Tailored costume.

Hair up. Small hats.

Bodice molded tightly over top of hips. Long-waisted look.

Sleeve tight.

Bustle squared out. Lower than 1870s.

Skirt draping simpler.

Could clear floor. Long for evening.

1900 Tailor-made costume.

Hair up and soft. Hats large.

Corseted figure emphasizes full bosom and hips.

Slimmer silhouette.

Skirt fits hips smoothly, flares lower.

Trains in back.

completely shed the layers of clothing and rigid boning that had confined them for centuries, but in the 1890s those restrictive elements were still very much in evidence. The accent was on the horizontal in the middle of the decade, and more vertical by the turn of the century when the ideal figure was somewhat S-shaped: the bosom curved out above the waist and the hip line curved out behind below the waist.

◆ Appendix B

Source Lists

The chronological list of source materials and the list of useful costume source books are provided to start the designer on more extensive research in particular periods. The chronological list gives the dates of the periods, including some of the people and events of the time, and the type of source material available for primary research. From the thirteenth century on, some of the painters who worked with clothed figures are listed with their nationality and birth- and death dates, to give the designer an idea of the range of material that was painted by each. Some of the painters were associated with more than one country, but are only included here once.

The book list should guide the designer toward the many types of sources that are available for research. Included are general costume surveys, specialty books, and specific sources for the periods of history. An indication of the time span of the material covered is also included with each entry. The books cited can guide designers to the sections of the library and bookstore that have potential for their purposes, and they can easily search out other related books that may be useful. A purposeful browse can be extremely rewarding for the designer. A number of these books are published in paperback editions. A good personal library can slowly but surely be acquired at moderate prices if designers keep their eyes open whenever they are in a bookstore or read a book sale catalog.

◆ Chronological List of Source Materials

Greek

Age of Pericles or Golden Age 480–400 B.C.
Fourth Century 400–320 B.C.
Hellenistic 320–100 B.C.
Sculpture
Vase painting

Roman

Monarchy 750–500 B.C.
Republic 500–31 B.C.
Empire 31 B.C.–A.D. 323
Sculpture
Painting
Mosaics
Coins

Early Christian 323–604

Mosaics

Byzantine 400–1100

Sack of Rome by Alaric 410
Charlemagne crowned emperor at Rome 800
Alfred the Great 870–901
Norman Conquest 1066
Crusades 1095–1103
Ivory carvings
Manuscript miniatures
Romanesque churches
Sculpture
Tapestries
Frescoes

Romanesque 900–1200

Thirteenth Century

Early Gothic 1200–1350

Richard the Lionhearted 1189–1199
Magna Carta 1215
Marco Polo's voyages 1260–1295
Manuscript miniatures
Stained glass
Small wood, ivory, and stone carvings
Statuary
Frescoes

Painters—Italian

Cimabue 1240–c.1302
Duccio c. 1255–1318
Giotto c. 1266–1337
Simone Martini 1284–1344
Pietro Lorenzetti active 1320–1345
Ambrogio Lorenzetti active 1319–1347

Francesco Traini active c. 1321–mid-1300s
Andrea Orcagna 1308–1368

Fourteenth Century
Middle Gothic 1350–1425

Edward III of England 1327–1377
Richard II of England 1377–1399
Henry IV of England 1399–1413
Henry V of England 1413–1422
Charles Vl of France 1380–1422
Medici power begins
Books of hours
Panel paintings
Brasses and rubbings
Tomb sculptures

Painters—Italian

Masaccio 1401–1428
Fra Angelico 1387–1455
Antonio Pisanello c. 1395–1455
Fra Filippo Lippi c. 1406–1469

Flemish

Jan van Eyck active 1422–1441

Fifteenth Century
Late Gothic 1425–1485

Joan of Arc martyred 1431
Edward IV of England d.1483
Richard III of England d.1485
Cosimo de Medici from 1434
Lorenzo de Medici d. 1492
Louis XI of France d. 1483

Painters—Italian

Andrea Verrocchio 1435–1488
Piero della Francesca c.1410/20–1492
Domenico Ghirlandaio 1449–1494
Cosimo Tura before 1431–1495
Ercoli Roberti c. 1450–1496
Piero Pollaiuoli 1441–1496
Antonio Pollaiuolo 1431–1498
Benozzo Gozzoli 1421–1497
Alesso Baldovinetti 1426–1499
Filippino Lippi 1457–1504

Andrea Mantegna 1431–1506
Gentile Bellini 1429–1507
Cosimo Rosselli 1437–1507
Sandro Botticelli 1447–1510
Giorgione 1476–1510
Bernardino Pinturicchio c. 1404–1513
Giovanni Bellini 1430–1516
Leonardo da Vinci 1452–1519

French

Jean Fouquet c. 1420–1481

Flemish

Roger van der Weyden c. 1400–1464
Dirk Bouts c. 1415–1475
Hans Memling c. 1430–1495

Early Renaissance France
Early Tudor England   } *1485–1520*
High Renaissance Italy

Italian

Raphael 1483–1520
Luca Signorelli c. 1445–1523
Perugino c. 1445–1523
Vittore Carpaccio—active 1490–c. 1526
Andrea del Sarto 1486–1531
Lorenzo di Credi c. 1458–1537
Michelangelo Buonarroti 1475–c. 1564

German

Matthias Grünewald c. 1470/80–1528
Albrecht Dürer 1471–1528
Lucas Cranach 1472–1553

Flemish

Gerard David d. 1523
Quentin Metsys c. 1464–1530

French

Jean Clouet c. 1485–1540
François Clouet c . 1510–1572

Sixteenth Century

Tudor England 1520–1547

Henry VIII of England d. 1547

Renaissance France and Germany

Francois I of France d. 1547
Martin Luther of Germany d. 1546

Elizabethan 1545–1620

Elizabethan and Jacobean England
Late Valois and Early Bourbon France
Elizabeth I of England 1558–1603
James I of England 1603–1625
William Shakespeare 1564–1616
Sculpture
Brasses
Engravings
Miniatures
Tapestries
Renaissance Germany and Spain

Painters—Italian

Giovanni Baptista Rosso 1494–1540
Francesco Parmigianino 1503–1540
Sebastiano del Piombo 1485–1547
Jacopo Pontormo 1494–1556
Francesco Primiticcio c. 1504–1570
Paris Bordone 1500–1571
Agnolo Bronzino 1503–1572
Georgio Vasari 1511–1574
Titian 1487–c. 1576

Flemish/Dutch

Guillim Stretes—active 1530s to 1550s
Anthonis Mor c. 1517–1576
Pieter Bruegel c. 1525–1569

German

Barthel Bruyn c. 1492–1555
Christoph Amberger c. 1500–1561
Hans Holbein c. 1497–1543

Later Italian

Giovanni Battista Moroni 1525–1578
Paolo Veronese 1528–1588

Jacopo Tintoretto 1518–1594
Michelangelo Merisi de Caravaggio 1573–1610

English

Hans Eworth active c. 1545–1574
Federigo Zuccari c. 1540–1609
Isaac Oliver—active 1590–1617
Nicholas Hilliard 1547–1619
Marcus Gheeraerts 1561–1636

Flemish

Pieter Pourbus 1523–1584
Peter Paul Rubens 1577–1640

Spanish

Alonzo Sanches-Coello c. 1531–1588
El Greco 1548–1614

Seventeenth Century

Cavalier or Early Baroque 1620–1660

Charles I of England 1625–1649
Oliver Cromwell 1599–1658
Thirty Years' War

Painters—Flemish/Dutch

Adriaen Brouwer c. 1605–1638
Anthony van Dyck 1599–1641
Cornelis de Vos 1584–1651
Nicholaes Elias c. 1590–1654
Franz Hals 1580–1666
Jan Miensz Molenaer c. 1609–1668
Rembrandt van Rijn 1606–1669
Gerard ter Borch 1617–1681
Adriaen Ostade 1610–1684

French

Jacques Callot c. 1592–1635
Antoine Le Nain 1588–1648
Louis Le Nain 1593–1648
Simon Vouet 1590–1649
Georges de La Tour 1593–1652
Philippe de Champaigne 1602–1674
Abraham Bosse 1602–1676
Mathieu Le Nain 1607–1677
Jacob Jordaens 1593–1678

Spanish

Diego Velázquez 1599–1660

English

Daniel Mytens c. 1590–before 1648
Gerrit S. van Honthorst 1590–1656
Cornelius Johnson 1593–1661
Wenzel Hollar 1607–1677

Petticoat Breeches, Restoration, or Middle Baroque 1660–1685

Charles II of England 1630–1685
Louis XIV of France 1638–1715

Restoration and Late Baroque 1685–1715

James II of England 1685–1688
William and Mary of England 1688–1702
Anne of England 1702–1714

Painters—Italian

Carlo Dolci 1616–1686

Flemish/Dutch

Gabriel Metsu 1629–1667
Bartholomeus van der Helst 1613–1670
Jan Vermeer 1632–1674
Pieter de Hooch 1630–1677
Jan Steen 1626–1679
Gerard ter Borch 1617–1681

French

Charles Le Brun 1619–1690
Pierre Mignard 1612–1697

Spanish

Bartolomé Esteban Murillo 1617–1682

English

Sir Peter Lely 1618–1680
Jacob Pluysmans 1633–1696
Sir Godfrey Kneller c. 1646–1723

Eighteenth Century

Early Georgian England

George I of England 1714–1727
George II of England 1727–1760

Rococo France 1715–1755

Louis XV of France 1715–1774
Benjamin Franklin 1706–1790
George Washington 1732–1799
Catherine the Great of Russia 1729–1796

Painters—French

Antoine Watteau 1684–1721
Antoine Coypel 1661–1722
John-Baptiste-Joseph Pater 1695–1736
Nicholas Lancret 1660–1743
Hyacinthe Rigaud 1659–1743
Jean Baptiste van Loo 1684–1745
Nicholas de Largillière 1656–1746
Jean François de Troy 1679–1752
Carle van Loo 1705–1765
Jean-Marc Nattier 1685–1766
François Boucher 1703–1770
Louis-Michel Van Loo 1707–1771
François Hubert Drouais 1727–1775
Jean-Baptiste-Siméon Chardin 1699–1779
Jean-Baptiste Perroneau c. 1715–1783
Quentin de La Tour 1704–1788
Jean Baptiste Greuze 1725–1805
Jean-Honoré Fragonard 1732–1806

Italian

Giovanni Antonio Canaletto 1697–1768
Giovanni Battista Tiepolo 1696–1770
Pietro Longhi 1702–1785
Francesco Guardi 1712–1793

English

William Hogarth 1697- 1764
Francis Cotes 1725–1770
Joseph Highmore 1692–1780
Allan Ramsey 1713–1784
Arthur Devis c. 1711–1787
Thomas Gainsborough 1727–1788
Sir Joshua Reynolds 1723–1792
George Romney 1734–1802
Johann Zoffany 1733–1810

German

Daniel Chodowiecki 1726–1801

Flemish

Anton Raphael Mengs 1728–1779

Swedish

Alexander Roslin 1718–1793

American Colonies and United States

Robert Feke 1705–1750
Joseph Blackburn 1700–1765
Joseph Badger 1708–1765
John Hesselius 1728–1778
Ralph Earle 1751–1801
John Singleton Copley 1737–1815
Benjamin West 1738–1820

Middle to Late Georgian

George III of England 1760–1820
Louis XVI of France 1774–1792

Painters—French

Jean-Michel Moreau (le Jeune) 1741–1814
Pierre-Paul Prud'hon 1758–1823
Théodore Géricault 1791–1824
Jacques-Louis David 1748–1825
Antoine-Jean Gros 1771–1835
Francois Gerard 1770–1837
Louise Elisabeth Vigée-Lebrun 1755–1842
Jean-Auguste-Dominique Ingres 1780–1867

Spanish

Francisco de Goya 1746–1828

England—Regency
France—Directoire and Empire   } *1790–1815*
Germany—Biedermeier
United States—Federal

Painters—English

George Morland 1764–1804
John Opie 1761–1807
John Hoppner 1758–1810
Robert Dighton 1752–1814
Samuel Cotes 1734–1818
Thomas Rowlandson 1756–1827
Sir Thomas Lawrence 1769–1830

Scots

Sir Henry Raeburn 1756–1823

United States

Edward Savage 1761–1817
Charles Wilson Peale 1741–1827
Gilbert Stuart 1755–1828
John Trumbull 1756–1843

Nineteenth Century—Victorian Era

Romantic Age 1815–1848

Daguerreotype invented 1839 (Louis Daguerre 1789–1851)

Crinoline Period 1845–1868

Bustle Period 1868–1890

Fin de siècle 1890–1900

Painters—French

Horace Vernet 1789–1863
Eugène Delacroix 1798–1863
Jean-François Millet 1814–1875
Gustave Courbet 1819–1877
Honoré Daumier 1808–1879
Èdouard Manet 1832–1883
Constantin Guys 1802–1892

English

Henry Alken 1784–1851
George Cruikshank 1792–1878
John Leech 1817–1864
George Cruikshank 1792–1878
H. K. Browne (Phiz) 1815–1882
Aubrey Beardsley 1872–1898

United States

Thomas Sully 1783–1872
Samuel Morse 1791–1872

French

Henri-Marie-Raymond de Toulouse-Lautrec 1864–1901
Edgar Degas 1834–1917
Pierre-Auguste Renoir 1841–1919
Claude Monet 1840–1926

United States

Thomas Nast 1840–1902
James McNeil Whistler 1854–1903
Winslow Homer 1836–1910
Thomas Eakins 1844–1916
John Singer Sargent 1856–1925
Charles Dana Gibson 1867–1944

◈ Useful Costume Source Books

Coverage in some of these volumes extends to the periods preceding and following the time span noted.

General Costume Surveys

Baclawski, Karen. *The Guide to Historic Costume.* New York: Drama Book Publishers, 1995.

Barton, Lucy. *Historic Costume for the Stage.* Boston: Walter H. Baker (revised), 1961. Ancient Egypt to 1914.

Barsis, Max. *The Common Man Through the Centuries.* New York: Frederick Unger, 1973.

Batterberry, Michael, and Ariane. *Mirror, Mirror.* New York: Holt, Rinehart and Winston, 1977. Ancient Near East through twentieth century.

Bigelow, Marybelle S. *Fashion in History, Apparel in the Western World.* Minneapolis: Burgess, 1986. Ancient Egypt to 1970, including fashion design and illustration section.

Boucher, François. *20,000 Years of Fashion.* New York: Harry N. Abrams, 1967. Prehistoric times to 1914.

Braun and Schnieder. *Historic Costume in Pictures: 1450 Costumes on 125 Plates.* Magnolia, MA: Peter Smith, 1990. Antiquity to nineteenth century.

Bruhn, Wolfgang, and Max Tilke. *A Pictorial History of Costume.* New York: Praeger, 1955. Antiquity through nineteenth century, including national costumes.

Chenoun, Farid. *A History of Men's Fashions.* Paris: Flammarion, 1993. 1760–1990.

Contini, Mila. *Fashion from Ancient Egypt to the Present Day.* New York: Odyssey, 1965.

Cunnington, C. Willett and Phillis, and Charles Beard. *A Dictionary of English Costume: 900–1900.* New York: Barnes & Noble, 1960.

Cunnington, Phillis. *Costume in Pictures.* New York: Dutton, 1964. Middle Ages through first half of the twentieth century.

Cunnington, Phillis, and Catherine Lucas. *Costume for Births, Marriages & Deaths.* London: Adam & Charles Black, 1972.

Davenport, Millia. *The Book of Costume.* New York: Crown, 1948. Antiquity to the 1860s.

Dorner, Jane. *Fashion*. London: Octopus Books, 1974. Fourteenth century to modern day.

Garland, Madge. *The Changing Face of Beauty*. New York: M. Barrows and Company, 1957. Ancient Crete to twentieth century.

Gorsline, Douglas. *What People Wore*. New York: Bonanza Books, 1952. Antiquity to twentieth century.

Hansen, Henny Harald. *Costumes and Styles*. New York: Dutton, 1956. Antiquity to twentieth century.

Hill, Margot Hamilton, and Peter A. Bucknell. *The Evolution of Fashion: 1066–1930*. New York: Drama Book Specialists, 1967.

Huyghe, René (ed.). *Larousse Encyclopedia of Renaissance and Baroque Art*. London: Hamlyn, 1964. Thirteenth through eighteenth centuries.

Kelly, Francis M., and Randolphe Schwabe. *Historic Costume: A Chronicle of Fashion in Western Europe*. 2nd Edition. Benjamin Blom, 1968. Reprint edition Salem, NH: Ayer, 1988. 1490–1790.

_____. *A Short History of Costume and Armor: 1066–1800*. North Stratford, NH: Ayer, 1972.

Kemper, Rachel H. *Costume*. New York: Newsweek Books, 1978. Antiquity to the 1970s.

Kohler, Carl. *A History of Costume*. New York: Dover, 1963. Antiquity to 1870.

Kybalova, Ludmila, Olga Herbenova, and Milena Lamarova. *Pictorial Encyclopedia of Fashion*. London: Hamlyn, 1968. Antiquity to the 1960s.

Laver, James. *The Concise History of Costume and Fashion*. New York: Harry N. Abrams, 1984. Antiquity to the 1960s.

_____. *Costume Through the Ages*. New York: Simon & Schuster, 1963. Ancient Rome to 1930.

Mansfield, Alan. *Ceremonial Costume*. Totowa, NJ: Barnes & Noble, 1980.

Nunn, Joan. *Fashion in Costume 1200–1980*. Franklin, NY: New Amsterdam Books, 1990.

Payne, Blanche, Jane Farrel-Beck, and Geitel Winakor. *The History of Costume*, Second Edition. New York: Harper Collins, 1992. From Ancient Mesopotamia through the twentieth century.

Pistolese, Rosana, and Ruth Horsting. *History of Fashions*. New York: Wiley, 1970. Antiquity to twentieth century.

Racinet, Albert. *The Encyclopedia of Costumes*. New York: Facts on File, 1992. Antiquity to early nineteenth century; includes national costumes.

Ribero, Aileen, and Valerie Cumming. *The Visual History of Costume*. London: B. T. Batsford, 1989. Fourteenth to twentieth centuries.

Rosenberg, Adolph. *Geschichte des Kostums*. New York: E. Weyhe, 1905–1923. Five volumes. Ancient Greece to twentieth century.

Rothstein, Natalie (ed.). *Four Hundred Years of Fashion*. London: William Collins Sons, 1984. Seventeenth through twentieth century.

Russell, Douglas A. *Costume History and Style*. Englewood Cliffs, NJ: Prentice-Hall, 1983. Prehistoric through the 1970s.

Schoeser, Mary, and Celia Rufey. *English and American Textiles: 1790 to the Present*. New York: Thames and Hudson, 1989.

Squire, Geoffery. *Dress and Society*. New York: Viking, 1974. 1560–1970.

Tortora, Phyllis, and Keith Eubank. *Survey of Historic Costume, A History of Western Dress*. Second Edition. New York: Fairchild, 1994. About 3000 B.C. to 1990.

Wilcox, R. Turner. *The Dictionary of Costume*. New York: Scribner, 1969.

_____. *The Mode in Costume*. New York: Scribner, 1958. Ancient Egypt to 1947.

Yarwood, Doreen. *The Encyclopedia of World Costume*. New York: Scribner, 1978.

_____. *European Costumes: 4000 Years of Fashion*. New York: Bonanza Books, 1982.

General Survey Specialty Books

Arms and Heraldry

Allcock, Hubert. *Heraldic Design*. New York: Tudor, 1962.

Fox-Davis, Arthur Charles. *The Art of Heraldry: An Encyclopaedia of Armory*. New York: Arno Press, 1976.

_____. *A Complete Guide to Heraldry*. New York: Bonanza Books, 1978.

Hart, Harold H. (ed.). *Weapons and Armor*. Compiled by Robert Sietsema. New York: Hart Publishing, 1978.

Nickel, Helmut, Stuart W. Pyhrr, and Leonid Tarassuk. *The Art of Chivalry*. New York: Metropolitan Museum of Art, 1982.

Norman, Vesey. *Arms and Armor*. London: Octopus Books, 1972.

Reid, William. *Arms Through the Ages*. New York: Harper, 1976. Neolithic Age to modern times.

Stone, George Cameron. *A Glossary of the Construction, Decoration and Use of Arms and Armor*. New York: Jack Brussel, 1961. Antiquity to twentieth century.

Children

Cunnington, Phillis, and Anne Buck. *Children's Costume in England*. London: A. & C. Black, 1965. Fourth through nineteenth centuries.

Rose, Claire. *Children's Clothes*. London: B. T. Batsford, 1989. 1750–1985.

Sichel, Marion. *Costume Reference. History of Children's Costume*. New York: Chelsea House, 1983.

Worrell, Estelle Ansley. *Children's Costume in America 1607–1910*. New York: Scribner, 1980.

Church

Haverstick, John. *The Progress of the Protestant*. New York: Holt, Rinehart and Winston, 1968. Fifteenth to twentieth centuries.

Mayo, Janet. *A History of Ecclesiastical Dress*. New York: Holmes & Meier, 1984. From early Christian to the 1980s.

Rice, Edward. *The Church: A Pictorial History*. New York: Farrar, Straus and Cudahy, 1961. Early Christian era through nineteenth century.

Collars

Colle, Doriece. *Collars, Stocks, Cravats*. Emmaus, PA.: Rodale Press, 1972. Men's neckpieces from 1655 to 1900.

Corsets and Underwear

Carter, Alison. *Underwear. The Fashion History.* New York: Drama Books, 1992. From 1490 to 1990.

Ewing, Elizabeth. *Dress and Undress: A History of Women's Underwear.* New York: Drama Book Specialists, 1978.

_____. *Underwear: A History.* New York: Theatre Arts Books, 1972.

Saint-Laurent, Cecil. *The History of Ladies' Underwear.* London: Michael Joseph, 1968. Early times to 1960s.

Shep, R. L. *Corsets: A Visual History.* Mendocino, CA: R. L. Shep, 1993.

Waugh, Norah. *Corsets and Crinolines.* New York: Theatre Arts Books, 1970. Sixteenth century to 1925.

Everyday Life

Brosse, Jacques, Paul Chaland, and Jacques Ostier. *100,000 Years of Daily Life.* New York: Golden Press, 1961.

Cunnington, Phillis, and Catherine Lucas. *Occupational Costume in England.* London: A. & C. Black, 1967. Eleventh through ninteenth centuries.

Ewing, Elizabeth. *Everyday Dress 1650–1900.* New York: Chelsea House, 1984.

Lister, Margot. *Costumes of Everyday Life: An Illustrated History of Working Clothes.* Boston: Plays, Inc. 1972.

Marly, Diana de. *Working Dress.* New York: Holmes & Meier, 1986. Before 1600 to 1945.

Eye Wear

Corson, Richard. *Fashions in Eyeglasses From the 14th Century to the Present Day.* London: Peter Owen, 1980.

Marly, Pierre. *Spectacles and Spyglasses.* France: Editions Hoebeke, 1988.

Hats, Hair, and Makeup

Amphlett, Hilda. *Hats: A History of Fashions in Headwear.* Chalfont St. Giles, England: Sadler, 1974. First millennium A.D. to twentieth century.

Corson, Richard. *Fashions in Hair: The First Five Thousand Years.* London: Peter Owen, 1971.

_____. *Fashions in Makeup from Ancient to Modern Times.* New York: Universe Books, 1972

Cox, J. Stevens. *An Illustrated Dictionary of Hairdressing and Wigmaking.* London: Batsford Academic and Educational, 1984.

Ginsburg, Madeleine. *The Hat: Trends and Traditions.* New York and Toronto: Barron's Educational Series, 1990. Medieval times to present day.

Kilgour, Ruth Edwards. *A Pageant of Hats Ancient and Modern.* New York: Robert M. McBride, 1958.

McDowell, Colin. *Hats: Status, Style and Glamour.* New York: Rizzoli, 1992.

Sevens, Bill. *The Long and Short of It: Five Thousand Years of Fun and Fury Over Hair.* New York: David McKay, 1971.

Wilcox, R. Turner. *The Mode in Hats and Headdresses.* New York: Scribner, 1959. Antiquity to 1944.

Jewelry

Black, J. Anderson. *A History of Jewelry: Five Thousand Years*. New York: Park Lane, 1981.

Frank, Joan. *The Beauty of Jewelry*. New York: Crescent Books, 1979. Primarily eighteenth, nineteenth, and twentieth centuries.

Fregnac, Claude. *Jewelry: From Renaissance to Art Nouveau*. London: Octopus Books, 1973.

Hart, Harold H. (ed.). *Jewelry*. Revised edition by Robert Sietsma. Text by Nancy Goldberg. New York: Hart, 1978.

Law

Robbins, Sara (ed.). *Law, A Treasury of Art and Literature*. New York: Macmillan. 1990. Ancient beginnings to modern day.

Medicine

Margotta, Roberto. *The Story of Medicine*. New York: Golden Press, 1968. Primitive man to modern times.

Military Uniforms

Kannik, Preban. *Military Uniforms in Color*. London: Blandford, 1968.

Knotel, Richard, and Herbert Knotel, Jr. *Uniforms of the World: A Compendium of Army, Navy and Air Force Uniforms 1700–1937 with 1600 illustrations*. New York: Charles Scribner's Sons, 1980.

Mollo, Andrew, and Digby Smith. *World Army Uniforms Since 1939*. Poole, Dorset: Blandford Press, 1983.

Mollo, Boris. *Uniforms of the Imperial Russian Army*. Poole, Dorset: Blandford Press, 1979.

Mollo, John. *Uniforms of the American Revolution in Color*. New York: Macmillan, 1975.

Schick, I. T. (ed.). *Battledress. The Uniforms of the World's Great Armies 1700 to the Present*. Boston: Little Brown, 1978.

Windrow, Martin, and Gerry Embleton. *Military Dress of North America. 1665–1970*. New York: Charles Scribner's Sons, 1973.

Shoes

Trasko, Mary. *Heavenly Soles, Extraordinary Twentieth-Century Shoes*. New York: Abbeville Press, 1989.

Wilcox, R. Turner. *The Mode in Footwear*. New York: Charles Scribner's Sons, 1948.

Wilson, Eunice. *A History of Shoe Fashion*. London: Pitman, 1969. Pre-Roman Britain to 1960s.

Sport

Arlott, John, and Arthur Daley. *The Pageantry of Sport*. New York: Hawthorn, 1968. Fourteenth through nineteenth centuries.

Cunnington, Phillis, and Alan Mansfield. *English Costume for Sports and Outdoor Recreation from the 16th to the 19th Centuries*. London: Adam and Charles Black, 1969.

Tapestries

Hulst, Roger Adolf d', A. *Flemish Tapestries from the 15th to 18th Centuries.* New York: Universe Books, 1967.

Jarry, Madelein. *World Tapestry from Its Origins to the Present.* New York: Putman, 1969. Primarily fourteenth through eighteen centuries.

Jobe, Joseph. *The Art of Tapestry.* London: Thames and Hudson, 1965. Primarily fourteenth through eighteenth centuries.

Thomson, Francis Paul. *Tapestry: Mirror of History.* New York: Crown, 1980. Primarily eleventh through eighteenth centuries.

Ancient Greece to the Twelfth Century

Amiet, Pierre. *Art in the Ancient World: a Handbook of Styles and Forms.* New York: Rizzoli, 1981. Ancient Mesopotamia to Rome.

Bonfante, Larissa. *Greek-Etruscan Dress.* Baltimore: Johns Hopkins, 1975.

Chamoux, François. *Greek Art.* Greenwich, CT: New York Graphic Society, 1966.

Charbonneaux, Jean, Roland Martin, and François Villard. *Classical Greek Art.* New York: Braziller, 1972.

Field, D. M. *Greek and Roman Mythology.* New York: Chartwell Books, 1977.

Graber, André. *Byzantine Painting.* Geneva: Skira, 1953. Fifth to fourteenth centuries.

_____. *Early Medieval Painting from the 4th to 11th Centuries.* New York: Skira, 1957.

Hale, William Harlan (ed.). *The Horizon Book of Ancient Greece.* New York: American Heritage, 1965.

Hanfmann, George M. A. *Roman Art.* Greenwich, CT: New York Graphic Society, 1964.

Heuzey, Leon. *Histoire du Costume Antique.* Paris: Librarie Ancienne Honoré. Champion, 1922. Greek and Roman costumes.

Hope, Thomas. *Costume of the Greeks and Romans.* New York: Dover, 1962.

Huyghe, Rene (ed.). *Larousse Encyclopedia of Byzantine and Medieval Art.* London: Hamlyn, 1963.

Laver, James. *Costume in Antiquity.* New York: Clarkson N. Botter, 1964. From 3000 B.C. to sixth century A.D.

Maiuri, Amedeo. *Roman Painting.* Geneva: Skira, 1953.

Oakeshott, Walter. *The Mosaics of Rome, from the Third to the Fourteenth Centuries.* Greenwich, CT: New York Graphic Society, 1967.

Rice, Talbot. *The Art of Byzantine.* New York: Harry N. Abrams, 1959.

Richter, Gisela M. A. *Attic Red Figured Vases.* New Haven: Yale University Press, 1958.

Robertson, Martin. *Greek Painting.* Geneva: Skira, 1959.

_____. *A Shorter History of Greek Art.* New York: Cambridge University Press, 1981.

Robinson, H. Russell. *The Armor of Imperial Rome.* New York: Scribner, 1975.

Shoder, Raymond V. *Masterpieces of Greek Art.* Greenwich, CT: New York Graphic Society, 1960.

Twelfth Through Fifteenth Centuries: Gothic

Baker, John. *English Stained Glass.* London: Thames and Hudson, 1960. Twelfth to sixteenth centuries.

Bise, Gabriel. *Medieval Hunting Scenes.* Geneva: Minerva, 1978. Fourteenth century.

Boehn, Max von. *Modes and Manners. Volume I. From the Decline of the Ancient World to the Renaissance.* London: George G. Harrap, 1932.

Clayton, Muriel. *Brass Rubbings.* London: Victoria and Albert Museum, 1968.

Cunnington, C. Willett, and Phillis. *The Handbook of English Medieval Costume.* Boston: Plays, Inc., 1969.

Cunnington, Phillis. *Medieval and Tudor Costume.* Boston: Plays, Inc., 1972. Eleventh to sixteenth centuries.

Delaisse, L. M. J. *Medieval Miniatures.* New York: Harry N. Abrams, 1965. Eleventh through sixteenth centuries.

DuPont, Jacques. *Gothic Painting.* Geneva: Skira, 1954. Fourteenth and fifteenth centuries.

Evans, Joan (ed.). *The Flowering of the Middle Ages.* New York: McGraw-Hill, 1966. Eleventh through fifteenth centuries.

Formaggio, Dino, and Carlo Passo. *A Book of Miniatures.* New York: Tudor, 1962. Eleventh through fifteenth centuries.

Gaborit, Jean Rene. *Great Gothic Sculpture.* New York: William Morrow, 1978. Twelfth through fourteenth centuries.

Graber, André. *Romanesque Painting from the 11th to 13th Century.* New York: Skira, 1958.

Houston, Mary. *Medieval Costume in England and France.* London: A. & C. Black, 1939. Thirteenth, fourteenth, and fifteenth centuries.

Lacroix, Paul. *The Arts in the Middle Ages and the Renaissance.* New York: Frederick Ungar, 1964. Thirteenth to sixteenth centuries.

_____. *France in the Middle Ages.* New York: Frederick Ungar, 1963. Twelfth to sixteenth centuries.

_____. *Military and Religious Life in the Middle Ages and the Renaissance.* New York: Frederick Ungar, 1964. Twelfth to sixteenth centuries.

Lassaigne, Jacques and Giulio Carlo Argan. *The Fifteenth Century.* New York: Skira, 1955.

Laver, James. *Early Tudor: 1485–1558.* London: Harrap, 1951.

Meiss, Millard. *French Painting in the Time of Jean de Berry.* London: Phaedon, 1969. Late fourteenth century.

Meiss, Millard. *The Great Age of Fresco.* New York: Braziller, 1970. Primarily fourteenth, fifteenth, and early sixteenth centuries.

Newton, Stella Mary. *Fashion in the Age of the Black Prince: a Study of the Years 1340–1365.* Woodbridge, England: Boydell Press, 1980.

Platt, Colin. *The Atlas of Medieval Man.* New York: St. Martin's Press, 1980. Eleventh through fifteenth centuries.

Porcher, Jean. *Medieval French Miniatures.* New York: Harry N. Abrams, 1960. 11th through 15th centuries.

Scott, Margaret. *The History of Dress Series. Late Gothic Europe. 1400–1500.* New Jersey: Humanities Press, 1980.

Stirton, Paul. *Renaissance Painting.* New York: Mayflower Books, 1979.

Sixteenth Century

Blum, André. *The Last Valois: 1515–90.* London: Harrap, 1951.

Boehn, Max von. *Modes and Manners. Volume II. The Sixteenth Century.* London: George G. Harrap, 1932.

Cunnington, C. Willett, and Phillis. *Handbook of English Costume in the 16th Century.* Boston: Plays, Inc., 1970.

Hay, Denys (ed.). *The Age of the Renaissance.* New York: McGraw-Hill, 1967. Primarily fifteenth and sixteenth centuries.

Laver, James (ed.) *Le Costume des Tudor à Louis XIII.* Paris: Horizon de France, 1950. From 1485 to 1643.

Morse, H. K. *Elizabethan Pageantry.* London: The Art Book Co., 1980. From 1560 to 1620.

Norris, Herbert. *Costume and Fashion, Vol. III. Book 1, 1485–1547. Book 2, 1547–1603.* New York: Dutton, 1938.

Ross, Josephine. *The Tudors.* New York: Putnam, 1979. From 1485 to 1603.

Sichel, Marion. *Costume Reference. Volume II. Tudors and Elizabethans.* London: B. T. Batsford, 1977.

Vecellio, Cesare. *Vecellio's Renaissance Costume Book.* New York: Dover, 1977.

Venturi, Lionello. *The Sixteenth Century.* New York: Skira, 1956.

Williams, Neville. *All the Queen's Men.* New York: Macmillan, 1972. From 1533 to 1603.

_____. *Life and Times of Elizabeth I.* Garden City, NY: Doubleday, 1972.

Seventeenth and Eighteenth Centuries

Bernier, Olivier. *The Eighteenth Century Woman.* Garden City, NY: Doubleday & Company, Inc., 1981.

Blum, André. *Early Bourbon. 1590–1643.* London: George G. Harrap, 1951.

Boehn, Max von. *Modes and Manners. Volume III. The Seventeenth Century.* London: George G. Harrap, 1932.

_____. *Modes and Manners. Volume IV. The Eighteenth Century.* London: George G. Harrap, 1932

Cumming, Valerie. *A Visual History of Costume. The Seventeenth Century.* New York: Drama Books, 1984.

Cunnington, C. Willett, and Phillis. *Handbook of English Costume in the 18th Century.* Boston: Plays, Inc., 1972.

_____. *Handbook of English Costume in the 17th Century.* Boston: Plays, Inc., 1972.

Daniel, Howard, (ed.). *Callot's Etchings.* New York: Dover, 1974.

DuPont, Jacques, and François Mathey. *The Seventeenth Century.* New York: Skira, 1951.

Earle, Alice Morse. *Two Centuries of Costume in America. 1620–1820.* New York: Dover, 1970.

Fosca, François (George de Traz). *The Eighteenth Century.* Geneva: Skira, 1952.

George, M. Dorothy. *Hogarth to Cruikshank: Social Change in Graphic Satire.* New York: Walker, 1967. Eighteenth and nineteenth centuries.

Grafton, John. *The American Revolution: A Picture Sourcebook.* New York: Dover, 1975.

Hesketh, Christian. *Tartans*. New York: Putnam, 1961. Primarily eighteenth and nineteenth centuries.

Hibbert, Christopher (ed.). *Twilight of Princes: Milestones of History*. New York: Newsweek Books, 1974. From 1713 to 1799.

Hogg, Ian V., and John H. Batchelor. *Armies of the American Revolution*. Englewood Cliffs, NJ: Prentice-Hall, 1975.

Ketchum, Richard M (ed.). *The American Heritage Book of the Revolution*. New York: American Heritage, 1971.

Kinnaird, Clark. *George Washington: The Pictorial Biography*. New York: Hastings House, 1967.

Laver, James (intro). *17th and 18th Century Costume*. London: Victoria and Albert Museum, 1951.

Masters, John. *Casanova*. New York: Bernard Geis Associates, 1969.

Mollo, John, and Malcolm McCregor. *Uniforms of the American Revolution*. New York: Macmillan, 1975.

Peterson, Harold L. *The Book of the Continental Soldier*. Harrisburg, PA.: Stackpole, 1968.

Preston, Antony, David Lyon, and John H. Batchelor. *The Navies of the American Revolution*. Englewood Cliffs, NJ: Prentice-Hall, 1975.

Ribero, Aileen. *Dress in Eighteenth-Century Europe. 1715–1789*. New York: Holmes & Meier, 1985.

_____. *Fashion in the French Revolution*. New York: Holmes & Meier, 1988.

_____. *A Visual History of Costume*. New York: Drama Book, 1983. Eighteenth century.

Schönberger, Arno, and Halldor Soehner. *The Rococo Age*. New York: McGraw-Hill, 1963. Eighteenth century.

Sichel, Marion. *Costume Reference. Volume V. The Regency*. London: B. T. Batsford, 1978.

Walker, Stella A. *Sporting Art*. New York: Clarkson N. Potter, 1972. England 1700–1900.

Warwick, Edward, Henry C. Pitz, and Alexander Wyckoff. *Early American Dress*. New York: Bonanza Books, 1965. Seventeenth and eighteenth centuries.

Weigert, Roger-Armand. *Personnages de Qualité*. Paris: Editions Rombaldi, 1956. From 1680 to 1715.

Nineteenth Century

Beebe, Lucius, and Charles Clegg. *The American West*. New York: Dutton,1955.

Blay, John S. *After the Civil War: A Pictorial Profile of America from 1865 to 1900*. New York: Bonanza Books, 1960.

_____. *The Civil War: A Pictorial Profile*. New York: Bonanza Books, 1958.

Bloomingdale Brothers. *Bloomingdale's Illustrated 1886 Catalog: Fashions, Dry Goods and Housewares*. New York: Dover, 1988.

Blum, Stella (ed.). *Ackerman's Costume Plates: Women's Fashions in England 1818–1828*. New York: Dover, 1978.

_____ (ed.). *Eighteenth Century French Fashion Plates in Full Color*. New York: Dover, 1982.

_____. *Victorian Fashions and Costumes from Harper's Bazaar: 1867–98*. New York: Dover, 1974.

Boehn, Max von. *Modes and Manners of the l9th Century*. Reprint, four volumes in two. New York: Benjamin Blom, 1970.

Brander, Michael. *The Victorian Gentleman*. London: Gordon Cremonesi, 1972.

Byrde, Penelope. *Nineteenth Century Fashion*. London: B. T. Batsford, 1992.

Cone, Polly (ed.). *The Imperial Style: Fashions of the Hapsburg Era*. New York: Metropolitan Museum of Art, 1980. Primarily nineteenth century.

Cunnington, C. Willett. *English Women's Clothing in the Nineteenth Century*. New York: Dover, 1990.

Cunnington, C Willett, and Phillis. *Handbook of English Costume in the 19th Century*. Boston: Plays, Inc., 1970.

Evans, Hilary and Mary. *The Victorians*. New York: Arco, 1974. Mid- to late nineteenth century.

Gibbs-Smith, Charles H. *The Fashionable Lady in the 19th Century*. London: Victoria and Albert Museum, 1960.

Holland, Vyvyan. *Hand Colored Fashion Plates*. London: Batsford, 1955. From 1770 to 1899.

Kraus, Michael and Vera. *Family Album for Americans*. New York: Grosset & Dunlap, 1961. Late eighteenth and nineteenth centuries.

Kulaciov, Robert. *Mr. Godey's Ladies*. New York: Bonanza Books, 1971. From 1830s to 1870s.

Laver, James. *Manners and Morals in the Age of Optimism. 1848–1914*. New York: Harper, 1966.

Lucie-Smith, Edward and Celestine Dars. *How the Rich Lived*. London: Paddington Press, 1976. From 1870 to 1914.

_____. *Work and Struggle*. London: Paddington Press, 1977. From 1870 to 1914.

Peacock, John. *Men's Fashion: The Complete Sourcebook*. London: Thames and Hudson, 1996. French Revolution to present day.

Pitz, Henry C. *The Gibson Girl and Her America*. New York: Dover, 1969.

Pyne, W. H. *Rural Occupations in Early 19th Century England*. New York: Dover, 1977.

Sears, Stephen W. (ed.). *Century Collection of Civil War Art*. New York: American Heritage, 1974.

Simpson, Jeffrey. *The American Family: A History in Photographs*. New York: Viking, 1976. Late Victorian to modern times.

Weymouth, Lally. *America in 1876: The Way We Were*. New York: Vintage Books, 1976.

Nineteenth- and Twentieth-Century Periodicals

American Magazine (1876–1956)
Bon Ton and Le Moniteur de la Mode (1851–1927)
Bon Ton, Journal des Modes (1834–1881)
Butterick's Home Catalogue (1959–present)
Coutoure (1988–present)
Elle (French, 1945–; English 1985–present)
Esquire (1933–present)

Flare (was *Miss Chatelaine* 1840–) (1964–present)
Gallery of Fashion (1794–1803)
The Gentleman's Magazine (1828–1894)
Gentleman's Quarterly or *G.Q.* (1957–present)
Godey's Lady's Book (1830–1898)
Good Housekeeping (1885–present)
Harper's Weekly (1857–1916)
Harper's Bazaar (1867–present)
Illustrated London News (1842–present)
L'Illustration (1843–1944)
Ladies Home Journal (1883–present)
Life Magazine (1936–1972, 1978–present)
Mirabella (1989–present)
Mode Illustré (1843–1873)
Peterson's Magazine (1846–1898)
Vogue (1892–present)
Women's Wear Daily or *W* (1892–present)

Twentieth Century

Baker, Patricia. *Fashions of a Decade: The 1940s.* New York: Facts on File, Inc., 1992.

Byrde, Penelope. *A Visual History of Costume. The Twentieth Century.* New York: Drama Books, 1986.

Constantino, Maria. *Fashions of a Decade. The 1930s.* New York: Facts on File, Inc., 1994.

Ewing, Elizabeth, and Alice Mackrell. *History of 20th Century Fashion.* Lanham, MD: Barnes & Noble, 1992.

Gimbel Brothers. *Gimbel's Illustrated 1915 Fashion Catalogue.* New York: Dover, 1994.

Hochswender: Woody. *Men in Style: the Golden Age of Fashion from Esquire.* New York: Rizzoli, 1993.

Mansfield, Alan, and Phillis Cunnington. *Handbook of English Costume in the 20th Century 1900–1950.* Boston: Plays, Inc., 1973.

Milbank, Caroline Rennolds. *New York Fashion, The Evolution of American Style.* New York: Harry N. Abrams, 1989. From 1860s to the 1980s.

Mitchell, Jon. J. *Men's Fashion Illustration from the Turn of the Century.* New York: Dover 1990.

Peacock, John. *20th Century Fashion. A Complete Sourcebook.* London: Thames and Hudson, 1993.

Rolley, Katrina, and Caroline Aise. *Fashion in Photographs 1900–1920.* London: B.T. Batsford, 1992.

Sichel, Marion. *Costume Reference. Volume 7. The Edwardians.* London: B. T. Batsford, 1978.

_____. *Costume Reference. Volume 8. 1918–1939.* London: B. T. Batsford, 1978.

_____. *Costume Reference. Volume 10. 1950 to the Present Day.* London: B. T. Batsford, 1979.

Yapp, Nick. *150 Years of Photo Journalism.* Volumes I and II. Hulton Deutsch Collection: Konemann, 1995.

Bibliography

General Theatre and Basic Design Approach

Adams, J. Donald. *Naked We Came.* New York: Holt, Rinehart and Winston, 1967.

Bailey, Margaret J. *Those Glorious Glamour Years.* Secaucus, N.J.: The Citadel Press, 1982. Hollywood costume design of the 1930s.

Bell, Quentin. *On Human Finery,* 2nd ed. New York: Schocken Books, 1978.

Bevlin, Marjorie Elliott. *Design Through Discovery, The Elements and Principles.* New York: Holt, Rinehart and Winston, 1984.

Bland, Alexander. *A History of Ballet and Dance.* New York: Praeger, 1976.

Burian, K. V. *Story of World Opera.* London: Peter Nevill, 1961.

Clark, Kenneth. *The Nude.* Princeton, N.J.: Princeton University Press, 1956.

Clark, Mary and Clement Crisp. *Design for Ballet.* New York: Hawthorne, 1978.

Davis, Fred. *Fashion, Culture and Identity.* Chicago: University of Chicago Press, 1992.

Dodd, Craig. *Ballet and Modern Dance.* New York: Elsevier-Dutton, 1980.

Hollander, Anne. *Seeing Through Clothes.* New York: Viking, 1975.

Horn, Marilyn J. *The Second Skin,* 2nd ed. Boston: Houghton Mifflin, 1975.

Jones, Robert Edmund. *The Dramatic Imagination.* New York: Theatre Arts, 1941.

Komisarjevsky, Theodore. *The Costume of the Theatre.* New York: Benjamin Blom, 1968.

Laver, James. *Clothes.* London: Burke, 1952.

———. *Costume in the Theatre.* London: Harrap, 1964.

———. *Drama: Its Costumes and Decor.* London: Studio Publications, 1951.

———. *Taste and Fashion.* London: Harrap, 1945.

Levine, W. Robert. *In a Glamorous Fashion.* New York: Charles Scribner's Sons, 1980. Early 20th century to the 1970s.

Los Angeles County Museum of Art. *Hollywood and History, Costume Design in Film.* Los Angeles: Museum Associates, 1987.

Lurie, Alison. *The Language of Clothes.* New York: Random House, 1981.

Nagler, A. M. *A Source Book in Theatrical History.* New York: Dover, 1959.

Newton, Stella Mary. *Health, Art and Reason: Dress Reformers of the 19th Century.* London: John Murray, 1974.

Nicholl, Allardyce. *Mimes, Masks and Miracles.* London: Harrap, 1931.

———. *Stuart Masques and the Renaissance Stage.* London: Harrap, 1937.

Orrey, Leslie (ed.). *The Encyclopedia of Opera.* New York: Scribner, 1976.

Pecktal, Lynn. *Costume Design. Techniques of Modern Masters.* New York: Backstage Books, 1993.

Strong, Roy. *Festival Designs by Inigo Jones: Drawings for Scenery and Costume.* International Exhibition Foundation, 1967–1968.

Veblen, Thorstein. *The Theory of the Leisure Class.* New York: New American Library, 1953.

Methods and Materials

Albers, Josef. *Interaction of Color.* New Haven, Conn.: Yale University Press, 1975.

Baker, Georgia O'Daniel. *A Handbook of Costume Drawing.* Boston: Focal Press, 1992.

Berry, William A. *Drawing the Human Form.* New York: Van Nostrand Reinhold, 1977.

Birren, Faber. *Color: A Survey in Words and Pictures.* New Hyde Park, N.Y.: University Books, 1963.

———. *Creative Color.* New York: Van Nostrand Reinhold, 1961.

———. *Light, Color and Environment.* New York: Van Nostrand Reinhold, 1982.

Bridgman, George B. *Bridgman's Complete Guide to Drawing from Life.* New York: Sterling, 1952.

Cody, John. *Visualizing Muscles: A New Écorché Approach to Surface Anatomy.* Lawrence, Kans.: University Press of Kansas, 1990.

Cunningham, Rebecca. *Principles of Costume Design.* New York: Longman, 1989.

Dalley, Terence (ed.). *The Complete Guide to Illustration and Design: Techniques and Materials.* Secaucus, N.J.: Chartwell Books, 1980.

De Grandis, Luigina. *Theory and Use of Color.* New York: Harry N. Abrams, 1986.

Dobkin, Alexander. *Principles of Figure Drawing.* Cleveland: World, 1948.

Edwards, Betty. *Drawing on the Right Side of the Brain.* Los Angeles: J. P. Tarcher, 1979.

Eiseman, Leatrice and Lawrence Herbert. *The Pantone Book of Color.* New York: Harry N. Abrams, 1990.

Gillette, J. Michael. *Designing with Light,* 2nd ed. Mountain View, Calif.: Mayfield, 1989.

Harrison, Hazel. *The Encyclopedia of Watercolor Techniques.* Philadelphia: Running Press, 1990

Hogarth, Burne. *Drawing Dynamic Hands.* New York: Watson-Guptill, 1988.

———. *Dynamic Anatomy.* New York: Watson-Guptill, 1990.

———. *Dynamic Figure Drawing.* New York: Watson-Guptill, 1990.

———. *Dynamic Wrinkles and Drapery.* New York: Watson-Guptill, 1995.

Hollen, Norma and Jane Saddler. *Textiles,* 6th ed. New York: Macmillan, 1988.

Ingham, Rosemary and Liz Covey. *The Costume Designer's Handbook: A Complete Guide for Amateur & Professional Costume Designers.* Portsmouth, N.H.: Heinemann, 1992.

Itten, Johannes. *The Elements of Color.* New York: Van Nostrand Reinhold, 1970.

Jerde, Judith. *Encyclopedia of Textiles.* New York: Facts on File, 1992.

Laidman, Hugh. *Figures/Faces.* New York: Greenwich House, 1983.

Leveille, Paul. *Drawing Expressive Portraits.* Cincinnati, Ohio: North Light Books, 1996.

Mayer, Ralph. *The Artist's Handbook of Materials and Techniques.* New York: Viking Press, 1982.

———. *The Painter's Craft.* New York: Van Nostrand, 1948.

Orsini, Nicholas. *The Language of Drawing.* Garden City, N.Y.: Doubleday, 1982.

Parker, W. Oren and R. Craig Wolf. *Scene Design and Stage Lighting,* 6th ed. Orlando, Fla.: Harcourt Brace, 1991.

Peck, Stephen Rogers. *Atlas of Human Anatomy for the Artist.* New York: Oxford University Press, 1982.

Pecktal, Lynn. *Designing and Painting for the Theatre.* New York: Holt, Rinehart and Winston, 1975.

Pope, Arthur. *The Language of Drawing and Painting.* Cambridge, Mass.: Harvard University Press, 1931.

Raynes, John. *Human Anatomy for the Artist.* New York: Crescent Books, 1979.

Richmond, L. and J. Littlejohns. *Fundamentals of Water Color Painting.* New York: Watson-Guptill, 1978.

Ruby, Erik A. *The Human Figure: A Photographic Reference for Artists.* New York: Van Nostrand Reinhold, 1974.

Russell, Douglas A. *Stage Costume Design: Theory, Technique and Style.* Englewood Cliffs, N.J.: Prentice-Hall, 1985.

Schueser, Mary and Celie Rufey. *English and American Textiles: From 1790 to the Present.* New York: Thames and Hudson, 1989.

Sheppard, Joseph. *Bringing Textures to Life.* Cincinnati, Ohio: North Light Books, 1993.

Smith, Stan and Professor H. F. Ten Holt (eds.). *The Painter's Handbook.* New York: Gallery Books, 1984.

Fabrics and Construction

Arnold, Janet. *A Handbook of Costume.* London: Macmillan, 1973.

———. *Patterns of Fashion.* Volume 1: 1660–1860; Volume 2: 1860–1940. New York: Drama Book Specialists, 1972.

Baker, Patsy. *Wigs & Make-up.* Oxford: Focal Press, 1993.

Barazani, Gail Coningsby. *Safe Practices in the Arts and Crafts: A Studio Guide.* The College Art Association of America, 1978.

Basic Tailoring. New York: Time-Life Books, 1974.

Baygan, Lee. *Makeup for Theatre, Film & Television.* New York: Drama Book Publishers, 1982.

Bernstein, Aline. *Masterpieces of Women's Costume of the 18th and 19th Centuries.* New York: Crown, 1959.

Butterick, E. & Company. *American Dress Pattern Catalogues, 1873–1909.* New York: Dover, 1988.

Cabrera, Roberto and Patricia Flaherty Meyers. *Classic Tailoring Techniques, A Construction Guide for Men's Wear.* New York: Fairchild, 1983.

Corson, Richard. *Stage Makeup,* 8th ed. Englewood Cliffs, N.J.: Prentice-Hall, 1990.

Croonborg, Frederick T. *The Blue Book of Men's Tailoring.* New York: Van Nostrand Reinhold, 1977.

Davis, R. I. *Men's Garments, 1830–1890: A Guide to Pattern Cutting & Tailoring.* Studio City, Calif.: Players Press, 1995.

Dreher, Denise. *From the Neck Up, An Illustrated Guide to Hatmaking.* Minneapolis, Minn.:Madhatter Press, 1981.

Dryden, Deborah M. *Fabric Painting and Dyeing for the Theatre.* Portsmouth, N.H.: Heinemann, 1993.

Hecklinger, Charles. *Dress and Cloak Cutter.* Mendocina, Calif.: R. L. Shep, 1987. Originally published in 1881.

Ingham, Rosemary and Liz Covey. *The Costume Technician's Handbook.* Portsmough, N.H.: Heinemann, 1992.

James, Thurston. *The Prop Builder's Mask-Making Handbook.* Cincinnati, Ohio: Betterway Books, 1990.

McCann, Michael. *Artist Beware.* New York: Watson-Guptill, 1979.

Rossol, Monona. *The Artist's Complete Health and Safety Guide.* New York: Allworth Press, 1990.

———. *Stage Fright: Health and Safety in the Theatre.* New York: Alworth Press, 1991.

Taylor, Al and Sue Roy. *Making a Monster.* New York: Crown, 1980.

Vincent, W. E. F. *Tailoring of the Belle Epoque.* Mendocino, Calif.: R. L. Shep, 1991.

Waugh, Norah. *The Cut of Men's Clothes: 1600–1900.* London: Faber & Faber, 1964.

———. *The Cut of Women's Clothes: 1600–1930.* New York: Theatre Arts Books, 1968.

Index